D0854547

British Rail 1981

MOTIVE POWER

COMBINED VOLUME

LONDON

IAN ALLAN LTD

CONTENTS

TRACTION SCENE

During the first half of 1980 withdrawals were confined to shunters and locomotives written off due to accident damage or general condition. However, by the summer BR was feeling the effects of the economic recession and the cut-back in industrial output and a serious decline in freight traffic caused a surplus of motive power. Arrangements were made to store serviceable and unserviceable locomotives at BREL Swindon Works and this resulted in a new category of withdrawal. These locomotives are shown officially as "Withdrawn from operating stock" and are indicated in this book by the letter "S" after the number. They are stored pending a decision on their future, when they will either be returned to traffic or condemned. During the autumn of 1980 the last members of Classes 24, 31/0, 44, and 84 were withdrawn.

New deliveries were again confined to Class 56 locomotives and power cars (DMBs) for IC 125 units. These included the first Class 253 DMBs with GEC equipment and some teething troubles resulted in the substitution of locomotive-hauled trains on some WR services. The Class 56 locomotives continued to widen their area of operation, and the re-engined 47 901 returned to traffic initially on tests in South Wales.

On the Southern Region, four Class 33 locomotives and one Class 73 were named, the first SR locomotives to be so treated since the end of steam. The experimental revised livery with yellow cabs and large logo and numbers was approved by the BRB for standard use but because of financial constraints few locomotives were repainted. A number of unofficial names of local significance were applied to shunters (these are not shown in this book) and the Railway Technical Centre repainted its Class 24 locomotive in standard RTC red and blue livery and named it *Experiment*.

In an attempt to reduce track wear, a number of Class 86/0 locomotives were fitted with Sab resilient wheels and reclassified Class 86/3. A few more Class 86/2s received nameplates. Declining coal traffic on the Woodhead line brought a further purge of Class 76 locomotives, while the proposed closure of this line in June 1981 will mean the end of this line.

British Rail diesel locomotives are listed in this publication in numerical order and under the numerical classification system introduced in 1968. Each locomotive carries a five-digit number, the first two digits of which indicate the class of locomotive (generally, the lower numbers indicate the least powerful locomotives). The remaining three digits are the individual locomotive identification; the first of these three often indicates a sub-class (thus 47 401 is Class 47/4). Such a sub-class would incorporate detail differences from the main batch. Locomotives reclassified from one section to another receive new numbers.

The headings give the main details of each class, showing manufacturer of diesel engine, power control equipment, and mechanical parts. The power rating is shown in b.h.p. and in the kW equivalent. The headings also indicate the type of train brake and heating fitted, and the original "D" prefix number series. It should be noted that some classes were modified or renumbered at random from the original number series, and in many instances the first locomotive in the class list was not originally the first locomotive. Weights of locomotives in the same class may vary due to differing braking or heating equipment.

Diesel and electric locomotive wheel arrangements are described by a development of the continental system. This calculates by axles and uses letters to denote driving axles and numerals to denote non-powered carrying axles. A locomotive with two bogies each having two powered axles is a B-B (three axles—C-C, etc.). If the axles on a bogie or frame are individually powered, such as in a diesel-electric by one traction motor per axle, the suffix letter "o" is added. Thus the Class 55 is a Co-Co, and the former Class 52 a C-C. Shunting locomotives with a rigid frame and coupled wheels follow steam locomotive pattern and are known by the Whyte system as 0-4-0, 0-6-0, etc.

The information shown in each class heading follows a style similar to that used on the standard information panel applied to BR locomotives. The layout of this panel is shown below:

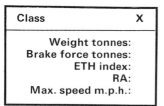

The code A, V, or X in the top right-hand corner indicates air, vacuum, or dual braking. Class, weight (always in working order) and maximum speed are all self-explanatory. The brake force is an indication of the locomotive's stopping power. It is shown in tonnes and calculated by a formula dependent on weight and certain other factors. All BR routes have a classification code which indicates their ability to carry concentrated weight (the lower the number, the lighter the weight). The RA (route availability) number is based on the weight per axle of the locomotive, and no locomotive may work over a route with a lower RA number than itself. Locomotives fitted with electric train heating equipment will also show an ETH index on this panel. Each coach has an ETH rating, and the total of all the coach ratings in a train must not exceed the ETH index figure on the locomotive. Original names of locomotives are shown where appropriate, although nameplates may have been removed subsequently.

Further technical data, information and photographs showing detail differences between individual locomotive types will be found in Volume 1 of the Ian Allan *Motive Power Recognition* series to be published during 1981. Volume 1 covers diesel and electric locomotives currently in service.

The numbers of locomotives in service are correct to the time of going to press. See also "Late Information" section.

Information in this booklet has been checked against BR TOPS Records.

This booklet shows the latest known stock position at the time of going to press. To allow readers to keep their records up to date, motive-power changes (new building, withdrawals, reallocations, reclassifications, renumberings, etc.) are published every month in the Ian Allan magazines *Railway World* and *Modern Railways*. Notification of any errors found in the booklet should be sent to The Editor, BR Locomotives, Ian Allan Ltd. The publishers cannot enter into correspondence about individual locomotive types or about more general railway topics.

N.B. British Rail High Speed Train power cars are listed individually in this publication, and the unit formations in the *ABC BR Multiple-Units*.

COUPLING OF DIESEL LOCOMOTIVES

Main-line diesel locomotives of most classes are equipped to operate in multiple with locomotives having similar control systems. In order to distinguish locomotives which can operate in this way, a colour code symbol is painted above each buffer and repeated in miniature on the plug and socket covers.

Type of Locomotive	*Coupling symbol*
All diesel-electric locomotives with electro-pneumatic control.	★ BLUE STAR
All diesel-electric locomotives with electro-magnetic control.	● RED CIRCLE
Class 50 diesel-electric locomotives	■ ORANGE SQUARE

Cover: Class 56 No 56 044 leaves Wath yard./*A. Wynn*

SAFETY FIRST

Travel by rail has an excellent and envied safety record and in two recent consecutive years—1976 and 1977—no passengers were killed travelling on British Rail trains.

Inevitably each year a number of people are killed whilst playing or trespassing on the lines—sadly, even experience and trained railway staff become involved in mishaps, demonstrating the inherent dangers even for those whose duties take them to the wrong side of the fence.

British Rail welcomes the interest in its operations shown by railway enthusiasts using this book. But railway lines, maintenance depots, sidings and sheds are dangerous places unless your visit is by invitation and properly supervised.

Otherwise your presence there is probably illegal, certainly not welcome and could be FATAL.

British Railways Board

Class 01   0-4-0

Diesel mechanical shunter built 1956
Engine: Gardner 6L3 of 153 b.h.p. (114 kW)
Mechanical parts: Barclay
Weight: 25 tons
Brake force: 15 tonnes. No train brake
Maximum tractive effort: 12,750 lb
Transmission: Mechanical. Vulcan-Sinclair rigid type hydraulic coupling. Wilson S.E. 4 type four-speed epicyclic gearbox. Wiseman type 15 RLGB reverse and final drive unit
Route availability: 1
Maximum speed: 14 m.p.h.
No train heating
Previous no. series:
D2953–2954

01 002

TOTAL: 1

Class 03   0-6-0

Diesel mechanical shunter built 1957–61
Engine: Gardner 8L3 of 204 b.h.p. (152 kW)
Mechanical parts: BR
Weight: 30–31 tons
Brake force: 13 tonnes. Vacuum braked (¶ dual braked)
Maximum tractive effort: 15,300 lb
Transmission: Mechanical. Vulcan-Sinclair type 23 fluid coupling. Wilson-Drewry C.A.5 type five-speed epicyclic gearbox. Type RF 11 spiral bevel reverse and final drive unit
Route availability: 1
Maximum speed: 28 m.p.h.
No train heating
Previous no. series:
D2000–2199

03 017	03 022	03 034
03 021	03 026	

03 059¶	03 094¶	03 161
03 060	03 107	03 162¶
03 061s	03 112¶	03 168
03 062s	03 119	03 170¶
03 063¶	03 120	03 175
03 064	03 121	03 179¶
03 066¶	03 129	03 180¶
03 067	03 141	03 189
03 069	03 142	03 196¶
03 072	03 144	03 197¶
03 073¶	03 145	03 370
03 078¶	03 149	03 371¶
03 079	03 151	03 382
03 080	03 152	03 389
03 081s	03 154	03 397¶
03 084¶	03 158¶	03 399¶
03 086¶	03 160	
03 089¶		

Nos. 03 119/30/41/2/4/5/51/2 have cut-down cab for working on the BPGV line

TOTAL: 56

Class 05   0-6-0

Diesel mechanical shunter built 1955
Engine: Gardner 8L3 of 204 b.h.p. (152 kW)
Mechanical parts: Hunslet
Weight: 32 tons
Brake force: 13 tonnes. Vacuum brake
Maximum tractive effort: 14,500 lb
Transmission: Mechanical. Hunslet patent friction clutch. Hunslet four-speed gearbox incorporating reverse and final drive gears
Route availability: 2
Maximum speed: 18 m.p.h.
No train heating
Previous no. series:
D2550–2618

05 001

TOTAL: 1

Class 06   0-4-0

Diesel mechanical shunter built 1958–60
Engine: Gardner 8L3 of 204 b.h.p. (152 kW)
Mechanical parts: Barclay
Weight: 37 tons
Brake force: 15 tonnes. Vacuum brake
Maximum tractive effort: 19,800 lb
Transmission: Mechanical Vulcan-Sinclair type 23 fluid coupling. Wilson-Drewry C.A.5 type five-speed epicyclic gearbox. Wiseman type 15 RLGB reverse and final drive unit
Route availability: 5
Maximum speed: 23 m.p.h.
No train heating
Previous no. series: D2410–2444

06 002	06 005	06 008
06 003		

TOTAL: 4

Class 08   0-6-0

Built 1952–62 to standard design adopted for 350 h.p. shunter
Engine: English Electric 6-cyl. 6KT of 350 b.h.p. (261 kW)
Mechanical parts: BR
Weight: 49–50 tons
Brake force: 19 tonnes. Vacuum brake (¶ dual braked) (● air braked)
Maximum tractive effort: 35,000 lb
Power/control equipment: English Electric. Two EE 506 traction motors. Double reduction gear drive
Route availability: 5
Maximum speed: 15/20 m.p.h.
No train heating

Previous no. series: D3000–3116, D3127–3136, D3167–3438, D3454–3472, D3503–3611, D3652–3664, D3672–3718, D3722–4048, D4095–8, D4115–4186/91/2

08 004	08 069	08 123
08 008	08 075	08 124
08 011	08 078	08 125
08 018	08 079	08 127s
08 019	08 083	08 128s
08 021	08 085	08 129
08 022	08 086s	08 130
08 023	08 087	08 131
08 024	08 088	08 132
08 026		
08 028	08 091	08 134
08 030	08 093	08 136
08 031	08 094	08 137
08 033	08 095	08 141
08 035	08 096	08 142
08 036	08 097	08 146s
	08 098	08 147
08 045	08 099	08 148
	08 100	08 149s
08 047	08 101	08 150
08 049	08 102	08 152
08 050	08 103	08 153
08 051	08 104	08 159
08 052	08 105	08 160
08 053	08 106	08 161
	08 107	08 163
	08 108	08 164
08 056	08 109	08 166
08 058	08 110	08 168
	08 112	08 169
08 060	08 113	08 170
08 061	08 114	08 171
08 062	08 115	08 172
08 063	08 116	08 174
08 064		08 176
08 067	08 120	08 177
08 068	08 121	08 178
		08 180

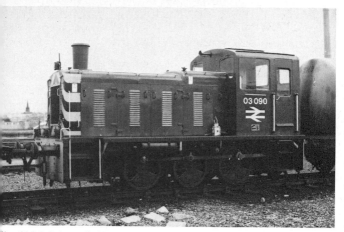

Class 03 0-6-0 shunter No 03 090   [*J. E. Augustson*

Class 06 0-4-0 shunter No 06 005   [*J. E. Augustson*

Class 98.6 & 0 shunter No.98 704 (unofficially named Chopwell)

T.J. C. Hillmer

08 181	08 231	08 284	08 337	08 389●	08 440
08 182	08 232	08 285	08 338	08 390●	08 441●
08 183	08 233	08 286	08 339	08 391	08 442●
08 184	08 234	08 287	08 340	08 392s	08 443
08 185	08 235	08 288	08 341	08 393●	08 444
08 186	08 237	08 289	08 342	08 394	08 445●
08 187	08 238	08 290	08 343	08 395	08 446
08 188	08 239	08 291	08 344	08 396	08 447
08 189	08 240	08 292	08 345	08 397●	08 448●
08 190	08 241	08 293	08 346	08 398	08 449
08 191	08 242		08 347	08 399●	08 450
08 192	08 243●	08 295	08 348	08 400	08 451
08 193	08 244	08 296	08 349	08 401●	08 452
08 194	08 245	08 297	08 350	08 402●	08 453s
08 195	08 246	08 298	08 351	08 403	08 454
08 196	08 247	08 299	08 352	08 404	08 455
08 197	08 248	08 300	08 353	08 405●	08 456
08 198s	08 249	08 301	08 354	08 406	08 457
08 199	08 250	08 302	08 355	08 407●	08 458
08 200	08 251s	08 303	08 356	08 408	08 459
08 201	08 252	08 304	08 359	08 409	08 460●
08 202	08 253	08 305	08 360	08 410●	08 461
08 203	08 254		08 361	08 411●	08 462
08 204	08 255		08 362	08 412	08 463
08 205	08 256	08 308	08 363	08 413●	08 464
08 206	08 257	08 309	08 364	08 414●	08 465
08 207s	08 258	08 311		08 415	08 466
08 208	08 259s	08 312	08 366	08 416	08 467
08 209	08 260	08 313	08 367	08 417	08 468
08 210	08 261	08 314	08 368	08 418●	08 469
08 211	08 262		08 369	08 419	08 470
08 212	08 263		08 370	08 420	08 471
	08 264	08 317	08 371	08 421	08 472
08 214	08 265	08 319	08 372	08 422	08 473
08 215	08 266	08 320	08 373	08 423	08 474
		08 321	08 374	08 424	08 475
08 217	08 268	08 322	08 375	08 425	08 476
	08 269	08 323	08 376	08 427	08 477
08 219	08 270	08 324	08 377	08 428●	08 478
08 220	08 271	08 325	08 378	08 429	08 479
08 221	08 272	08 326	08 379	08 430	08 480●
08 222	08 273	08 327	08 380	08 431	08 481
	08 274	08 328	08 381	08 432	08 482
08 224	08 275	08 329	08 382	08 433	08 483●
08 225	08 277	08 330	08 383	08 434	08 484●
08 226	08 279	08 331	08 384	08 435	08 485●
08 227	08 280	08 332	08 385	08 436	08 486
08 228	08 281	08 333	08 386	08 437	08 487
		08 334	08 387	08 438	08 488
		08 335	08 388●	08 439	08 489●
08 230s	08 283	08 336			

08 490	08 540¶	08 591	08 642¶	08 693	08 743¶
08 491	08 541¶	08 592	08 643¶	08 694	08 744¶
08 492●	08 542¶	08 593	08 644¶	08 695	08 745¶
08 493●	08 543¶	08 594	08 645¶	08 696	08 746¶
08 494	08 544¶	08 595	08 646¶	08 697	08 747¶
08 495	08 545s	08 597	08 647¶	08 698	08 748¶
08 496	08 546	08 598	08 648¶	08 699	08 749¶
08 497	08 547	08 599	08 649¶	08 700●	08 750¶
08 498	08 548	08 600●	08 650¶	08 701	08 751¶
08 499●	08 549	08 601	08 651¶	08 702	08 752¶
08 500	08 550	08 602	08 652¶	08 703●	08 753¶
08 501	08 551	08 603	08 653¶	08 704	08 754¶
08 502●	08 552	08 604	08 654¶	08 705	08 755¶
08 503●	08 553	08 605	08 655¶	08 706	08 756¶
08 504●	08 554	08 606	08 656	08 707	08 757¶
08 505	08 555	08 607	08 657	08 708	08 758¶
08 506●	08 556	08 608	08 658	08 709	08 759¶
08 507●	08 557	08 609	08 659	08 710	08 760¶
08 508	08 558	08 610	08 660	08 711	08 761¶
08 509●	08 559	08 611	08 661●	08 712	08 762¶
08 510●	08 560	08 612	08 662	08 713	08 763¶
08 511●	08 561	08 613	08 663	08 714	08 764¶
08 512●	08 562	08 614	08 664	08 715	08 765¶
	08 563	08 615	08 665	08 716	08 766¶
08 514●	08 564	08 616	08 666	08 717	08 767¶
08 515	08 565	08 617	08 667	08 718	08 768¶
08 516●	08 567	08 618	08 668	08 719	08 769
08 517●	08 568	08 619	08 669	08 720	08 770
08 518●	08 569	08 620	08 670	08 721	08 771
08 519	08 570	08 621●	08 671	08 722	08 772
08 520	08 571	08 622	08 672	08 723	08 773
08 521●	08 572	08 623	08 673	08 724	08 774
08 522	08 573	08 624	08 674	08 725	08 775
08 523	08 574	08 625	08 675	08 726	08 776
08 524	08 575	08 626	08 676	08 727	08 777
08 525¶	08 576	08 627●	08 677	08 728	08 778
08 526¶	08 577	08 628	08 678●	08 729	08 779
08 527¶	08 578	08 629	08 680	08 730	08 780
08 528¶	08 579	08 630	08 681	08 731	08 781
08 529¶	08 580	08 631	08 682	08 732	08 782
08 530¶	08 581	08 632	08 683	08 733	08 783
08 531¶	08 582	08 633	08 684	08 734	08 784
08 532¶	08 583	08 634	08 685	08 735	08 785
08 533¶	08 584	08 635	08 686	08 736	08 786
08 534¶	08 585		08 687	08 737¶	08 787
08 535¶	08 586	08 637	08 688●	08 738¶	08 788
08 536¶	08 587	08 638	08 689	08 739¶	08 789
08 537¶	08 588	08 639	08 690	08 740¶	08 790
08 538¶	08 589	08 640¶	08 691	08 741¶	08 791
08 539¶	08 590	08 641¶	08 692	08 742¶	08 792

Class 09 0-6-0 shunter No 09 001

[C. Burnham

Class 13 0-6-0+0-6-0 shunter No 13 001

[B. J. Nicolle

08 793	08 843¶	08 893¶	08 943¶	08 949¶	08 954¶
08 794	08 844¶	08 894¶	08 944¶	08 950¶	08 955¶
08 795	08 845¶	08 895¶	08 945¶	08 951¶	08 956¶
08 796	08 846¶	08 896¶	08 946¶	08 952¶	08 957¶
08 797	08 847¶	08 897¶	08 947¶	08 953¶	08 958¶
08 798	08 848¶	08 898¶	08 948¶		
08 799	08 849¶	08 899¶			

TOTAL: 854

08 800	08 850¶	08 900¶
08 801	08 851¶	08 901¶
08 802	08 852¶	08 902¶
08 803	08 853¶	08 903¶
08 804	08 854¶	08 904¶
08 805	08 855¶	08 905¶
08 806●	08 856¶	08 906¶
08 807	08 857¶	08 907¶
08 808	08 858¶	08 908¶
08 809	08 859¶	08 909¶
08 810●	08 860	08 910¶
08 811●	08 861	08 911¶
	08 862s	08 912¶
08 813	08 863s	08 913¶
08 814●	08 864	08 914¶
08 815	08 865	08 915¶
08 816●	08 866	08 916¶
08 817	08 867	08 917¶
08 818	08 868	08 918¶
08 819	08 869	08 919¶
08 820	08 870	08 920¶
08 821	08 871	08 921¶
08 822	08 872¶	08 922¶
08 823●	08 873¶	08 923¶
08 824●	08 874¶	08 924¶
08 825●	08 875¶	08 925¶
08 826	08 876¶	08 926¶
08 827●	08 877¶	08 927¶
08 828●	08 878¶	08 928¶
08 829●	08 879¶	08 929¶
08 830¶	08 880¶	08 930¶
08 831¶	08 881¶	08 931¶
08 832¶	08 882¶	08 932¶
08 833¶	08 883¶	08 933¶
08 834¶	08 884¶	08 934¶
08 835¶	08 885¶	08 935¶
08 836¶	08 886¶	08 936¶
08 837¶	08 887¶	08 937¶
08 838¶	08 888¶	08 938¶
08 839¶	08 889¶	08 939¶
08 840¶	08 890¶	08 940¶
08 841¶	08 891¶	08 941¶
08 842¶	08 892¶	08 942¶

Class 09   0-6-0

Uprated version of 08, built 1959–62
Engine: English Electric 6-cyl. 6KT of 400 b.h.p. (298 kW)
Mechanical parts: BR
Weight: 50 tons
Brake force: 19 tonnes. Dual braked
Maximum tractive effort: 25,000 lb
Power/control equipment: English Electric. Two EE 506 traction motors. Double reduction gear drive
Route availability: 5
Maximum speed: 27 m.p.h.
No train heating
Previous no. series: D3665–3771, D3719–3721, D4099–4114

09 001	09 010	09 019
09 002	09 011	09 020
09 003	09 012	09 021
09 004	09 013	09 022
09 005	09 014	09 023
09 006	09 015	09 024
09 007	09 016	09 025
09 008	09 017	09 026
09 009	09 018	

TOTAL: 26

Class 13   0-6-0+0-6-0

Permanently coupled "master" and "slave" units, converted in 1965 from Class 08 0-6-0 diesels for hump shunting in Tinsley Yard. The cab of the "slave" unit has been removed and both units are specially weighted

Engine: Two English Electric 6-cyl. 6KT. Total 800 b.h.p. (597 kW)

Mechanical parts: BR

Weight: 120 tons

Brake force: 38 tonnes. Vacuum brake

Maximum tractive effort: 70,000 lb

Power/control equipment: English Electric. Four EE 506 traction motors. Double reduction gear drive

Route availability: 8

Maximum speed: 20 m.p.h.

No train heating

Previous no. series: D4500–4502

13 001   13 002   13 003

TOTAL: 3

Class 20   Bo-Bo★

Single cab design built 1957–67. Adopted as standard 1000 b.h.p. design

Engine: English Electric 8 SVT Mk. 2 of 1,000 b.h.p. (746 kW)

Mechanical parts: English Electric

Weight: 72–73 tons

Brake force: 35 tonnes. Vacuum brake (¶ dual braked)

Maximum tractive effort: 42,000 lb

Power/control equipment: English Electric. Four EE 526/5D or 526/8D traction motors

Route availability: 5

Maximum speed: 75 m.p.h.

No train heating

Previous no. series: D8000–8199, D8300–8327

20 001	20 057	20 110
20 002¶	20 058	20 111¶
20 003	20 059	20 112
20 004	20 060	20 113
20 005	20 061	20 114¶
20 006	20 063	20 115¶
20 007	20 064¶	20 116¶
20 008	20 065	20 117
20 009¶	20 066¶	20 118¶
20 010	20 067	20 119
20 011¶	20 068	20 120
20 013	20 069	20 121
20 015¶	20 070	20 122¶
20 016	20 071	20 123¶
20 017	20 072	20 124¶
20 019	20 073	20 125¶
20 020	20 075	20 126
20 021	20 076¶	20 127
20 022	20 077	20 128
20 023	20 078s	20 129
20 025	20 080	20 130
20 026	20 081	20 131
20 027	20 082	20 132
20 028	20 083¶	20 133
20 029	20 084	20 134
20 030	20 085	20 135
20 031	20 086¶	20 136
20 032	20 087	20 137¶
20 034	20 088	20 138¶
20 035¶	20 089¶	20 139
20 036¶	20 090	20 140
20 037		20 141
20 039¶	20 092	20 142
20 040	20 093	20 143
20 041	20 094	20 144¶
20 042	20 095	20 145¶
20 043	20 096	20 146¶
20 044	20 097	20 147
20 045	20 098	20 148
20 046	20 099	20 149¶
20 047	20 100	20 150¶
20 048	20 101	20 151
20 049	20 102	20 152¶
20 050s	20 103	20 153¶
20 051	20 104	20 154¶
20 052	20 105	20 155¶
20 053	20 106	20 156¶
20 054	20 107	20 157
20 055	20 108	20 158
20 056	20 109	20 159

Class 20 Bo-Bo No 20 082

[B. J. Nicolle]

18

20 160	20 183	20 206¶
20 161	20 184¶	20 207¶
20 162¶	20 185	20 208
20 163	20 186	20 209
20 164¶	20 187	20 210
20 165¶	20 188	20 211
20 166	20 189	20 212
20 167¶	20 190	20 213
20 168	20 191¶	20 214
20 169	20 192	20 215
20 170	20 193	20 216¶
20 171	20 194	20 217¶
20 172	20 195	20 218¶
20 173	20 196	20 219¶
20 174¶	20 197	20 220¶
20 175¶	20 198	20 221¶
20 176	20 199	20 222¶
20 177		20 223¶
20 178	20 201¶	20 224¶
20 179¶	20 202¶	20 225¶
20 180	20 203¶	20 226¶
20 181	20 204¶	20 227¶
20 182	20 205¶	20 228

TOTAL: 217

Class 25   Bo-Bo★

1961 development of now extinct Class 24 design with higher power, and styling changes

Engine: Sulzer 6-cyl. 6LDA 28-B of 1,250 b.h.p. (933 kW)
Mechanical parts: BR
Weight: 74 tons
Brake force: 38 tonnes. Vacuum brake (¶ dual braked)
Maximum tractive effort: 39,000 lb
Power/control equipment: AEI. Four AEI 137 BX traction motors
Route availability: 5
Maximum speed: 90 m.p.h.
No train heating
Previous no. series: D5151–5175

Class 25/0

25 002	25 007s	25 011
25 005	25 010	25 025
25 006s		

TOTAL: 7

Class 25/1   **Bo-Bo★**
As class 25/0 with detail modifications
Power/control equipment: GEC series 1. Four AEI 253 AY traction motors

Class 20 Bo-Bo No 20 215   [*N. E. Preedy*

19

[B. J. Nicolle]

Class 25/0 Bo-Bo No 25 054

Weight: 71–75 tons
Maximum tractive effort:
45,000 lb
Steam heating, except 25 031/2
Previous no. series: D5176–5232

25 027	25 048¶	25 065
25 028	25 049¶	25 066
	25 050¶	25 067
25 032¶	25 051¶	25 069
25 033¶	25 052	25 071
25 034¶	25 053¶s	25 072
25 035¶	25 054¶	25 073
25 036¶		
25 037¶	25 056	25 075
25 038	25 057¶	25 076¶
25 039	25 058¶	
25 040	25 059¶	25 078
25 041	25 060¶	25 079¶
25 042		25 080
25 043	25 062	25 081
25 044¶		25 082¶
25 046	25 064¶	

TOTAL: 44

Class 25/2   **Bo-Bo★**
Further detail differences
Power/control equipment: GEC
series 2. Four AEI 253 AY traction
motors
Weight: 71–76 tons
25 083–7 and 25 218–41 and
25 243–7 fitted with steam heating
Previous no. series: D5233–5299,
D7500–7597

25 083		25 113¶
25 084	25 099¶s	25 114
25 085	25 100	25 115
25 086	25 101	25 117¶
25 088¶	25 102	25 118
25 089¶		25 119
25 090	25 104	25 120¶
25 093	25 105	25 123
25 094	25 106¶	25 124
25 095¶	25 107	25 125
25 097¶	25 108	25 126

25 129	25 169	25 209¶
25 130	25 170	25 210¶
25 131		25 211¶
25 132	25 172	25 212¶
25 133	25 173¶	25 213¶
25 134	25 175¶	25 214
25 135	25 176¶	25 215
25 136	25 177	25 216
25 138	25 178¶	25 217
25 139	25 179	25 218¶
25 140	25 180	25 219
25 141	25 181¶	25 220
25 142	25 182¶	25 221¶
25 143	25 183¶s	25 222¶
25 144	25 184¶	25 223
25 145¶	25 185¶	25 224
25 146	25 186	25 225
	25 187	25 226¶
25 148	25 188	25 227
25 149	25 189¶	25 228¶
25 150		25 229¶
25 151	25 191¶	25 230¶
25 152	25 192¶	25 231¶
25 153	25 193¶	25 232¶
25 154¶	25 194¶	25 233¶
25 155¶s	25 195	25 234¶
25 156	25 196¶	25 235¶
25 157	25 197¶s	25 236¶
25 158	25 198¶	25 237¶
	25 199¶	25 238
25 160	25 200¶	25 239¶
25 161	25 201¶	25 240¶
25 162	25 202¶	25 241¶
25 163	25 203¶s	25 242¶
25 164		25 243¶
	25 205¶	25 244¶
	25 206¶	25 245¶
25 167	25 207¶	25 246¶
25 168	25 208¶	25 247¶

TOTAL: 140

Class 25/3   **Bo-Bo★**
Final development of Class 25
Power/control equipment: GEC
Series 3. Four AEI 253 AY traction
motors
Weight: 71 tons

Mechanical parts: Beyer Peacock/BR
No train heating
Previous no. series: D7598–7677

25 248	25 276¶	25 303¶
25 249¶	25 277¶	25 304
25 250¶	25 278¶	25 305¶
25 251¶	25 279¶	25 306
	25 280	25 307¶
25 253	25 281	25 308¶
25 254¶	25 282¶	25 309¶
25 256¶	25 283¶	25 310¶
25 257¶	25 284¶	25 311¶
25 258¶	25 285¶	25 312¶
25 259¶	25 286¶	25 313¶
25 260	25 287¶	25 314¶
25 261	25 288¶	25 315¶
25 262¶	25 289¶	25 316¶
25 263	25 290	25 317¶
25 264	25 291	25 318¶
25 265¶	25 292	25 319¶
25 266¶	25 293	25 320¶
25 267	25 294	25 321¶
25 268¶		25 322¶
25 269¶	25 296¶	25 323¶
25 270	25 297¶	25 324¶
25 271	25 298¶	25 325¶
25 272	25 299	25 326¶
25 273	25 300¶	25 327¶
25 274	25 301¶	
25 275	25 302	

TOTAL: 77

Class 26 Bo-Bo★

Introduced 1958 as design alternative to Class 24
Engine: Sulzer 6-cyl. 6LDA28 of 1,160 b.h.p. (865 kW)
Mechanical parts: Birmingham RC & W
Weight: 73–79 tons
Brake force: 35 tonnes. Vacuum brake (26 001–7 dual braked)
Maximum tractive effort: 42,000 lb
Power/control equipment: Crompton Parkinson. Four CP C171 traction motors

Route availability: 6
Maximum speed: 80 m.p.h. (nos. 26 001–7 75 m.p.h.)
26 008–20 fitted steam heating
Previous no. series: D5300–5319

Class 26/0

26 001	26 007	26 013
26 002	26 008	26 014
26 003	26 010	26 015
26 004	26 011	26 018
26 005	26 012	26 019
26 006		

TOTAL: 16

Class 26/1 Bo-Bo★

As class 26/0 but all fitted with vacuum brake and steam heating
Power/control equipment: Crompton Parkinson. Four CP C171 D3 traction motors
Weight: 73 tons
Route availability: 5
Previous no. series: D5320–5346

26 021	26 030	26 039
26 022	26 031	26 040
26 023	26 032	26 041
26 024	26 033	26 042
26 025	26 034	26 043
26 026	26 035	26 044
26 027	26 036	26 045
26 028	26 037	26 046
26 029	26 038	

TOTAL: 26

Class 27 Bo-Bo★

1961 development of Class 26
Engine: Sulzer 6-cyl. 6LDA28-B of 1,250 b.h.p. (933 kW)
Mechanical parts: Birmingham RC & W
Weight: 71–76 tons
Brake force: 35 tonnes. Vacuum brake (¶dual braked)
Maximum tractive effort: 40,000 lb

Class 25/3 Bo-Bo No 25 281

[*J. E. Augustson*

Class 26 Bo-Bo No 26 031

[*J. E. Augustson*

Class 27/1 Bo-Bo No 27 108

[J. E. Augustson]

24

Power/control equipment:
GEC. Four GEC WT 459 traction motors
Route availability: 5
Maximum speed: 90 m.p.h.
Steam heating, except 27 024–31
Previous no. series:
Random from D5347–5415

Class 27/0

27 001	27 017	27 030
27 002	27 018	
27 003	27 019	27 032
27 004	27 020	27 033
27 005	27 021	27 034¶
27 007	27 022	27 036
27 008	27 023	27 037
27 009	27 024	27 038¶
27 010	27 025	27 040
27 011	27 026	27 041¶
27 012	27 027	27 042¶
27 014	27 028	
27 016	27 029	

TOTAL: 36

Class 27/1   Bo-Bo★
As Class 27/0
Weight: 76 tons
Dual braked
Steam heating
Previous no. series:
Random from D5374–5413

Fitted for push-pull working

27 101¶	27 105¶	27 109¶
27 102¶	27 106¶	27 110¶
27 103¶	27 107¶	27 111¶
27 104¶	27 108¶	27 112¶

TOTAL: 12

Class 27/2   Bo-Bo★
As Class 27/1 but without steam heating
Dual braked
Electric train heating
Previous no. series:
Random from D5384–5412

27 203¶	27 207¶	27 210¶
27 204¶	27 208¶	27 211¶
27 205¶	27 209¶	27 212¶
27 206¶		

TOTAL: 10

Class 31   AIA-AIA ●
Built 1957–62. Prototype now at NRM, York. Currently on loan to North Yorkshire Moors Railway
Engine: English Electric 12-cyl. 12SV of 1,470 b.h.p. (1,097 kW)
Mechanical parts: Brush
Weight: 109 tons
Brake force: 49 tonnes. Vacuum brake
Maximum tractive effort:
42,800 lb
Power/control equipment:
Brush. Four TM 73-68 traction motors
Route availability: 5
Maximum speed: ‡80 m.p.h., 90 m.p.h.
Steam heating
Previous no. series: D5500–5519

Class 31/0: Fitted with electro-magnetic control equipment
31 004‡s   31 008‡s   31 019‡s
Scheduled for early withdrawal

TOTAL: 3

Class 31/1   AIA-AIA★
Development of 31/0
Weight: 107–11 tons
Vacuum brake (¶dual braked)

[J. Scrace]

Class 31/4 A1A-A1A No 31 413

Previous no. series:
Random from D5518–5862

31 101‡	31 152¶	31 203¶	31 251	31 277	31 302¶
31 102‡	31 153¶	31 204	31 252¶	31 278¶	31 303
31 103‡s	31 154¶	31 205¶	31 253	31 279	31 304¶
31 105‡¶	31 155¶	31 206¶	31 254	31 280•	31 305
31 106‡¶	31 156¶	31 207	31 255¶	31 281¶	31 306
31 107‡¶	31 158¶	31 208¶	31 256¶	31 282¶	31 307¶
31 108‡	31 159¶	31 209¶	31 257¶	31 283¶	31 308
31 109‡¶	31 160	31 210¶	31 258¶	31 284¶	31 309
31 110‡¶	31 161	31 211	31 259¶	31 285¶	31 311¶
31 111‡	31 162¶	31 212¶	31 260	31 286¶	31 312
31 112¶	31 163¶	31 213¶	31 261	31 287	31 313
31 113‡¶	31 164	31 214	31 262	31 288	31 314¶
31 114	31 165¶	31 215	31 263¶	31 289	31 315
31 115‡	31 166¶	31 216	31 264s	31 290	31 316
31 116‡¶	31 167	31 217¶	31 265	31 291	31 317
31 117¶	31 168¶	31 218¶	31 266	31 292¶	31 318
31 118¶	31 169	31 219¶	31 268¶	31 293	31 319
31 119¶	31 170¶	31 220¶	31 269	31 294¶	31 320¶
31 120	31 171¶	31 221¶	31 270	31 295	31 321
31 121¶	31 173¶	31 222¶	31 271	31 296¶	31 322¶
31 122	31 174¶	31 223¶	31 272¶	31 297	31 323¶
31 123¶	31 175¶	31 224¶	31 273¶	31 298	31 324
31 124	31 176¶	31 225¶	31 274s	31 299	31 325
31 125	31 177	31 226¶	31 275	31 300	31 326
31 126	31 178¶	31 227¶	31 276¶	31 301¶	31 327¶
31 127¶	31 179	31 228			
31 128¶	31 180¶	31 229			**TOTAL: 218**
31 129	31 181¶	31 230¶			
31 130¶	31 182	31 231¶			
31 131¶	31 183	31 232¶			
31 132	31 184¶	31 233¶			
31 133	31 185¶	31 234			
31 134	31 186¶	31 235¶			
31 135¶	31 187¶	31 236			
	31 188¶	31 237			
31 137¶	31 189¶	31 238¶			
31 138¶	31 190¶	31 239			
31 139	31 191¶	31 240			
31 141¶	31 192¶	31 241¶			
31 142¶	31 193	31 242¶			
31 143¶	31 194	31 243¶			
31 144¶	31 195¶	31 244			
31 145¶	31 196¶	31 245¶			
31 146	31 198¶	31 246			
31 147¶	31 199¶	31 247¶			
31 148	31 200	31 248			
31 149¶	31 201¶	31 249¶			
31 151	31 202¶	31 250¶			

Class 31/4   AIA-AIA★
Development of 31/1
Weight: 108–12 tons
Steam and electric train heating
(31 424 ETH only)
Dual braked.
Previous no. series:
Random from D5522–5856

31 401¶	31 414¶
31 402¶	31 415¶
31 403¶	31 416¶
31 404¶	31 417¶
31 405¶	31 418‡¶
31 406¶	31 419¶
31 407¶	31 420¶ (31 172)
31 408¶	31 421¶ (31 140)
31 409¶	31 422¶ (31 310)
31 410¶	31 423¶ (31 197)
31 411¶	31 424¶ (31 157)
31 412¶	
31 413¶	**TOTAL: 24**

Class 33/0 Bo-Bo No 33 056 The Burma Star

[*Chris Leigh*

Class 33/1 Bo-Bo No 33 110

[*B. J. Nicolle*

Class 33   Bo-Bo★

Built 1960–2 for Southern Region
Engine: Sulzer 8-cyl. 8LDA28 pressure-charged of 1,550 b.h.p. (1,156 kW)
Mechanical parts: Birmingham RC & W
Weight: 77 tons
Brake force: 35 tonnes. Dual braked
Maximum tractive effort: 45,000 lb
Power/control equipment: Crompton Parkinson. Four CP C171 C2 traction motors
Route availability: 6
Maximum speed: 85 m.p.h.
Fitted with electric train-heating equipment only
Previous no. series: Random from D6500–6585

Class 33/0

33 001	33 004	33 006
33 002	33 005	33 007
33 003		

33 008 Eastleigh

33 009	33 015	33 021
33 010	33 016	33 022
33 011	33 017	33 023
33 012	33 018	33 024
33 013	33 019	33 025
33 014	33 020	33 026

33 027 Earl Mountbatten of Burma

Class 33/2 Bo-Bo No 33 206   [*J. E. Augustson*

29

33 028	33 037	33 046
33 029	33 038	33 047
33 030	33 039	33 048
33 031	33 040	33 049
33 032	33 042	33 050
33 033	33 043	33 051
33 034	33 044	33 052
33 035	33 045	

33 053 Ashford

33 054	33 055

33 056 The Burma Star

33 057	33 060	33 063
33 058	33 061	33 064
33 059	33 062	33 065

TOTAL: 63

Class 33/1 Bo-Bo★

Class 33 locomotives fitted for push-pull operation with MU stock
Buckeye couplers
Weight: 77½ tons
Previous no. series:
Random from D6511–6580

33 101	33 108	33 114
33 102	33 109	33 115
33 103	33 110	33 116
33 104	33 111	33 117
33 105	33 112	33 118
33 106	33 113	33 119
33 107		

TOTAL: 19

Class 33/2 Bo-Bo★

Class 33 locomotives with narrow (8' 8") body for Hastings line
Weight: 76½ tons
Previous no. series: D6586–6597

33 201	33 205	33 209
33 202	33 206	33 210
33 203	33 207	33 211
33 204	33 208	33 212

TOTAL: 12

Class 37 Co-Co★

Built 1960–65
Engine: English Electric 12-cyl. 12CSVT of 1,750 b.h.p. (1,306 kW)
Mechanical parts: English Electric
Weight: 101–6 tons
Brake force: 50 tonnes. Vacuum brake (¶dual braked)
Maximum tractive effort: 55,500 lb
Power/control equipment: English Electric. Six EE 538 traction motors
Some fitted with steam heating
Route availability: 5
Maximum speed: 90 m.p.h.
Previous no. series: D6600–6608, D6700–6999

37 001¶	37 007¶	37 013
37 002¶	37 008¶	37 014¶
37 003	37 009¶	37 015¶
37 004¶	37 010¶	37 016¶
37 005	37 011	37 017
37 006¶	37 012¶	37 018¶

37 019¶	37 069¶	37 119¶	37 169¶	37 216¶	37 263¶
37 020¶	37 070¶	37 120¶	37 170¶	37 217	37 264¶
37 021¶	37 071	37 121¶	37 171¶	37 218	37 265¶
37 022¶	37 072¶	37 122¶	37 172¶	37 219¶	37 266¶
37 023	37 073¶	37 123¶	37 173¶	37 220	37 267¶
37 024¶	37 074¶	37 124¶	37 174¶	37 221¶	37 268¶
37 025	37 075	37 125¶	37 175¶	37 222	37 269¶
37 026¶	37 076¶	37 126¶	37 176¶	37 223	37 270¶
37 027¶	37 077¶	37 127¶	37 177¶	37 224¶	37 271¶
37 028	37 078¶	37 128¶	37 178¶	37 225	37 272¶
37 029¶	37 079¶	37 129¶	37 179¶	37 226¶	37 273¶
37 030¶	37 080¶	37 130¶	37 180¶	37 227	37 274¶
37 031¶	37 081¶	37 131¶	37 181¶	37 228	37 275¶
37 032¶	37 082	37 132¶	37 182¶	37 229	37 276¶
37 033¶	37 083	37 133¶	37 183¶	37 230	37 277¶
37 034¶	37 084¶	37 134¶	37 184¶	37 231¶	37 278¶
37 035	37 085¶	37 135¶	37 185¶	37 232¶	37 279¶
37 036	37 086¶	37 136¶	37 186¶	37 233¶	37 280¶
37 037¶	37 087	37 137¶	37 187¶	37 234¶	37 281¶
37 038¶	37 088¶	37 138¶	37 188¶	37 235	37 282¶
37 039¶	37 089¶	37 139¶	37 189¶	37 236¶	37 283¶
37 040	37 090	37 140¶	37 190¶	37 237¶	37 284¶
37 041¶	37 091¶	37 141¶	37 191¶	37 238	37 285¶
37 042¶	37 092¶	37 142¶	37 192¶	37 239	37 286¶
37 043¶	37 093¶	37 143¶	37 193¶	37 240	37 287¶
37 044¶	37 094¶	37 144¶	37 194¶	37 241¶	37 288¶
37 045¶	37 095¶	37 145¶	37 195¶	37 242¶	37 289¶
37 046	37 096¶	37 146¶	37 196	37 243¶	37 290¶
37 047¶	37 097	37 147¶	37 197¶	37 244¶	37 291¶
37 048¶	37 098¶	37 148¶	37 198¶	37 245¶	37 292¶
37 049¶	37 099	37 149¶	37 199¶	37 246¶	37 293¶
37 050¶	37 100	37 150¶	37 200¶	37 247¶	37 294¶
37 051	37 101¶	37 151¶	37 201¶	37 248	37 295¶
37 052¶	37 102¶	37 152¶	37 202¶	37 249¶	37 296¶
37 053¶	37 103¶	37 153¶	37 203¶	37 250¶	37 297¶
37 054¶	37 104	37 154¶	37 204¶	37 251	37 298¶
37 055¶	37 105¶	37 155¶	37 205¶	37 252¶	37 299¶
37 056¶	37 106¶	37 156¶	37 206¶	37 253	37 300¶
37 057¶	37 107¶	37 157¶	37 207¶	37 254¶	37 301¶
37 058	37 108¶	37 158¶	37 208¶	37 255¶	37 302¶
37 059¶	37 109	37 159¶	37 209¶	37 256¶	37 303¶
37 060¶	37 110¶	37 160¶	37 210¶	37 257¶	37 304¶
37 061	37 111¶	37 161¶	37 211¶	37 258¶	37 305¶
37 062	37 112¶	37 162	37 212¶	37 259¶	37 306¶
37 063¶	37 113	37 163¶	37 213	37 260¶	37 307¶
37 064¶	37 114	37 164¶	37 214	37 261¶	37 308¶
37 065	37 115¶	37 165¶	37 215¶	37 262¶	
37 066	37 116¶	37 166¶			
37 067¶	37 117	37 167¶			
37 068¶	37 118¶	37 168¶			

TOTAL: 308

31

Class 37 Co-Co No 37 032   [*B. J. Nicoll*

Class 37 Co-Co No 37 145   [*N. E. Preed*

Class 40   1 Co-Co1 ★

Built 1958–62
Engine: English Electric 16-cyl. 16SVT Mk. 2 of 2,000 b.h.p. (1,492 kW)
Mechanical parts: English Electric
Weight: 128–34 tons
Brake force: 51 tonnes. Vacuum brake (¶dual braked)
Maximum tractive effort: 52,000 lb
Power/control equipment: English Electric. Six EE 526/5D traction motors
Route availability: 6
Maximum speed: 90 m.p.h.
Steam heating (some removed)
Previous no. series: D200–399

40 001¶	40 004¶	40 008
40 002¶	40 006¶	40 009
40 003	40 007¶	

40 010 Empress of Britain
40 011 Mauretania (s)
40 012¶ Aureol
40 013¶ Andania
40 014¶ Antonia
40 015¶ Aquitania
40 016 Campania
40 017 Carinthia
40 018 Carmania
40 019 Caronia
40 020 Franconia
40 022¶ Laconia
40 023 Lancastria
40 024¶ Lucania
40 025 Lusitania
40 027¶ Parthia
40 028¶ Samaria
40 029¶ Saxonia
40 030¶ Scythia
40 031 Sylvania
40 032 Empress of Canada
40 033¶ Empress of England
40 034¶ Accra
40 035¶ Apapa

40 036	40 038¶	40 042
40 037		40 044¶

40 046	40 100s	40 150¶
40 047¶	40 101	40 151¶
40 049	40 103	40 152¶
40 050¶	40 104¶	40 153¶
	40 105s	40 154¶
40 052¶	40 106	40 155¶
	40 107	
40 055¶		40 157¶
40 056¶	40 109s	40 158¶
40 057¶	40 110¶	40 159¶
40 058¶	40 111¶	40 160¶
40 060¶	40 112	40 161
40 061¶	40 113¶	40 162¶
40 062	40 114s	40 163¶
40 063¶	40 115	40 164¶
40 064¶	40 116	40 165¶
40 065	40 117¶	40 166¶
40 066¶	40 118¶	40 167¶
40 067¶	40 119¶	40 168¶
40 068¶	40 120	40 169¶
40 069¶	40 121	40 170¶
40 070	40 122¶	40 171¶
40 071¶		40 172¶
40 073¶	40 124¶	40 173
40 074¶	40 125	40 174¶
40 075	40 126¶	40 175
40 076¶	40 127¶	40 176¶
40 077¶	40 128¶	40 177¶
40 078¶	40 129¶	40 178¶
40 079¶	40 130¶	40 179
40 080¶	40 131¶	40 180¶
40 081¶	40 132¶	40 181¶
40 082¶	40 133¶	40 182¶
40 083¶	40 134¶	40 183
40 084¶	40 135¶	40 184
40 085¶	40 136¶	40 185¶
40 086¶	40 137¶	40 186¶
40 087	40 138	40 187
40 088	40 139	40 188¶
40 090¶	40 140¶	40 191¶
40 091¶	40 141¶	40 192¶
40 092		40 193¶
40 093¶	40 143¶	40 194¶
40 094	40 144	40 195¶
40 095¶	40 145¶	40 196¶
40 096¶	40 146¶s	40 197¶
40 097¶	40 147¶	40 198
40 098¶	40 148	40 199¶
40 099¶	40 149¶	

TOTAL: 178

Class 44   1Co-Co1★

"Peak" Class. Introduced 1959
Engine: Sulzer 12-cyl. 12LDA28-A
of 2,300 b.h.p. (1,715 kW)
Mechanical parts: BR
Weight: 133 tons
Brake force: 63 tonnes. Vacuum
brake
Maximum tractive effort:
50,000 lb
Power/control equipment:
Crompton Parkinson. Six CP171 B1
traction motors
Route availability: 7
Maximum speed: 90 m.p.h.
No train heating
Previous no. series: D1–10

44 004 Great Gable
44 007 Ingleborough
44 008 Penyghent
Scheduled for early withdrawal

TOTAL: 3

Class 45   1Co-Co1★

Uprated development of "Peak"
Class, built 1960-2
Engine: Sulzer 12-cyl. 12LDA28-B
of 2,500 b.h.p. (1,865 kW)
Mechanical parts: BR
Weight: 135 tons
Brake force: 63 tonnes. Dual
braked
Maximum tractive effort:
55,000 lb
Power/control equipment:
Crompton Parkinson. Six CP C172
A1 traction motors
Route availability: 7
Maximum speed: 90 m.p.h.
Steam heating (some isolated)
Previous no. series:
Random from D11–137

Class 45/0

45 001	45 002	45 003

45 004 Royal Irish Fusilier

45 005

45 006 Honourable Artillery
       Company

45 007	45 010	45 012
45 008	45 011	45 013
45 009		

45 014 The Cheshire Regiment

45 015	45 018	45 020
45 016	45 019	45 021s
45 017		

45 022 Lytham St. Annes
45 023 The Royal Pioneer Corps

45 024s	45 029	45 034
45 025	45 030	45 035
45 026	45 031	45 036
45 027	45 032s	45 037
45 028	45 033	45 038

45 039 The Manchester Regiment
45 040 King's Shropshire Light
       Infantry
45 041 Royal Tank Regiment

45 042

45 043 The King's Own Royal
       Border Regiment
45 044 Royal Inniskilling Fusilier
45 045 Coldstream Guardsman
45 046 Royal Fusilier

45 047s

45 048 The Royal Marines
45 049 The Staffordshire
       Regiment (The Prince of
       Wales's Own)

45 050	45 052	45 054
45 051	45 053	

45 055 Royal Corps of Transport

45 056	45 057	45 058

45 059 Royal Engineer
45 060 Sherwood Forester

45 061	45 064	45 068
45 062	45 065	45 069
45 063	45 066	45 070

Class 40 1Co-Co1 No 40 018 Carmania   [*J. E. Augustson*

Class 40 1Co-Co1 No 40 131   [*N. E. Preedy*

35

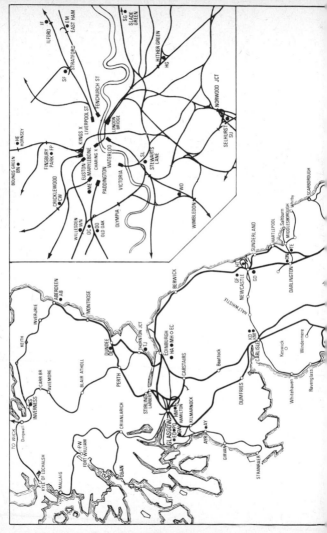

36

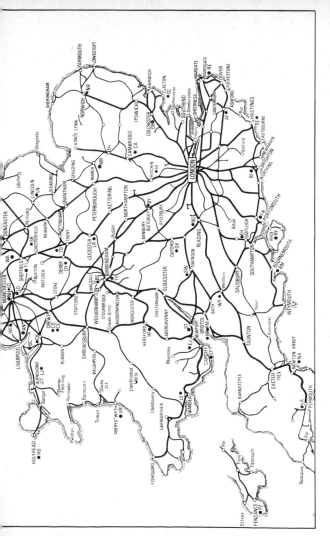

45 071	45 074	45 076	45 145	45 148	
45 072	45 075	45 077	45 146	45 149	
45 073			45 147	45 150	

TOTAL: 76   TOTAL: 50

Class 45/1   1 Co-Co1 ★

Class 45/0 without steam heating
Weight: 133 tons
Dual braked
Electric train heating equipment
Previous no. series:
Random from D11–137

45 101	~~45 102~~	45 103

45 104 The Royal Warwickshire
       Fusilier

45 105	45 107	45 109
45 106	45 108	45 110

45 111 Grenadier Guardsman
45 112 Royal Army Ordnance
       Corps

~~45 113~~	~~45 115~~ ✓	45 117
45 114	45 116	

45 118 The Royal Artilleryman

45 119	45 121	45 122
45 120		

45 123 The Lancashire Fusilier

45 124	45 128	45 132
45 125	45 129	45 133
~~45 126~~	45 130	45 134
45 127	45 131	

45 135 3rd Carabinier

45 136

45 137 The Bedfordshire and
       Hertfordshire Regiment
       (T.A.)

45 138	45 140	45 142
45 139	45 141	

45 143 5th Royal Inniskilling
       Dragoon Guards
45 144 Royal Signals

Class 46   1 Co-Co1 ★

Introduced 1961. Final development
of "Peak" Class
Engine: Sulzer 12-cyl. 12LDA28-B
of 2,500 b.h.p. (1,865 kW)
Mechanical parts: BR
Weight: 138 tons
Brake force: 63 tonnes. Dual
braked
Maximum tractive effort:
55,000 lb
Power/control equipment:
Brush. Six TM 73–68 Mk. 3 traction
motors
Route availability: 7
Maximum speed: 90 m.p.h.
Steam heating
Previous no. series: D138–193

46 001	46 010	46 019
46 002	46 011	46 020
	46 014	46 021
46 004	46 015	46 022
	46 016	46 023
46 006	46 017	
46 007	46 018	46 025s
46 008		
46 009		

46 026 Leicestershire and
       Derbyshire Yeomanry (s)

46 027s	46 037s	46 047
46 028s	46 038s	46 048
46 029	46 039	46 049
46 030s	46 040s	46 050s
46 031	46 041	46 051
46 032	46 042s	46 052
46 033	46 043	46 053
46 034s	46 044	46 054s
46 035	46 045	46 055
46 036	46 046	46 056

TOTAL: 51

Class 44 1Co-Co1 No 44 008 Penyghent

[B. J. Nicolle

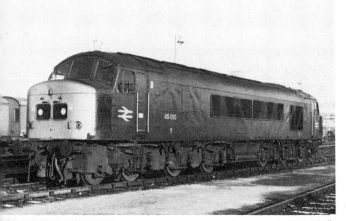

Class 45/0 1Co-Co1 No 45 010

[B. J. Nicolle

Class 47   Co-Co

Built 1962-7
Engine: Sulzer 12-cyl. 12LDA28-C of 2,580 b.h.p. (1,925 kW) (not 47 601)
Weight: 109-23 tons
Brake force: 60 tonnes. Dual braked
Maximum tractive effort:
62,000 lb (47 401-20 55,000 lb) (47 601 57,325 lb)
Power/control equipment:
Brush. Six TM 64-68 Mk. 1 or Mk. 1A traction motors
Route availability: 6
Maximum speed: 95 m.p.h.
Steam heating. Some isolated
Previous no. series:
Random from D1500-1999, D1100-1111
Further members of this class are to be converted and renumbered into Class 47/4

Class 47/0

47 001	47 026	47 048
47 002	47 027	47 049
47 003	47 028	47 050
47 004	47 029	47 051
47 005	47 030	47 052
47 006		47 053
47 007	47 032	47 054
47 008	47 033	47 055
47 009		47 056
47 010	47 035	47 059
47 011	47 036	47 060
47 012		47 061
47 013	47 038	47 063
47 014	47 039	47 064
47 015	47 040	47 066
47 016	47 041	47 068
47 017	47 042	47 069
47 018		47 070
47 019		47 072
47 020	47 045	47 074
	47 047	47 075

47 076 City of Truro
47 077 North Star
47 078 Sir Daniel Gooch
47 079 G. J. Churchward

47 080 Titan	47 087 Cyclops
47 081 Odin	47 088 Samson
47 082 Atlas	47 089 Amazon
47 083 Orion	47 090 Vulcan
47 085 Mammoth	47 091 Thor
47 086 Colossus	

47 093	47 115	47 142
47 094	47 116	47 143
47 095	47 117	47 144
47 096	47 118	47 145
47 097	47 119	47 146
47 098	47 120	47 147
47 099	47 121	47 148
47 100	47 122	47 149
47 101	47 123	47 150
47 102	47 124	47 151
47 103	47 125	47 152
47 104	47 128	47 155
47 105	47 129	47 156
47 106	47 130	47 157
47 107	47 131	47 158
47 108	47 134	47 159
47 109	47 135	47 160
47 110	47 136	47 162
47 111	47 137	47 163
47 112	47 138	
47 113	47 140	47 165
47 114	47 141	47 166

47 168

47 170 County of Norfolk
47 171
47 172 County of Hertfordshire

47 173	47 177	47 178
47 174		47 179
47 175		

47 180 County of Suffolk

47 181	47 182	47 183

47 184 County of Cambridgeshire

47 185	47 187	47 189
47 186	47 188	47 190

Class 46 1Co-Co1 No 46 021   [*B. J. Nicolle*

Class 47/3 Co-Co No 47 352   [*B. J. Nicolle*

41

Class 47/4 Co-Co No 47 510 Fair Rosamund

[R. W. Hinton]

47 191	47 226	47 265	47 322	47 342	47 362
47 192	47 227	47 266	47 323	47 343	47 363
47 193	47 228	47 267	47 324	47 344	47 364
47 194	47 229	~~47 268~~	47 325	47 345	47 365
47 195	47 230	47 269	47 326	47 346	47 366
47 196	47 231	47 270	47 327	47 347	47 367
47 197	47 232	47 271	47 328	47 348	47 368
47 198	47 233	47 272	47 329	47 349	47 369
47 199	47 234	47 273	47 330	47 350	47 370*
47 200	47 235	47 274	47 331	47 351	47 371
47 201	47 236	47 275	47 332	47 352	47 372
47 202	47 237	47 276	47 333	47 353	47 373†
47 203	47 238	47 277†	47 334	47 354	47 374
47 204	47 239	47 278	47 335	47 355	47 375
47 205	47 240	47 279	47 336	47 356	47 376
~~47 206~~	~~47 241~~	47 280	47 337	47 357	47 377
~~47 207~~	47 242	47 281	47 338	47 358	47 378
	47 243	47 282	47 339	47 359	47 379*
~~47 209~~	47 244	47 283	47 340	47 360	47 380
47 210	47 245	47 284	47 341	47 361	47 381
47 211	47 246	47 285			

Class 47/3 section:

47 212	47 247	47 286
47 213	47 248	47 287
47 214	47 249	47 288
47 215	47 250	47 289
47 216	47 251	47 290
47 217	47 252	47 291
47 218	47 254	47 292
47 219	47 255	47 293
47 220	47 256	47 294
47 221	47 257	47 295
47 222	47 258	47 296
47 223	47 262	47 297
47 224	47 263	47 298
~~47 225~~	47 264	

TOTAL: 263

Class 47/3   Co-Co

Class 47 locomotives without train heating

Weight: 112 tons (*fitted with mu control gear) (†fitted with remote slow speed control)
Previous no. series: D1782–1900

47 301	47 308	47 315
47 302	47 309	47 316
47 303	47 310	47 317
47 304	47 311	47 318
47 305	47 312	47 319
47 306	47 313	47 320
47 307	47 314	47 321

TOTAL: 81

Class 47/4   Co-Co

Class 47 locomotives with electric or dual train heating. Twelve locomotives to be converted to Class 47/7 and further conversions from Class 47/0 to be added to Class 47/4.

Weight: 120–5 tons
Previous no. series:
Random from D1500–1999

47 401	47 418	47 435
47 402	47 419	47 436
47 403	47 420	47 437
47 404	47 421	47 438
47 405	47 422	47 439
47 406	47 423	47 440
47 407	~~47 424~~	47 441
47 408	47 425	47 442
47 409	47 426	47 443
47 410	47 427	47 444
47 411	47 428	47 445
47 412	~~47 429~~	47 446
47 413	47 430	47 447
47 414	47 431	47 448
47 415	47 432	47 449
47 416	47 433	47 450
47 417	47 434	47 451

Class 47/7 Co-Co No 47 702 Saint Cuthbert

[*N. E. Preed*

Class 47/9 Co-Co No 47 901

[*B. J. Nicoll*

44

47 452	47 462	47 472
47 453	47 463	47 473
47 454	47 464	47 474
47 455	47 465	47 475
47 456	47 466	47 476
47 457	47 467	47 477
47 458	47 468	47 478
47 459	47 469	47 479
47 460	47 470	
47 461	47 471	

47 480 Robin Hood

| 47 481 | 47 482 | 47 483 |

47 484 Isambard Kingdom Brunel

47 485	47 489	47 496
47 486	47 490	47 497
47 487	47 491	47 498
47 488	47 492	47 499

47 500 Great Western

| 47 501 | 47 503 | 47 507 |
| 47 502 | 47 505 | |

47 508 Great Britain
47 509 Albion
47 510 Fair Rosamund
47 511 Thames
47 512
47 513 Severn

47 515	47 523	47 531
	47 524	47 532
47 517	47 525	47 533
47 518	47 526	47 534
47 519	47 527	47 535
47 520	47 528	47 536
47 521	47 529	47 537
47 522	47 530	

47 538 Python

47 539	47 544	47 550
47 540	47 545	47 551
47 541	47 546	47 552
47 542	47 547	47 553
47 543	47 549	

Class 50 Co-Co No 50 003 Temeraire [*B. J. Nicolle*

47 555–50 016

47 555 The Commonwealth Spirit
47 556 (47 020)
47 557
47 558 (47 026)
47 559 (47 028)
47 560
47 561
47 562 (47 036)
47 563
47 564 (47 038)
47 565 (47 039)
47 566
47 567
47 568 (47 045)
47 569 (47 047)
47 570 (47 048)
47 571
47 572 (47 168)
47 573 (47 173)
47 574 (47 174)
47 575 (47 175)
47 576
47 577 (47 179)
47 578 (47 181)
47 579 (47 183)
47 580 County of Essex
47 581 Great Eastern
47 582 (47 170)
47 583 (47 172)
47 584 (47 180)
47 585 (47 184)   **TOTAL: 185**

Class 47/7   Co-Co

Introduced: 1979
Locomotives modified for push-pull working. To be converted from Class 47/4 locomotives
Previous no. series: In sequence 47 493, 47 504/14, 47 495, 47 554, 47 494, 47 506, 47 516

47 701 St. Andrew
47 702 St. Cuthbert
47 703 St. Mungo
47 704 Dunedin
47 705 Lothian
47 706 Strathclyde
47 707 Holyrood
47 708 Waverley
47 709 The Lord Provost

47 710 Sir Walter Scott
47 711 William Wallace
47 712 Prince Charles Edward
                            TOTAL: 12

Class 47/9   Co-Co

Class 47 locomotive re-engined
Engine: GEC 12 RK 3 ACT of 3,300 h.p.
Weight: 116 tons
Previous no. series: D1628, 47 901

                            TOTAL: 1

Class 50   Co-Co ■
Built 1967–8. Originally leased to BR.
Engine: English Electric 16-cyl. 16CSVT of 2,700 b.h.p. (2,014 kW)
Mechanical parts: English Electric
Weight: 115 tons
Brake force: 59 tonnes. Dual braked
Maximum tractive effort: 48,500 lb
Power/control equipment: English Electric. Six 538/5A traction motors
Route availability: 6
Maximum speed: 100 m.p.h.
Electric train heating only
Previous no. series: D400–49

50 001 Dreadnought
50 002 Superb
50 003 Temeraire
50 004 St. Vincent
50 005 Collingwood
50 006 Neptune
50 007 Hercules
50 008 Thunderer
50 009 Conqueror
50 010 Monarch
50 011 Centurion
50 012 Benbow
50 013 Agincourt
50 014 Warspite
50 015 Valiant
50 016 Barham

Class 55 Co-Co No 55 018 Ballymoss [*J. E. Augustson*

Class 56 Co-Co No 56 062 [*Brian Morrison*

50 017 Royal Oak
50 018 Resolution
50 019 Ramillies
50 020 Revenge
50 021 Rodney
50 022 Anson
50 023 Howe
50 024 Vanguard
50 025 Invincible
50 026 Indomitable
50 027 Lion
50 028 Tiger
50 029 Renown
50 030 Repulse
50 031 Hood
50 032 Courageous
50 033 Glorious
50 034 Furious
50 035 Ark Royal
50 036 Victorious
50 037 Illustrious
50 038 Formidable
50 039 Implacable
50 040 Leviathan
50 041 Bulwark
50 042 Triumph
50 043 Eagle
50 044 Exeter
50 045 Achilles
50 046 Ajax
50 047 Swiftsure
50 048 Dauntless
50 049 Defiance
50 050 Fearless

TOTAL: 50

Class 55   Co-Co

Introduced 1961. Production version of "Deltic" prototype locomotive
Engines: Two 18-cyl. Napier "Deltic" 18–25 of 1,650 b.h.p. Total 3,300 b.h.p. (2,462 kW)
Mechanical parts: English Electric
Weight: 103 tons
Brake force: 51 tonnes. Dual braked
Maximum tractive effort: 50.000 lb

Power/control equipment:
English Electric. Six EE 538 traction motors
Route availability: 5
Maximum speed: 100 m.p.h.
Fitted with dual train-heating equipment
Previous no. series: D9000–9021

55 002 The King's Own Yorkshire Light Infantry
55 003 Meld
~~55 004~~ Queen's Own Highlander
55 005 The Prince of Wales's Own Regiment of Yorkshire
~~55 006~~ The Fife & Forfar Yeomanry
55 007 Pinza
~~55 008~~ The Green Howards
55 009 Alycidon
~~55 010~~ The King's Own Scottish Borderer
55 011 The Royal Northumberland Fusiliers
55 012 Crepello
55 013 The Black Watch
55 014 The Duke of Wellington's Regiment
55 015 Tulyar
55 016 Gordon Highlander
55 017 The Durham Light Infantry
55 018 Ballymoss
~~55 019~~ Royal Highland Fusilier

55 021 Argyll & Sutherland Highlander
55 022 Royal Scots Grey

TOTAL: 20

Class 56   Co-Co

Introduced 1976. Still in production. Nos. 56 001–30 built in Romania; 56 031–120 built BREL
Engine: GEC Diesels 16-cyl. 16RK3CT of 3,250 b.h.p. (2,460 kW)
Mechanical parts:
BR/Brush/Electroputere
Weight: 126 tons

Brake force: 60 tonnes. Air braked
Maximum tractive effort:
49,456 lb
Power/control equipment:
Brush. Six TM 76–32 traction motors
Route availability: 7
Maximum speed: 80 m.p.h.
No train heating

56 001	56 041	56 081
56 002	56 042	56 082
56 003	56 043	56 083
56 004	56 044	56 084
56 005	56 045	56 085
56 006	56 046	56 086
56 007	56 047	56 087
56 008	56 048	56 088
56 009	56 049	56 089
56 010	56 050	56 090
56 011	56 051	56 091
56 012	56 052	56 092
56 013	56 053	56 093
56 014	56 054	56 094
56 015	56 055	56 095
56 016	56 056	56 096
56 017	56 057	56 097
56 018	56 058	56 098
56 019	56 059	56 099
56 020	56 060	56 100
56 021	56 061	56 101
56 022	56 062	56 102
56 023	56 063	56 103
56 024	56 064	56 104
56 025	56 065	56 105
56 026	56 066	56 106
56 027	56 067	56 107
56 028	56 068	56 108
56 029	56 069	56 109
56 030	56 070	56 110
56 031	56 071	56 111
56 032	56 072	56 112
56 033	56 073	56 113
56 034	56 074	56 114
56 035	56 075	56 115
56 036	56 076	56 116
56 037	56 077	56 117
56 038	56 078	56 118
56 039	56 079	56 119
56 040	56 080	56 120

TOTAL: 120

Class 253

Power cars for High Speed Train. Built 1976–7 for Western Region London–Bristol/South Wales services and 1979–80 for West of England services. Used as pairs with Mk. III coaches coupled between them in units 253 001–27. Complete units listed in DMU section.
Engine: Paxman Valenta 12-cyl. 12RP200L V-type of 2,250 b.h.p. (1,680 kW).
Mechanical parts: BREL
Weight: 66 tons
Power/control equipment:
Brush. Four traction motors driving through a cardan shaft with flexible couplings and single reduction gearing
Maximum speed: 125 m.p.h.

W43002	W43020	W43038
W43003	W43021	W43039
W43004	W43022	W43040
W43005	W43023	W43041
W43006	W43024	W43042
W43007	W43025	W43043
W43008	W43026	W43044
W43009	W43027	W43045
W43010	W43028	W43046
W43011	W43029	W43047
W43012	W43030	W43048
W43013	W43031	W43049
W43014	W43032	W43050
W43015	W43033	W43051
W43016	W43034	W43052
W43017	W43035	W43053
W43018	W43036	W43054
W43019	W43037	W43055

TOTAL: 54

Class 254

Power cars for High Speed Train. Introduced 1977 for Eastern Region East Coast main line services. Used in

Class 253 IC 125 unit with power car No. W43121 leading.

[C. J. Marsden

pairs with Mk. III coaches coupled between them in units 254 001–32 Complete units listed in DMU section

Engine: Paxman Valenta 12-cyl. 12RP200L V-type of 2,250 b.h.p. (1,680 kW).

Mechanical parts: BREL

Weight: 66 tons

Power/control equipment: Brush. Four traction motors driving through a cardan shaft with flexible couplings and single reduction gearing

Maximum speed: 125 m.p.h.

E43056	E43079	E43102
E43057	E43080	E43103
E43058	E43081	E43104
E43059	E43082	E43105
E43060	E43083	E43106
E43061	E43084	E43107
E43062	E43085	E43108
E43063	E43086	E43109
E43064	E43087	E43110
E43065	E43088	E43111
E43066	E43089	E43112
E43067	E43090	E43113
E43068	E43091	E43114
E43069	E43092	E43115
E43070	E43093	E43116
E43071	E43094	E43117
E43072	E43095	E43118
E43073	E43096	E43119
E43074	E43097	W43120*
E43075	E43098	W43121*
E43076	E43099	E43122†
E43077	E43100	E43123†
E43078	E43101	

*Spare power cars for WR Class 253 sets delivered 1977
†Spare power cars for Class 254 units

TOTAL: 68

Class 253

Further power cars for WR Paddington–West of England services.

Introduced: 1979
*Spare vehicle
Power/control equipment: GEC

W43124*	W43134	W43144
W43125	W43135	W43145
W43126	W43136	W43146
W43127	W43137	W43147
W43128	W43138	W43148
W43129	W43139	W43149
W43130	W43140	W43150
W43131	W43141	W43151
W43132	W43142	W43152
W43133	W43143	

TOTAL: 29

Class 254

Further power cars for ER services
Introduced: 1980
Power control equipment: Brush

E43153	E43156	E43159
E43154	E43157	E43160
E43155	E43158	

Class 253

Further power cars for NE/SW services
To be introduced

W43161	W43173	W43185
W43162	W43174	W43186
W43163	W43175	W43187
W43164	W43176	W43188
W43165	W43177	W43189
W43166	W43178	W43190
W43167	W43179	W43191
W43168	W43180	W43192
W43169	W43181	W43193
W43170	W43182	W43194
W43171	W43183	W43195
W43172	W43184	W43196

Class 254 DMB No Sc43090

[J. E. Augustson]

DEPARTMENTAL LOCOMOTIVES

Departmental locomotives are not shown in official stock change lists. These notes represent the latest known position. Departmental locomotives are being renumbered under Class 97 for TOPS purposes. Units which are not self-propelled are not being renumbered. *Former numbers in brackets.*

Class 42   B-B

Former "Warship" Class diesel hydraulic locomotive built at Swindon in 1958. Retained for static display at BREL, Swindon

Weight: 80 tons
Vacuum braked
818 Glory

Class 24 (97/2*)   Bo-Bo★

For details see Class 24

Test-train locomotive for Tribology Department, Railway Technical Centre, Derby
97 201* Experiment (RDB968007, 24 061)

Train pre-heating units
TDB968008 (24 054)
TDB968009 (24 142)

Class 35   B-B △

Former "Hymek" Class diesel hydraulic locomotives built by Beyer-Peacock in 1961. Not self-propelled. Stored awaiting disposal
7076   7096

Class 15   Bo-Bo

Non-powered carriage-heating units, converted from Class 15 locomotives

DB968000 (8243)
DB968001 (8233)
DB968002 (8237)
DB968003 (8203)

Class 31   AIA-AIA

Non-powered carriage heating unit converted from Class 31 locomotives

ADB968013 (31 013)
ADB968015 (31 014)

Ruston & Hornsby 0-4-0 Shunter (Class 97/0)

Introduced: 1957
Engine: Ruston & Hornsby 4-cyl. of 88 b.h.p. (68 kW)
Weight: 17 tons.
Maximum tractive effort: 9,500 lb
Transmission: Mechanical. Chain driven from gear-box
Route availability: 1

97 020 (20)

Ruston & Hornsby 0-6-0 Shunter (Class 97/0)

Introduced: 1953
Engine: Ruston & Hornsby 6-cyl. of 165 b.h.p. (124 kW)
Weight: 30 tons
Maximum tractive effort: 17,000 lb
Transmission: Electric: One BTH nose-suspended traction motor
Route availability: 1

97 650 (PWM650)
97 651 (PWM651)
97 652 (PWM652)
97 653 (PWM653)
97 654 (PWM654)

NOW IS THE TIME TO JOIN THE

RAILWAY ENTHUSIASTS SOCIETY

One of our six societies will cater for you wherever you may reside in England, Scotland or Wales, providing a regular programme of visits and tours for the young and not so young enthusiast to railway installations throughout the country.

All societies are unique in that their principal mode of travel is by *rail* from each area, allowing generous discounts to members under 18 years of age, those holding railcards and privilege tickets. Public transport and coaches are used from railheads in order to visit as many locations as possible on each tour, and with valid permits.

Our printed and illustrated journal, 'Terminus', is despatched free of charge to all members eight times per year at 6/7 weekly intervals and provides details of all society visits and railtours, visit reports, notes and news, articles, competitions, besides the very latest British Rail locomotive stock alterations.

Ordinary Membership during 1981 is £3.50 for twelve months after joining.

Family Membership (2 or more at same address) is £2.45 each for twelve months.

School Membership (5 or more joining together at the same school, youth club or similar group) is only £1.75 each for twelve months.

Complete the membership form and send away to your nearest secretary:

Cymru Enthusiasts for South Wales and the West of England:
99 Cefn Fforest Avenue, Cefn Fforest, Blackwood, Gwent NP2 1JX.

Midlands Enthusiasts for East Anglia, Central Wales and the Midlands:
7 Old Manor Close, Woodborough, Notts NG14 6DJ.

North West Enthusiasts for North Wales, the North West and Scotland (West):
22 Rochford Avenue, Whitefield, Manchester M25 7PS.

Termini Enthusiasts for Greater London and the South East:
33 High Acres, Abbots Langley, Watford WD5 0JB.

Tyne Tees Enthusiasts for North East and Scotland (East):
34 Kettleness Avenue, Dormanstoun, Redcar, Cleveland TS10 5EP.

Yorkshire Enthusiasts for Yorkshire and Humberside:
15 Exley Lane, Elland, West Yorkshire HX5 0SW.

Membership Form

Please detach or make a copy

Name in full ....

Address ....

.... Postcode ....

Telephone .... Occupation ....

Age .... Signed ....

Please make cheques and postal orders payable to The Railway Enthusiasts Society Limited. If you require additional membership forms for your friends please indicate the number required here.................

De Luxe society badges available for an additional fee of only 65p.

Class 97/1   0–6–0

For details see Class 08

RDB968020 Pluto (08 267)
97 801 (08 600)

Class 08   0–6–0

Former Class 08 locomotives converted to non-powered snowploughs

ADB968010 (08 117)
ADB968011 (08 119)
ADB968012 (08 111)
ADB968017 (08 048)
ADB968018 (08 065)
ADB968019 (08 066)

Mobile Load Bank

Former Class 84 electric locomotive.
Not self-propelled

ADB968021 (84 009)

Class 97/7
Battery-electric service locomotives

Former Class 501 vehicles converted for use in tunnel electrification work
Equipment: Four 170 h.p. axle-mounted traction motors powered from 160 battery cells or from live rail. Vehicles work in pairs
Weight: 58 tons

97 701	97 703	97 705
97 702	97 704	97 706

Clas 97/2 Bo-Bo departmental locomotive No 97 201 Experiment   [A. O. Wynn

ELECTRIC LOCOMOTIVES

Electric locomotives on BR were originally numbered in two series. Those built to BR designs were numbered from E3000 for a.c. units and from E5000 for d.c. units. Earlier locomotives built to pre-Nationalisation designs were numbered in the 20000 series. To allow for computerisation, an entirely new five figure numbering scheme was introduced in 1972.

In this new system, the locomotive class number is followed by an individual identification number and the book lists locomotives in the new number order.

The headings to each class show the type designation or class the manufacturers of main components, the type of train heating, and the previous number series.

Wheel arrangements of electric (and diesel) locomotives are described by a development of the Continental notation. This calculates by axles and not by wheels, and uses letters instead of numerals to denote driving axles (''A''=1, ''B''=2, ''C''=3, etc.) and numerals only for non-powered axles.

If all axles on a bogie or frame unit are individually powered, a suffix letter ''o'' is added to the descriptive letter. Thus BR electric locomotive No. 73 001 is shown as a Bo-Bo, indicating that it has two four-wheel bogies, each axle of which has an individual traction motor.

Class 86/0 Bo-Bo No 86 019

[R. L. Sewell]

Class 73 Bo-Bo

Electro-diesel locos built 1962* (1965) to operate from SR 750 V. d.c. third rail or on diesel engine
Equipment: English Electric 4-cyl. type 4 SRKT Mk.2 600 b.h.p. diesel engine; four English Electric 542A traction motors
Total h.p.: Electric 2,450, Diesel 600
Mechanical parts: BR, English Electric
Weight: *75 tons, 76 tons
Brake force: 31 tons. Dual braked and EP braking
Maximum tractive effort: 42,000 lb
Route availability: 6
Maximum speed: *80, 90 m.p.h.

*Class 73/0

73 001	73 003	73 005
73 002	73 004	73 006

TOTAL: 6

Class 73/1

73 101	73 115	73 129
73 102	73 116	73 130
73 103	73 117	73 131
73 104	73 118	73 132
73 105	73 119	73 133
73 106	73 120	73 134
73 107	73 121	73 135
73 108	73 122	73 136
73 109	73 123	73 137
73 110	73 124	73 138
73 111	73 125	73 139
73 112	73 126	73 140
73 113	73 127	73 141
73 114	73 128	

73 142 Broadlands

TOTAL: 42

Class 73/1 Bo-Bo electro-diesel No 73 107 *[J. E. Augustson*

Class 76 Bo-Bo No 76 016

[B. J. Nicolle]

58

Class 76   Bo-Bo

Built 1950 for Manchester–Sheffield
1,500 V. d.c. overhead electrification.
Locomotives fitted with train air
brakes (¶ or ●) are also equipped for
multiple-unit operation with other
Class 76 locomotives
Equipment: Four Metro-Vick 186
traction motors of 1,300 h.p. (970
kW)
Mechanical parts: BR
Maximum rail h.p.: 3,300
Weight: 87/88 tons
Brake force: 43 tonnes. Vacuum
brake (¶ Dual braked. ● Air braked)
Maximum tractive effort:
45,000 lb
Route availability: 8
Maximum speed: 65 m.p.h.
No train heating
Previous no. series:
E26001–26057

76 003s		
76 006¶	76 013¶	76 024¶
76 007¶	76 014¶	76 025¶
76 008¶	76 015¶	76 026¶
76 009¶	76 016¶	76 027¶
76 010¶	76 021¶	76 028¶
76 011¶	76 022¶	76 029¶
76 012¶	76 023¶	76 030¶

76 031 ●		
76 032 ●	76 033 ●	76 034 ●
76 035 ●		
76 036 ●s		
76 037 ●		
76 038 ●		
76 039 ●		
76 040s	76 051	76 054

TOTAL: 34

Scheduled for early withdrawal aris-
ing from proposed closure of
Manchester–Sheffield (via Woodhead) route on 1 June 1981

Class 81   Bo-Bo

Introduced 1959 for LMR Western
Lines 25 kV overhead electrification
Equipment: A.E.I. (B.T.H.). Four
A.E.I. (B.T.H.) 189 spring-borne d.c.
traction motors driving through
Alsthom quill drive. 3,200 h.p.
(2,387 kW) continuous rating
Mechanical parts: BRCW
Weight: 78 tons.
Brake force: 40 tonnes. Dual
braked
Maximum tractive effort:
50,000 lb
Route availability: 6
Maximum speed: 100 m.p.h.
Electric train heating
Previous no. series:
E3001–3023, E3096/3097

81 001	81 009	81 016
81 002	81 010	81 017
81 003	81 011	81 018
81 004	81 012	81 019
81 005	81 013	81 020
81 006	81 014	81 021
81 007	81 015	81 022
81 008		

TOTAL: 22

Class 82   Bo-Bo

Introduced in 1960 for LMR Western
Lines 25 kV electrification
Equipment: A.E.I. (M.V.) Four
A.E.I. 189 d.c. traction motors driving
through Alsthom quill drive. 3,300
h.p. continuous (2,462 kW) rating
Mechanical parts: Metropolitan
Vickers
Weight: $78\frac{1}{2}$ tons
Brake force: 38 tonnes. Dual
braked
Maximum tractive effort:
50,000 lb
Route availability: 6
Maximum speed: 100 m.p.h.
Electric train heating
Previous no. series:
E3047–3054

82 001–85 040

82 001	82 004	82 007
82 002	82 005	82 008
82 003	82 006	

TOTAL: 8

Class 83   Bo-Bo

Introduced in 1960 for LMR Western Lines 25 kV electrification
Equipment: E.E. Four English Electric 535A spring-borne d.c. traction motors driving through S.L.M. resilient drives. 2,950 h.p. (2,200 kW) continuous rating
Mechanical parts: English Electric
Weight: 75 tons
Brake force: 38 tonnes. Dual braked
Maximum tractive effort: 38,000 lb
Route availability: 6
Maximum speed: 100 m.p.h.
Electric train heating
Previous no. series:
E3024–3035, E3098–3100

83 001	83 008	83 012
83 002	83 009	83 013
83 005	83 010	83 014
83 006	83 011	83 015
83 007		

TOTAL: 13

Class 84   Bo-Bo

Introduced in 1960 for LMR Western Lines 25 kV electrification
Equipment: G.E.C. Four G.E.C. WT 501 spring-borne d.c. traction motors driving through Brown-Boveri spring drives. 3,100 h.p. (2,313 kW) continuous rating
Mechanical parts: North British
Weight: 75½ tons
Brake force: 38 tonnes. Dual braked
Maximum tractive effort: 50,000 lb
Route availability: 6

Maximum speed: 100 m.p.h.
Electric train heating
Previous no. series:
E3036–3045

84 003	84 008	84 010

TOTAL: 3

Class now withdrawn

Class 85   Bo-Bo

Introduced in 1960 for LMR Western Lines 25 kV electrification
Equipment: A.E.I. Four A.E.I. (B.T.H.) 189 d.c. traction motors driving through Alsthom quill drive. 3,200 h.p. (2387 kW) continuous rating
Mechanical parts: BR
Weight: 81 tons
Brake force: 41 tonnes. Dual braked
Maximum tractive effort: 50,000 lb
Route availability: 6
Maximum speed: 100 m.p.h.
Electric train heating
Previous no. series:
E3056–3095

85 001	85 015	85 028
85 002	85 016	85 029
85 003	85 017	85 030
85 004	85 018	85 031
85 005	85 019	85 032
85 006	85 020	85 033
85 007	85 021	85 034
85 008	85 022	85 035
85 009	85 023	85 036
85 010	85 024	85 037
85 011	85 025	85 038
85 012	85 026	85 039
85 013	85 027	85 040
85 014		

TOTAL: 40

Class 81 Bo-Bo No 81 003   [*A. O. Wynn*

Class 82 Bo-Bo No 82 002   [*A. O. Wynn*

Class 86   Bo-Bo

Introduced 1965 for LMR Western Lines 25 kV a.c. system
Equipment: E.E./A.E.I. Four A.E.I. type 282AZ nose-suspended traction motors. 3,600 h.p. (2,686 kW) continuous rating (Class 86/0 only)
Mechanical parts: English Electric and B.R.
Weight: 81½–82½ tons
Brake force: 40 tonnes. Dual braked
Maximum tractive effort: 58,000 lb
Route availability: 6
Maximum speed: 100 m.p.h.
Electric train heating
Previous no. series:
Random from E3101–3200

*Locomotives equipped for multiple-unit operation

Class 86/0

86 001*	86 011	86 031
86 002*	86 012	86 032*
86 003	86 013	86 033*
86 004	86 014	86 034*
86 005*	86 016	86 035*
86 006	86 017*	86 036
86 007	86 018*	86 037
86 008*	86 019	86 038*
86 009	86 030	86 039*
86 010*		

TOTAL: 28

Class 86/1

Rebuilt 1972 with BP9 bogies and four spring-borne G.E.C. G412AZ traction motors and Flexicoil suspension. 5,000 h.p. (3,730 kW) continuous rating
Weight: 85½ tons

86 101 Sir William A. Stanier FRS
86 102
86 103

TOTAL: 3

Class 86/2

Rebuilt 1972 with Flexicoil suspension and four A.E.I. type 282BZ traction motors. 4,040 h.p. (3,014 kW) continuous rating. Some with resilient wheels
Weight: 83½ tons

86 204 City of Carlisle
86 205 City of Lancaster
86 206 City of Stoke on Trent
86 207 City of Lichfield
86 208 City of Chester
86 209 City of Coventry
86 210 City of Edinburgh
86 211 City of Milton Keynes
86 212 Preston Guild
86 213 Lancashire Witch
86 214 Sanspareil
86 215
86 216 Meteor
86 217 Comet
86 218 Planet
86 219 Phoenix
86 220 Goliath
86 221 Vesta
86 222 Fury
86 223 Hector
86 224 Caledonian
86 225 Hardwicke
86 226 Mail
86 227 Lady of the Lake
86 228 Vulcan Heritage

86 229	86 230	86 231

86 232 Harold Macmillan
86 233 Sir Laurence Olivier

86234

86 235 Novelty

86 236	86 238	86 239
86 237		

86 240 Bishop Eric Treacy
86 241 Glenfiddich

86 242	86 245	86 248
86 243	86 246	86 249
86 244	86 247	

Class 83 Bo-Bo No 83 007 *[Brian Morrison*

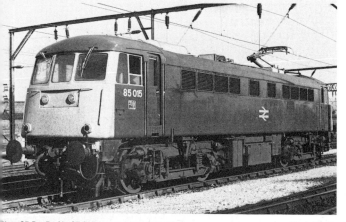

Class 85 Bo-Bo No 85 015 *[B. J. Nicolle*

86 250 The Glasgow Herald
86 251 The Birmingham Post

86 252   86 253

86 254 William Webb Ellis

86 255   86 257   86 258
86 256

86 259 Peter Pan

86 260   86 261

TOTAL: 58

Class 86/3

Introduced 1980. Class 86/0 locomotives. Fitted with Sab resilient
wheels

86 315 (86 015)*
86 320 (86 020)*
86 321 (86 021)*
86 322 (86 022)
86 323 (86 023)*
86 324 (86 024)
86 325 (86 025)*
86 326 (86 026)*
86 327 (86 027)
86 328 (86 028)*
86 329 (86 029)*

TOTAL: 11

Class 87/0   Bo-Bo

Built in 1973 for LMR West Coast
main line electrification to Glasgow.
25 kV a.c.
Equipment: G.E.C. Four G412AZ
traction motors with flexible drive.
5,000 h.p. (3,730 kW) continuous
rating
Mechanical parts: BREL
Weight: 82 tons
Brake force: 40 tonnes. Air braked
Maximum tractive effort:
58,000 lb
Route availability: 6
Maximum speed: 100 m.p.h.
Electric train heating

87 001 Royal Scot
87 002 Royal Sovereign
87 003 Patriot
87 004 Britannia
87 005 City of London
87 006 City of Glasgow
87 007 City of Manchester
87 008 City of Liverpool
87 009 City of Birmingham
87 010 King Arthur
87 011 The Black Prince
87 012 Coeur de Lion
87 013 John o'Gaunt
87 014 Knight of the Thistle
87 015 Howard of Effingham
87 016 Sir Francis Drake
87 017 Iron Duke
87 018 Lord Nelson
87 019 Sir Winston Churchill
87 020 North Briton
87 021 Robert the Bruce
87 022 Cock o' the North
87 023 Highland Chieftain
87 024 Lord of the Isles
87 025 Borderer
87 026 Redgauntlet
87 027 Wolf of Badenoch
87 028 Lord President
87 029 Earl Marischal
87 030 Black Douglas
87 031 Hal o' the Wynd
87 032 Kenilworth
87 033 Thane of Fife
87 034 William Shakespeare
87 035 Robert Burns

TOTAL: 35

Class 87/1   Bo-Bo

Class 87 locomotive built in 1974
with thyristor control equipment
Equipment: G.E.C. Four G412BZ
traction motors with flexible drive.
4,850 h.p. (3,628 kW) continuous
rating
Mechanical parts: BREL
Weight: 78 tons

87 101 Stephenson

TOTAL: 1

Class 86/1 Bo-Bo No 87 101 Stephenson

[*B. J. Nicol.*

Mobile Load Bank No ADB 968021 (formerly No 84 009)

[*E. Bulle*

LATE INFORMATION

DIESEL LOCOMOTIVES
Locomotives condemned: 06 005/8, 08 031, 08 152, 08 190/4, 08 280, 08 379, 08 789, 20 050, 25 002/5/6/7/11/28, 25 040/52/3/99, 25 163, 25 232/8/63, 44 044/7/8, 55 003, 25 155/83/97, 25 203/16/22/64, 40 042, 40 105/9/10/2/9/37, 45 008.

Withdrawn from operating stock: 03 080, 08 098, 08 435, 08 314, 08 726, 25 028, 31 265, 37 228, 40 038, 45 018/28/9, 45 030/9, 46 001/2/4/6/7/10/1/6/7/8/9/20/1/2/3, 46 015/43.

Renumbered: (new number in brackets) 47 172 (47 583), 47 139 (47 565), 47 180 (47 584), 47 047 (47 569), 47 168 (47 572), 47 174 (47 574).

ELECTRIC LOCOMOTIVES
Locomotives condemned: 84 003/10.
Renumbered: (new number in brackets) 86 011 (86 311), 86 013 (86 313) 73 101 (73 100).
Fitted mu operation: 86 313, 86 327.
Locomotives named: 73 100 Brighton Evening Argus, 86 234 J. B. Priestley O.M., 86 236 Josiah Wedgwood, 86 239 L. S. Lowry, 86 255 Penrith Beacon, 86 252 The Liverpool Daily Post, 86 253 The Manchester Guardian.

DIESEL and ELECTRIC MULTIPLE-UNITS

BR diesel multiple-units currently in service were mostly built between 1955 and 1963, and although body styles differ there is considerable mechanical standardisation. Some non-standard classes have been withdrawn in recent years, although a few odd examples survive in departmental use. Many dmu vehicles are likely to be retained until about 1990, and with this in mind, cars of several classes are being refurbished. Gloucester and Swindon-built cross-country units are having their BUT/AEC engines replaced with the more powerful Leyland 0680. Refurbished vehicles are denoted by a letter "R" adjacent to the number in this publication.

Withdrawals are confined in the main to accident-damaged vehicles or the removal of certain surplus types. In this latter category, Gloucester Class 100, and Park Royal Class 103 vehicles are likely to be withdrawn as soon as they become surplus. BRCW and Cravens Classes 104 and 105 are all scheduled for possible withdrawal before 1985. The Swindon-built Trans-Pennine units, some BRCW, Derby, Gloucester and Metro-Cammell units and all the SR diesel-electric units are likely to be replaced from 1985 to 1990. Work is in progress on the preparation of two types of possible replacement dmu, the Class 210 and the Leyland lightweight Class 140 railcar.

Unless otherwise stated, all multiple-unit trains are gangwayed within each set, with guard's and luggage compartment at the inner end of motor brake coaches, and seating is in open saloons with centre and/or end doors. The letter (L) in the headings indicates an open vehicle fitted with toilet facilities; (K) indicates a side corridor vehicle with toilet. Two standard lengths of underframe are in use, namely 56 ft. 11 in. and 63 ft. 5 in., but the actual body lengths vary by a few inches for the same type of underframe. The dimensions shown are the length over body and the overall width.

Cars are listed in numerical order by type and not by set formation. Several of the types listed are sub-divided by reason of detail or mechanical differences. For example, a certain number of cars in a class may have different seating arrangement or a different make of engine but are otherwise similar to the main batch. Such differences are noted in the heading to the class and given a reference mark by which the relevant dimensions or details and the cars concerned can be identified.

The type of set in which each class is usually formed, together with the principal manufacturer, is shown at the head of the details for that class, although it should be noted that changes may occur owing to varying operating conditions, even to the extent of coupling different makes of car in the same set or running power cars without intermediate trailers.

Most railcars are fitted with a standard mechanical transmission of a cardan shaft and freewheel to a four-speed epicyclic gearbox, and a further cardan shaft to the final drive. Where a non-standard transmission is employed, details are shown under the relevant heading. During 1979 changes have been made to the classification of dmus to bring them into line with other multiple unit stock. Thus, the Class codes for individual vehicles have been discontinued and a unit classification applied instead. For example a Pressed Steel 3-car unit is now a Class 117 unit and the vehicle codes 117/1, 117/2 and 176 no longer apply. The WR units which currently have a three-digit unit number are likely to be renumbered in due course in the standard BR six-digit unit numbering system, as now being applied to many a.c. electric units.

Electric multiple-unit trains are listed Region by Region and sub-divided into areas or lines or, in the case of the SR, into types of stock. Details of all coaches in each type of set are listed together. The dimensions shown are length and width over body and width overall. The standard coach descriptions have been used but some additional terms have been introduced to indicate detail differences. The term "semi-open" indicates a basically open vehicle divided into two smaller units by a solid transverse partition; the term "semi-compartment" indicates a vehicle with some open and some compartment accommodation. The term "saloon" has been reserved for low-density open vehicles with large windows to each seating bay, main line standard four-a-side seating and end doors, while the term "open" indicates a high density open vehicle with suburban five-a-side seating and doors to each seating bay or a high-density open vehicle with air-operated sliding doors. The letter (L) in the headings indicates an open vehicle fitted with toilet facilities, (K) indicates a side corridor vehicle with toilet and (H) indicates a vehicle with open or saloon second class accommodation, side corridor first class accommodation and a toilet. All motor coaches have driving facilities unless the heading specifically states otherwise.

Unit numbers, which are painted on the front and rear of each set, are listed where used by BR, together with the number series of individual coaches (these may have gaps due to scrapping, etc.). Where unit numbers are not used by BR, coach numbers only are shown.

The numbers of electric locomotives and multiple-units in service are correct to the time of going to press.

Information in this booklet has been checked against BR TOPS records.

Alterations to multiple-unit stock, together with information for updating this book, is shown in the Locomotive Stock Changes section of the Ian Allan monthly magazines *Modern Railways* and *Railway World*.

COUPLING CODES

Although several multiple-unit diesel sets can be coupled together and driven by one man in the leading cab, for various reasons it is not possible for all types of diesel unit to work together. In order to distinguish cars that can run together, all have painted at each end above the buffers a colour code symbol. A miniature symbol also appears on the plug socket covers. Only units bearing the same symbol may be coupled together.

- ♦ YELLOW DIAMOND
  (Departmental units only)
- ▲ RED TRIANGLE
- ● WHITE CIRCLE
- ■ BLUE SQUARE

Class 114   (2)■
Derby Works, B.R.
Motor Brake Second (DMBS)

Introduced: 1956
Engines:
Two B.U.T. (Leyland Albion) 6-cyl.
horizontal type of 230 b.h.p.
Body: 64' 6" × 9' 3"
Weight: 37 tons 10 cwt
Seats: 2nd, 62

E50001R	E50016R	E50033R
E50002R	E50017R	E50035R
E50003R	E50018R	E50036R
E50004R	E50019	E50037
E50005R	E50020R	E50038R
E50006	E50021	E50039
E50007R	E50022R	E50040R
E50008	E50023R	E50041R
E50009R	E50024R	E50042R
E50010	E50025R	E50043R
E50011R	E50026R	E50044
E50012	E50027R	E50045R
E50013R	E50030	E50046
E50014R	E50031R	E50047R
E50015R	E50032R	E50049R

Class 116 (†130)
    (3 Suburban)■
Derby Works, B.R.
Motor Brake Second (DMBS)

Introduced: 1957
Engines:
Two B.U.T. (Leyland) 6-cyl. hori-
zontal types of 150 b.h.p.
Body: 64' 0" × 9' 3". Non-
gangwayed (*gangwayed), with
side doors to each seating bay
(†converted for parcels traffic)
Weight: 36 tons
Seats: 2nd, 65

M50050R	M50051R	M50052R

M50053	M50066	M50079R
M50054	M50067R	W50080*R
M50055	M50068	M50081*
M50056	M50069R	M50082*
M50057R	M50070R	W50083*R
M50058R	M50071	W50084*R
M50059	M50072R	M50086*R
M50060	M50073	W50087*R
M50061R	M50074R	W50088*R
M50062R	M50075	W50089*R
M50063	M50076R	SC50090*
M50064R	M50077R	W50091*R
M50065R	M50078R	

Class 116 (†130)
    (3 Suburban)■
Derby Works, B.R.
Motor Second (DMS)

Introduced: 1957
Engines:
Two B.U.T. (Leyland) 6-cyl. hori-
zontal type of 150 b.h.p.
Body: 64' 0" × 9' 3". Non-
gangwayed (*gangwayed), with
side doors to each seating bay
(†converted for parcels traffic)
Weight: 36 tons
Seats: 2nd, 95 (*89)

M50092R	M50107R	M50120R
M50093R	M50108	M50121R
M50094R	M50109R	W50122*R
M50095R	M50110R	M50123*
M50097R	M50111	M50124*
M50098	M50112R	W50126*R
M50099R	M50113R	M50127
M50100	M50114	W50128*R
M50101		W50129*R
M50102	M50116	W50130*R
M50103	M50117R	W50131*R
M50104	M50118R	SC50132*
M50105R	M50119	W50133*R
M50106		

Class 111 (2)■
Metropolitan-Cammell
Motor Brake Second (DMBS)
Introduced: 1957
Engines:
Two Rolls-Royce 6-cyl. horizontal
type of 180 b.h.p.
Body: 57' 0" × 9' 3"
Weight: 33 tons
Seats: 2nd, 52

E50134R	E50136R	E50137R
E50135R		

Class 101 (4)■
Metropolitan-Cammell
Motor Composite (L) (DMC)
Introduced: 1956
Engines:
Two B.U.T. (A.E.C.) 6-cyl. horizontal
type of 150 b.h.p.
Body: 57' 0" × 9' 3"
Weight: 32 tons
Seats: 1st, 12; **2nd,** 53(45*) †2nd,
65

SC50138*	SC50143*	SC50148*
E50139*	SC50114*R	E50149*
E50140*R		E50150*
SC50141*R	SC50146*R	E50151*R
E50142*	SC50147*	

Class 101 (2)■
Metropolitan-Cammell
Motor Brake Second (DMBS)
Introduced: 1956
Engines:
Two B.U.T. (A.E.C.) 6-cyl. horizontal
type of 150 b.h.p.
Body: 57' 0" × 9' 3"
Weight: 32 tons
Seats: 2nd, 52

E50153	E50154R	E50156R
	E50155R	E50157

Class 101 (2)■
Metropolitan-Cammell
Motor Composite (DMC)
(†Second) (L) (DMS)
Introduced: 1956
For details see E50138

SC50158	E50160	E50162R
SC50159R	E50161R	SC50163

Class 101 (2)■
Metropolitan-Cammell
Motor Brake Second (DMBS)
Introduced: 1957
For details see E50152

E50164	E50166R	E50167R
E50165		

Class 101 (2‡ or 4)
Metropolitan-Cammell
Motor Composite (L) (DMC)
Introduced: 1957
For details see E50138

E50168‡	E50179R	E50188R
E50169†R	E50180	SC50189
E50170‡	E50181	E50191R
E50171‡R	E50182R	SC50192R
SC50172	E50183	E50193R
SC50174R	SC50184	SC50194
SC50175R	SC50185	E50195R
SC50176	SC50186R	E50196R
E50177	SC50187R	SC50197
E50178R		

Class 101 (2)■
Metropolitan-Cammell
Motor Brake Second (DMBS)
Introduced: 1957
For details see E50152

E50198R	M50203R	M50208R
E50199R	E50204R	E50209R
E50200	E50205	E50210
E50201R	M50206R	E50211
E50202R	E50207R	E50212

E50214R	E50221R	M50228
E50215R	M50222R	E50229R
E50216R	E50223	E50230R
E50217R	E50224R	E50231
E50218R	E50225R	E50232R
E50219R	E50226R	E50233R
E50220R	E50227R	

Class 101 (4) ▨
Metropolitan-Cammell
Motor Composite (L) (DMC)
Introduced: 1957
For details see E50138

SC50234*	SC50239*	SC50243*
E50235*R	E50240*R	E50244*
M50237	SC50241*	SC50245*
E50238*	SC50242*	

Class 101 (2) ■
Metropolitan-Cammell
Motor Brake Second (DMBS)
Introduced: 1957
For details see E50152

E50246R	E50247	E50248

Class 101 (2) ■
Metropolitan-Cammell
Motor Brake Second (DMBS)
Introduced: 1957
For details see E50152

E50250R	SC50254R	E50257R
E50251R	E50255R	E50258R
E50252R	E50256	E50259R
E50253		

Class 101 (2) ■
Metropolitan-Cammell
Motor Composite (L) (DMC)
Introduced: 1957
For details see E50138

SC50260	SC50264R	E50267R
E50261R	E50265	SC50268
E50262	E50266	SC50269
E50263R		

Class 111 (3) ■
Metropolitan-Cammell
Motor Composite (L) (DMC)
Introduced: 1957
Engines:
Two Rolls-Royce 6-cyl. horizontal type of 180 b.h.p.
Body: 57' 0" × 9' 3"
Weight: 33 tons
Seats: 1st, 12; 2nd, 53

E50270R	E50274R	E50277
E50271R	E50275	E50278
E50272	E50276R	E50279R
E50273R		

Class 111 (3) ■
Metropolitan-Cammell
Motor Brake Second (DMBS)
Introduced: 1957
For details see E50134

Gloucester Class 100 two-car unit at Guide Bridge.

[*B. J. Nicolle*

Park Royal Class 103 two-car unit at Towyn

[*J. Scrace*

E50280	E50283	E50287R
E50281R	E50284	E50288R
E50282	E50286R	E50289R

Class 101 (3 or 2*)■
Metropolitan-Cammell
Motor Brake Second (DMBS)
Introduced: 1957 (1958†)
For details see E50152

SC50290	M50305†R	M50313†
E50291	M50306†R	M50314†
SC50292	M50307†	M50315†
E50293*R	M50308†	M50316†
E50294*R	M50309†R	M50317†R
E50295*R	M50310†	M50318†
E50296*R	M50311†R	W50319R
M50303†R	M50312†	M50320†
W50304†R		

Class 101 (3)■
Metropolitan-Cammell
Motor Composite (DMC)
(†Second DMS) (L)
Introduced: 1958
For details see E50138

M50321†	M50327†R	M50333†
M50322R	M50328†R	M50334
M50323†	W50329†R	W50335†R
M50324†R	M50330R	M50336†R
M50325†	M50331†	M50337
M50326†R	M50332†	M50338†R

Class 100 (2)■
Gloucester R.C. & W. Co.
Motor Brake Second (DMBS)
Introduced: 1957
Engines:
Two B.U.T. (A.E.C.) 6-cyl. horizontal type of 150 b.h.p.
Body: 57' 6" × 9' 3"

Weight: 30 tons
Seats: 2nd, 52
*Fitted with C.A.V. Ltd. automatic gear change equipment

M50340	M50349	M50354
M50342	M50350	M50355
M50343	M50351	M50356
E50346	M50352	M50358*
M50348	M50353	

Class 105 (2)■
Cravens
Motor Brake Second (DMBS)
Introduced: 1956
Engines:
Two B.U.T. (Leyland) 6-cyl. horizontal type of 150 b.h.p.
Body: 57' 6" × 9' 2"
Weight: 29 tons
Seats: 2nd, 52

E50359	E50363	E50367
E50360	E50364	E50368
E50361	E50365	E50369
E50362	E50366	E50370

Class 105 (2)■
Cravens
Motor Brake Second (DMBS)
Introduced: 1956
For details see E50249

E50371*	E50379*	M50387*
M50372*	E50380*	M50388*
E50373*	E50381*	M50389*
M50374*	E50382*	M50390*
E50375*	E50383*	M50391*
E50376*	E50384*	M50392*
E50377*	M50385*	M50393*
E50378*	E50386*	

Class 103 (2) ■
Park Royal Vehicles
Motor Brake Second (DMBS)

Introduced: 1957
Engines:
Two B.U.T. (A.E.C.) 6-cyl. horizontal type of 150 b.h.p.
Body: 57' 6" × 9' 3"
Weight: 33 tons 10 cwt
Seats: 2nd, 52

M50395	M50402	M50405
M50398	M50403	M50408
M50399	M50404	M50409
M50400		

Class 104 (3) ■
Birmingham R. C. & W. Co.
Motor Brake Second (DMBS)

Introduced: 1957
Engines:
Two B.U.T. (Leyland) 6-cyl. horizontal type of 150 b.h.p.
Body: 57' 6" × 9' 3"
Weight: 31 tons
Seats: 2nd, 52

M50420	M50422	M50423
M50421		

Class 104 (3) ■
Birmingham R. C. & W. Co.
Motor Composite (DMC)
(*Second DMS) (L)

Introduced: 1957
Engines:
Two B.U.T. (Leyland) 6-cyl. horizontal type of 150 b.h.p.
Body: 57' 6" × 9' 3"
Weight: 31 tons
Seats: 1st, 12; 2nd, 54 (†51), *2nd, 66

M50424*	M50426*	M50427*
M50425*		

Class 104 (3) ■
Birmingham R. C. & W. Co.
Motor Brake Second (DMBS)

Introduced: 1957
For details see M50420

M50428	M50447	M50464
M50429	M50448	M50465
M50430	M50449	M50466
M50431	M50450	M50467
M50432	M50451	M50468
M50433	M50452	M50469
M50434	M50453	M50470
M50435	M50454	M50471
M50436	M50455	M50472
M50437	M50456	M50473
M50439	M50457	M50474
M50440	M50458	M50475
M50442	M50459	M50476
M50443	M50460	M50477
M50444	M50461	M50478
M50445	M50462	M50479
M50446	M50463	

Class 104 (3) ■
Birmingham R. C. & W. Co.
Motor Composite (DMC)
(*Second DMS) (L)

Introduced: 1957
For details see M50424

M50480*	M50491*	M50502
M50481*	M50492*	M50503
M50482*	M50493	M50504
M50483*	M50494	M50505
M50484*	M50496	M50506*
M50485*	M50497	M50507*
	M50498	M50508
M50487*	M50499	M50509
M50488*	M50500	M50510
M50490*	M50501	M50511

M50512	M50520	M50526
M50514	M50521	M50527
M50515	M50522	M50528
M50516	M50523	M50529
M50517	M50524	M50530
M50518	M50525	M50531
M50519		

Class 104 (2)■
Birmingham R. C. & W. Co.
Motor Brake Second (DMBS)
Introduced: 1958
For details see M50420

M50532	M50536	M50539
M50533	M50537	M50540
M50534	M50538	M50541
M50535		

Class 104 (4)■
Birmingham R. C. & W. Co.
Motor Composite (L) (DMC)
Introduced: 1958
For details see M50424

E50542*	E50560†	M50577†
E50543†	E50561†	E50578†
E50544†	E50562†	E50579†
E50545†	E50563†	E50580†
E50546†	E50564†	M50581†
E50547†	M50565†	E50582†
E50548†	E50566†	E50583†
E50549†	E50567†	E50584†
E50550†		E50585†
E50551†	E50570†	E50586†
	M50571†	E50587†
E50553†	E50572†	E50588†
E50554†	E50573†	E50589†
E50555†	E50574†	E50590†
E50556†	E50575†	E50591†
E50557†	E50576†	E50593†

Class 104 (2)■
Birmingham R. C. & W. Co.
Motor Brake Second (DMBS)
Introduced: 1958
For details see M50420

E50594	E50596	E50598
E50595	E50597	

Class 108 (2 or 3*)■
Derby Works, B.R.
Motor Brake Second (DMBS)
Introduced: 1958
Engines:
Two B.U.T. (Leyland) 6-cyl. horizontal type of 150 b.h.p.
Body: 57' 6" × 9' 2"
Weight: 29 tons
Seats: 2nd, 52

E50599	E50610R	E50621*R
E50601R	E50612R	E50622*R
E50602	E50613R	E50623*R
E50603R	E50614R	E50624*R
E50604R	E50616R	M50625
E50605R	E50617R	E50626
E50606R	E50618R	E50627
E50607R	E50619R	E50628
E50608R	E50620*R	E50629R
E50609R		

Class 108 (3* or 4)■
Derby Works, B.R.
Motor Composite (L) (DMC)
Introduced: 1958
Engines:
Two B.U.T. (Leyland) 6-cyl. horizontal type of 150 b.h.p.
Body: 57' 6" × 9' 2"
Weight: 28 tons
Seats: 1st, 12; 2nd, 50 (52†, 53‡)

E50630R	E50636	E50642*R
E50631R	E50637R	E50643*R
E50632R	E50638R	E50644*R
E50633R	E50639R	E50645*R
E50634	E50641R	E50646*R
E50635		

Weight: 36 tons (36 tons 7 cwt*)
Seats: 1st, 18; 2nd, 16

M50696	W50712	W50728
M50697	M50713	M50729
W50698	M50714	M50730
W50699	W50715	M50731
W50700	M50716	M50732
W50701	M50717	W50733
W50702	M50718	M50734
M50703	M50719	M50735
M50704	M50720	M50736R
W50705	M50721	M50737
W50706	W50722	M50738
W50707	W50723	M50739
W50708	M50724	M50741
M50709	M50725	M50742
W50710	M50726	M50743
W50711	M50727	M50744

Class 120   (3 Cross Country) ■
Swindon Works, B.R.
Motor Second (L) (DMBS)
Introduced: 1957
Engines:
Two B.U.T. (A.E.C.) (Leyland*) 6-cyl. horizontal type of 150 b.h.p.
Body: 64' 6" × 9' 3"
Weight: 36 tons 10 cwt
Seats: 2nd, 68

W50647	M50663	M50679
M50648	W50664	M50680
W50649	W50665	W50681
M50650	W50666	M50682
M50651	M50667	M50683
M50652	M50668	M50684
W50653	M50669	M50685
M50654R	M50670	W50686
M50655	M50671	M50687
M50656	W50672	M50688
M50657	M50673	M50689
W50658	W50674 *	W50691
W50659	M50675	M50692R
M50660	M50676	M50693
W50661	M50677	M50694
W50662	M50678	M50695

Class 101   (3‡ or 4) ■
Metropolitan-Cammell
Motor Composite (L) (DMC)
Introduced: 1957
For details see E50138

SC50746‡	SC50748	E50750R
SC50747‡R	SC50749R	E50751

Class 105   (2† or 3) ■
Cravens
Motor Brake Second (DMBS)
Introduced: 1957
For details see E50249

M50752	M50762	M50771†
M50754	M50763	M50772†
M50755	M50764	M50773†
M50756	M50765	M50776†
M50757	M50766	M50777†
M50758	M50767	M50778†
M50759	M50768	M50779†
	M50769	M50782†
M50761	M50770	M50784†

Class 120   (3 Cross Country) ■
Swindon Works, B.R.
Motor Brake Composite (DMBC)
Introduced: 1957
Engines:
Two B.U.T. (A.E.C.) 6-cyl. horizontal type of 150 b.h.p.
Body: 64' 6" × 9' 3"

Class 105 (2* or 3) ■
Cravens
Motor Composite (DMC)
(†Second DMS) (L)
Introduced: 1957 (1958*)
Engines:
Two B.U.T. (A.E.C.) 6-cyl. horizontal type of 150 b.h.p.
Body: 57' 6" × 9' 2"
Weight: 30 tons
Seats: 1st, 12; 2nd, 51, †2nd, 63

	M50794	M50804*
M50786†	M50795	M50805*
M50787	M50796	M50806*
M50788	M50797	M50807*
M50789	M50798	M50809*
M50790	M50800	M50810*
M50791	M50801	M50812*†
M50792	M50802	M50814*
M50793	M50803	M50815*

Class 116 (†130)
(3 Suburban) ■
Derby Works, B.R.
Motor Brake Second (DMBS)
Introduced: 1957
For details see M50050

M50818R	SC50836	M50854*R
M50819†R	M50837	W50855*R
SC50820	M50838	W50856*R
M50821R	SC50839	M50857*R
SC50822	M50840	W50858*
SC50823R	SC50841	SC50859
M50824	M50842*R	M50860R
SC50825	W50843*R	M50861R
E50826R	E50844*	M50862†R
M50827R	E50845*R	M50863*
M50828	SC50846	W50864*R
SC50829	W50847*R	E50865*
SC50830R	W50848*R	M50866*R
M50831R	M50849	E50867R
M50832R	M50850R	W50868*R
M50833R	M50851*R	W50869*R
M50834*R	M50852R	M50870
M50835R	SC50853	

Class 116 (†130)
(3 Suburban) ■
Derby Works, B.R.
Motor Second (DMS)
Introduced: 1957
For details see M50092

M50871R	M50890	M50907*R
M50872†R	M50891	W50908*R
SC50873	SC50892	W50909*R
M50875R	M50893	M50910*R
SC50876R	SC50894	W50911*
SC50877		M50912R
M50878R	W50896*R	M50913R
SC50879	E50897*	M50914R
M50880R	E50898*	M50915†*R
SC50881	SC50899	M50916*
SC50882	W50900*R	W50917*R
M50883R	W50901*R	W50918*R
M50884R	M50902	M50919*R
M50885R	M50903	E50920
M50886	M50904*R	M50921*
	M50905R	W50922*R
M50888R	M50906	M50923
SC50889		

Class 108 (2) ■
Derby Works, B.R.
Motor Brake Second (DMBS)
Introduced: 1959
For details see E50599

M50924R	M50928R	M50932
M50925	M50929	M50933
M50926	M50930	M50934R
M50927	M50931	M50935R

Class 126 (6 Inter-City) ●
Swindon Works, B.R.
Motor Second (L) (DMS)
Introduced: 1959
Engines:
Two B.U.T. (A.E.C.) 6-cyl. horizontal type of 150 b.h.p.
Body: 64' 6" × 9' 3". Gangwayed

both ends, side driving compartment at one end
Weight: 38 tons
Seats: 2nd, 64

SC50936

Class 108 (2)■
Derby Works, B.R.
Motor Brake Second (DMBS)
Introduced: 1959
For details see E50599

M50938	M50954	M50970R
M50939	M50955	M50971R
M50940R	M50956	M50973R
M50941R	M50957	M50974R
M50942R	M50958	M50975R
M50943R	M50959	M50976
M50944	M50960	M50977R
M50945R	M50962	M50978R
M50947R	M50963	M50980
M50948R	M50964	M50981R
M50949R	M50965	M50982
M50950	M50966	M50983R
M50951	M50967	M50985R
M50952	M50968	M50986R
M50953	M50969R	M50987

Class 126 (6 Inter-City)●
Swindon Works, B.R.
Motor Second (L) (DMS)
Introduced: 1959
For details see SC50936

SC51008	SC51016	SC51023
SC51009	SC51017	SC51024
SC51010	SC51018	SC51025
SC51012	SC51019	SC51026
SC51013	SC51020	SC51027
SC51014	SC51021	SC51029
SC51015	SC51022	

Class 126 (3 or 6 Inter-City)●
Swindon Works, B.R.
Motor Brake Second (L) (DMBS)
Introduced: 1959
Engines:
Two B.U.T. (A.E.C.) 6-cyl horizontal type of 150 b.h.p.
Body: 64' 6" × 9' 3". (Gangwayed at both ends, side driving compartment at one end*). Outer gangways have been removed from some vehicles
Weight: 38 tons
Seats: 2nd, 52

SC51030	SC51038	SC51045
	SC51039	SC51046
SC51032	SC51040	SC51047
SC51033	SC51041	SC51048
SC51034	SC51042	SC51049
SC51035	SC51043	SC51050
SC51036	SC51044	SC51051
SC51037		

Class 119 (3 Cross Country)■
Gloucester R. C. & W. Co.
Motor Brake Composite (DMBC)
Introduced: 1958
Engines:
Two B.U.T. (A.E.C.) (Leyland*) 6-cyl horizontal type of 150 b.h.p.
Body: 64' 6" × 9' 3"
Weight: 37 tons
Seats: 1st, 18; 2nd, 16

W51052*	W51063*	W51072*
W51054*	W51064	W51073*
W51055*	W51065*	W51074
W51056*	W51066*	W51075*
M51057*	W51067*	W51076*
W51058*	W51068*	W51077*
W51059	W51069*	W51078*
W51060*	W51070*'	W51079*
W51062*	W51071*	

Birmingham RC&W Class 104 three-car unit at Stockport [*B. J. Nicolle*

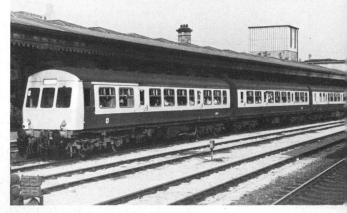

Metro-Cammell Class 111 three-car unit at Sheffield [*B. J. Nicolle*

Class 119 (3 Cross Country) ∎
Gloucester R. C. & W. Co.
Motor Second (L) (DMS)
Introduced: 1958
Engines:
Two B.U.T. (A.E.C.) (Leyland*) 6-cyl horizontal type of 150 b.h.p.
Body: 64' 6" × 9' 3"
Weight: 38 tons
Seats: 2nd, 68

W51080*	W51091*	M51100*
W51082*	W51092*	W51101*
W51083*	W51093*	W51102
W51084*	W51094*	W51103*
W51085*	W51095*	W51104*
W51086	W51096*	W51105*
W51087*	W51097*	W51106*
W51088*	W51098	W51107*
W51090*	W51099*	

Class 100 (2) ∎
Gloucester R. C. & W. Co.
Motor Brake Second (DMBS)
Introduced: 1957
For details see M50340

M51110	M51117	E51124
M51112	M51119	F51127
E51115		

Class 116 (3 Suburban)
Derby Works B.R.
Motor Brake Second (DMBS)
Introduced: 1958
For details see M50050

W51128ʀ	W51132ʀ	M51136
M51129ʀ	Mʋ1133	M51138ʀ
M51130	W51134ʀ	W51139ʀ
M51131ʀ	W51135ʀ	W51140*ʀ

Class 116 (3 Suburban) ∎
Derby Works, B.R.
Motor Second (DMS)
Introduced: 1958
For details see M50092

W51141ʀ	W51145ʀ	M51149
M51142ʀ	M51146	M51151ʀ
M51143ʀ	W51147ʀ	W51152ʀ
M51144ʀ	W51148ʀ	W51153*ʀ

Class 101 (2) ∎
Metropolitan-Cammell
Motor Brake Second (DMBS)
Introduced: 1958
For details see E50152

M51174	M51201ʀ	SC51227ʀ
M51175	M51202ʀ	SC51228
M51176	M51203ʀ	E51229ʀ
M51177ʀ	E51204ʀ	E51230ʀ
M51178ʀ	E51205	SC51231
M51179ʀ	E51206ʀ	SC51232ʀ
M51180	E51207	SC51233
M51181ʀ	E51208ʀ	SC51234
M51182ʀ	E51209ɴ	SC51235ʀ
M51183ʀ	E51210	E51236
M51184ʀ	E51211	SC51237ʀ
M51185	E51212ʀ	SC51239
M51186	E51213	SC51240
M51187ʀ	E51214ʀ	SC51241
M51188ʀ	E51215ʀ	SC51242
M51189ʀ	E51216ʀ	SC51243ʀ
M51190	E51217ʀ	SC51244
M51191	E51218	SC51245
M51192	E51219	E51246
M51193	E51220ʀ	E51247
M51194	E51221	SC51248ʀ
M51196	E51222ʀ	SC51249
M51197	E51223ɴ	SC51250ʀ
M51198ʀ	SC51224	SC51251
M51199	E51225ʀ	E51252
M51200ʀ	E51226	SC51253

Class 105 (2)■
Cravens
Motor Brake Second (DMBS)
Introduced: 1958
For details see E50249

E51254	E51271	E51286
E51255	E51272	E51287
E51256	E51273	E51288
E51257	E51274	E51289
E51258	E51275	E51290
E51259	E51276	E51291
E51260	E51277	E51292
E51261	E51278	E51293
E51262	E51279	E51294
E51263	E51280	E51295
E51265	E51281	E51296
E51266	E51282	E51297
E51267	E51283	E51298
E51268	E51284	E51299
E51269	E51285	E51301
E51270		

Class 118 (3 Suburban)■
Birmingham R. C. & W. Co.
Motor Brake Second (DMBS)
Introduced: 1960
Engines:
Two B.U.T. (Leyland) 6-cyl horizontal type of 150 b.h.p.
Body: 64' 0" × 9' 3". Gangwayed, with side doors to each seating bay
Weight: 36 tons
Seats: 2nd, 65

W51302	W51307	W51312
W51303	W51308	W51313
W51304	W51309	W51314
W51305	W51310	W51315
W51306	W51311	W51316

Class 118 (3 Suburban)■
Birmingham R. C. & W. Co.
Motor Second (DMS)
Introduced: 1960
Engines:
Two B.U.T. (Leyland) 6-cyl horizontal type of 150 b.h.p.
Body: 64' 0" × 9' 3". Gangwayed, with side doors to each seating bay
Weight: 36 tons
Seats: 2nd, 89

W51317	W51322	W51327
W51318	W51323	W51328
W51319	W51324	W51329
W51320	W51325	W51330
W51321	W51326	W51331

Class 117 (3 Suburban)■
Pressed Steel Co.
Motor Brake Second (DMBS)
Introduced: 1959
Engines:
Two B.U.T. (Leyland) 6-cyl. horizontal type of 150 b.h.p.
Body: 64' 0" × 9' 3". Gangwayed, with side doors to each seating bay
Weight: 36 tons
Seats: 2nd, 65

W51332R	W51346R	W51361R
W51333	W51347R	W51362
W51334R	W51348R	W51363R
W51335R	W51349R	W51364R
W51336R	W51350R	W51365R
W51337R	W51351R	W51366R
W51338R	W51352R	W51367R
W51339R	W51353R	W51368R
W51340R	W51354R	W51369R
W51341R	W51355R	W51370R
W51342R	W51356R	W51371R
W51343R	W51358R	W51372R
W51344R	W51359R	W51373R
W51345R	W51360R	

Class 117 (3 Suburban) ■
Pressed Steel Co.
Motor Second (DMS)
Introduced: 1959
Engines:
Two B.U.T. (Leyland) 6-cyl. horizontal type of 150 b.h.p.
Body: 64′ 0″×9′ 3″. Gangwayed, with side doors to each seating bay
Weight: 36 tons
Seats: 2nd. 89

W51374R	W51388R	W51402R
W51375	W51389R	W51403R
W51376R	W51390R	W51404R
W51377R	W51391R	W51405
W51378R	W51392R	W51406R
W51379R	W51393R	W51407R
W51380R	W51394R	W51408R
W51381R	W51395R	W51409R
W51382R	W51396R	W51410R
W51383R	W51397R	W51411R
W51384R	W51398R	W51412R
W51385R	W51399R	W51413R
W51386R	W51400R	W51414R
W51387R	W51401R	W51415R

Class 108 (2) ■
Derby Works, B.R.
Motor Brake Second (DMBS)
Introduced: 1960
For details see E50599

M51416	M51419	M51422R
M51417	M51420R	M51424R
M51418	M51421R	

Engines:
Two B.U.T. (Leyland) 6-cyl. horizontal type of 150 b.h.p.
Body: 57′ 0″×9′ 3″
Weight: 32 tons
Seats: 2nd, 52

E51425*	E51440†	SC51456
E51426*R	E51441†	SC51457R
E51427*	E51442†R	SC51458R
E51428*	E51443†R	SC51459R
E51429*	E51444R	SC51460R
E51430*	W51445R	SC51461R
E51431*	W51446R	W51462
E51432*	SC51448R	W51463
E51433*	W51449R	SC51464R
E51434*	W51450R	SC51465R
E51435†	SC51451R	SC51466R
E51436†	W51452R	SC51467R
E51437†R	SC51453R	SC51468R
E51438†	SC51454R	SC51469R
E51439†	SC51455R	SC51470R

Class 105 (2) ■
Cravens
Motor Brake Second (DMBS)
Introduced: 1959
For details see E50249

E51471	SC51479	E51489
E51472	SC51480	M51490
SC51473	SC51481	
SC51474	E51482	M51492
SC51475	SC51483	E51493
SC51476	E51484	
SC51477	E51485	
E51478		

Class 101 (2*, 3 or 4†) ■
Metropolitan-Cammell
Motor Brake Second (DMBS)
Introduced: 1959

Class 101 (2*, 3 or 4†) ■
Metropolitan-Cammell
Motor Composite (L) (DMC)
Introduced: 1959

Derby Class 114 two-car unit at Selby

[*J. E. Oxley*

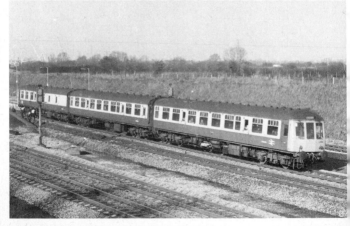

Gloucester Class 119 three-car cross country unit at Iver

[*Chris Leigh*

84

Engines:
Two B.U.T. (Leyland) 6-cyl. horizontal type of 150 b.h.p.
Body: 57' 0" × 9' 3"
Weight: 32 tons
Seats: 1st, 12; **2nd,** 53

W51495*	W51511†	SC51526R
E51496*	W51512†	SC51527R
E51497*	W51513†	SC51528R
E51498*	E51514†R	SC51529R
E51499*	W51515R	W51530
W51500*	SC51516R	SC51531
E51501*	W51517R	SC51532R
E51502*	SC51518R	W51533
E51503*	W51519	SC51534R
E51504*	SC51520R	SC51535R
W51505†	W51521R	SC51536R
E51506†R	W51522R	SC51537R
E51508†R	W51523 R	SC51538R
W51509†R	SC51524R	SC51539R
W51510†R	SC51525R	

Class 111 (3 or 2*)■
Metropolitan-Cammell
Motor Brake Second (DMBS)
Introduced: 1959 (1960*)
For details see E50134

F51541R	E51544	E51548*R
E51542	E51545R	E51549*
E51543	E51546R	E51550*R

Class 111 (3 or 2*)■
Metropolitan-Cammell
Motor Composite (L) (DMC)
Introduced: 1960
For details see E50270

E51551R	E51555R	E51558*R
E51552	E51556R	E51559*R
E51553	E51557R	E51560*R
E51554R		

Class 108 (2)■
Derby Works, B.R.
Motor Composite (L) (DMC)
Introduced: 1959
For details see E50630

M51561†R	M51566†	M51570†R
M51562†	M51567†	M51571†R
M51563†R	M51568†R	M51572†R
M51565†	M51569†	

Class 120 (3 Cross Country)■
Swindon Works, B.R.
Motor Brake Composite (L) (DMBC)
Introduced: 1961
For details see M50696

W51573*	W51576*	W51579*
W51574*	W51577*	W51580*
W51575*	W51578*	W51581*

Class 120 (3 Cross Country)■
Swindon Works, B.R.
Motor Second (L) (DMS)
Introduced: 1961
For details see W50647

W51582	W51585	W51588
W51583	W51586	W51589
W51584	W51587	W51590

Class 127 (4 Suburban)▲
Derby Works, B.R.
Motor Brake Second (DMBS)
Introduced: 1959
Engines:
Two Rolls-Royce 8-cyl horizontal type of 238 b.h.p.
Transmission:
Hydraulic. Torque converter
Body: 64' 0" × 9' 3". Non-gangwayed, side doors to each seating bay
Weight: 40 tons
Seats: 2nd, 78

M51591	M51613	M51633
M51592	M51614	M51634
M51593	M51615	M51635
M51595	M51616	M51636
M51596	M51617	M51637
M51597	M51618	M51638
M51598	M51619	M51639
M51599	M51620	M51640
M51600	M51621	
M51603	M51622	M51642
M51604	M51623	M51643
M51605	M51624	M51644
M51606	M51625	M51645
M51607	M51626	M51646
M51608	M51627	M51647
M51610	M51628	M51648
M51611	M51630	M51649
M51612		M51650

Class 115 (4 Suburban)■
Derby Works, B.R.
Motor Brake Second (DMBS)
Introduced: 1960
Engines:
Two B.U.T. (Leyland Albion) 6-cyl
horizontal type of 230 b.h.p.
Body: 64' 0" × 9' 3". Non-gang-
wayed, side doors to each seating
bay
Weight: 38 tons
Seats: 2nd, 78

M51651	M51661	M51671
M51652	M51662	M51672
M51653R	M51663	M51673
M51654	M51664R	M51674
M51655R	M51665R	M51675
M51656	M51666R	M51676
M51657	M51667	M51677R
M51658R	M51668	M51678
M51659R	M51669	M51679
M51660	M51670R	M51680R

Class 120 (3 Cross Country)■
Swindon Works, B.R.
Motor Brake Composite
(DMBC)
Introduced: 1959
For details see M50696

W51781*R SC51784* W51786*
W51782*R W51785*R SC51787*R
W51783*R

Class 120 (3 Cross Country)■
Swindon Works, B.R.
Motor Second (L) (DMS)
Introduced: 1960
For details see W50647

W51788R W51791R W51793R
SC51789R W51792R SC51794R
W51790R

Class 101 (3) ■
Metropolitan-Cammell
Motor Brake Second (DMBS)
Introduced: 1959
For details see E51425

SC51795R SC51798R SC51800
SC51796R W51799 W51801
SC51797R

Class 101 (3) ■
Metropolitan-Cammell
Motor Composite (L) (DMC)
Introduced: 1959
For details see E51495

SC51802R SC51805R SC51807R
SC51803R SC51806R W51808
SC51804R

Swindon Class 120 three-car cross country unit near Freshford [*J. R. Acton*

Swindon Class 123 motor second No E52105 leading a mixed rake [*Peter Harris*

Class 110 (3)■
Birmingham R. C. & W. Co.
Motor Brake Composite (DMBC)

Introduced: 1961
Engines:
Two Rolls-Royce Series 130D of 180 b.h.p.
Body: 57' 6" × 9' 3"
Weight: 32 tons
Seats: 1st, 12; 2nd, 33

E51809	E51816R	E51823
E51810R	E51817	E51824R
E51811	E51818R	E51825R
E51812	E51819R	E51826
E51813	E51820R	E51827
E51814	E51822	E51828
E51815R		

Class 110 (3)■
Birmingham R. C. & W. Co.
Motor Composite (L) (DMC)

Introduced: 1961
Engines:
Two Rolls-Royce Series 130D of 180 b.h.p.
Body: 57' 6" × 9' 3"
Weight: 31 tons 10 cwt
Seats: 1st, 12; 2nd, 54

E51829	E51836	E51843R
E51830	E51838R	E51844
E51831R	E51839R	E51845R
E51832R	E51840	E51846R
E51833R	E51841R	E51847
E51834	E51842	E51848
E51835		

Class 115 (4 Suburban)■
Derby Works, B.R.
Motor Brake Second (DMBS)

Introduced: 1960
For details see M51651

M51849	M51866	M51884R
M51850	M51867	M51885
M51851	M51868	M51886
M51852R	M51869	M51887R
M51853R	M51870	M51888
M51854	M51871	M51889
M51855	M51872	M51890
M51856R	M51873R	M51891R
M51857	M51874R	M51892R
M51858R	M51875	M51893
M51859	M51876	M51894
M51860	M51877	M51895
M51861	M51878	M51896
M51862	M51879R	M51897
M51863	M51880	M51898
M51864R	M51881	M51899
M51865	M51883	M51900R

Class 108 (2)■
Derby Works, B.R.
Motor Brake Second (DMBS)

Introduced: 1960
For details see E50599

M51901R	M51917	M51933
M51902R	M51918	M51934
M51903R	M51919	M51935R
M51904R	M51920	M51936R
M51905R	M51922	M51937R
M51906R		M51938R
M51907R	M51924R	M51939R
M51908R	M51925R	M51940
M51909R	M51926R	M51941
M51910	M51927	M51942R
M51911R	M51928	M51943
M51912	M51929R	M51945R
M51913R	M51930R	M51947
M51914R	M51931R	M51948R
M51916	M51932R	M51950R

Class 124 (5 Trans-Pennine)■
Swindon Works, B.R.
Motor Composite (DMC)

Introduced: 1960

Engines:
Two B.U.T. (Leyland Albion) 6-cyl
horizontal type of 230 b.h.p.
Body: 64' 6" × 9' 3"
Weight: 40 tons
Seats: 1st, 21; **2nd,** 36

E51951	E51957	E51963
E51952	E51958	E51964
E51953	E51960	E51965
E51954	E51961	E51966
E51955	E51962	E51967
E51956		

Class 124 (5 Trans-Pennine) ■
Swindon Works, B.R.
Motor Brake Second (K) (MBS)
(non-driving)
Introduced: 1960
Engines:
Two B.U.T.(Leyland Albion) 6-cyl
horizontal type of 230 b.h.p.
Body: 64' 6" × 9' 3"
Weight: 41 tons
Seats: 2nd, 48

E51969	E51976	E51981
E51973	E51978	E51982
E51974	E51979	E51983
E51975	E51980	E51984

Class 107 (3) ■
Derby Works, B.R.
Motor Brake Second (DMBS)
Introduced: 1960
Engines:
Two B.U.T. (A.E.C.) 6-cyl horizontal
type of 150 b.h.p.
Body: 58' 1" × 9' 3"
Weight: 34 tons 10 cwt

Seats: 2nd, 52

SC51985	SC51994R	SC52003
SC51986R	SC51996R	SC52004R
SC51987R	SC51997	SC52005R
SC51988	SC51998	SC52006
SC51989R	SC51999	SC52007R
SC51990R	SC52000	SC52008
SC51991R	SC52001R	SC52009R
SC51992	SC52002R	SC52010R
SC51993		

Class 107 (3) ■
Derby Works, B.R.
Motor Composite (L) (DMC)
Introduced: 1960
Engines:
Two B.U.T. (A.E.C.) 6-cyl horizontal
type of 150 b.h.p.
Body: 58' 1" × 9' 3"
Weight: 35 tons
Seats: 1st, 12; **2nd,** 53

SC52011R	SC52020R	SC52029
SC52012	SC52021	SC52030
SC52013	SC52022	SC52031R
SC52014R	SC52023R	SC52032R
SC52015	SC52024	SC52033R
SC52016R	SC52025	SC52034R
SC52017R	SC52026	SC52035R
SC52018R	SC52027R	SC52036
SC52019R	SC52028	

Class 108 (2) ■
Derby Works, B.R.
Motor Composite (L) (DMC)
Introduced: 1960
For details see E50630

M52037‡R	M52043‡R	M52049‡R
M52038‡R	M52044‡R	M52050‡R
M52039†R	M52045‡R	M52051‡R
M52040‡	M52046‡	M52052‡
M52041‡R	M52047‡R	M52053‡R
M52042‡R	M52048‡R	M52054‡R

Swindon Class 124 four-car Trans-Pennine unit at Doncaster

[*J. E. Oxley*

Swindon Class 126 unit, with end gangways removed, at Glasgow

[*C. J. M. Lofthu*

M52055‡R	M52059‡	M52063‡R
M52056‡	M52060‡R	M52064‡R
M52057‡	M52061‡	M52065‡
M52058‡	M52062‡	

Class 110 (3)■
Birmingham R.C. & W. Co.
Motor Brake Composite (DMBC)

Introduced: 1961
For details see E51809

E52066	E52069	E52072
E52067	E52070	E52073R
E52068	E52071	E52075

Class 110 (3)■
Birmingham R. C. & W. Co.
Motor Composite (L) (DMC)

Introduced: 1961
For details see E51829

E52076R	E52080	E52083
E52077	E52081	E52084
E52078R	E52082	E52085
E52079R		

Class 123 (3 or 4 Inter-City)■
Swindon Works, B.R.
Motor Brake Second (L) (DMBS)

Introduced: 1963
Engines:
Two B.U.T. (Leyland Albion) 6-cyl.
horizontal type of 230 b.h.p.
Body: 64' 11$\frac{1}{8}$" × 9' 3"
Weight: 41 tons 14 cwt
Seats: 2nd, 32

E52087	E52090	E52093
E52088	E52091	E52094
E52089	E52092	E52095

Class 123 (3 or 4 Inter-City)■
Swindon Works, B.R.
Motor Second (K) (DMS)

Introduced: 1963
Engines:
Two B.U.T. (Leyland Albion) 6-cyl.
horizontal type of 230 b.h.p.
Body: 64' 11$\frac{1}{8}$" × 9' 3"
Weight: 41 tons 9 cwt
Seats: 2nd, 56

E52096	E52099	E52103
E52097	E52100	E52104
E52098	E52102	E52105

Class 122 (*131) (1)■
Gloucester R. C. & W. Co.
Motor Brake Second (DMBS)
(DMLV*)

Introduced: 1958
Engines:
Two B.U.T. (A.E.C.) 6-cyl. horizontal
type of 150 b.h.p.
Body: 64' 6" × 9' 3". Non-
gangwayed, side doors to each
seating bay (*converted for parcels
traffic)
Weight: 36 tons
Seats: 2nd, 65

SC55000	M55006	M55012
SC55002	SC55007	SC55013*
M55003	M55009	
M55004	SC55011	SC55015*
SC55005		

Class 121 (1)■
Pressed Steel Co.
Motor Brake Second (DMBS)

Introduced: 1960

91

Engines:
Two B.U.T. (A.E.C.) (Leyland*) 6-cyl. horizontal type of 150 b.h.p.
Body: 64' 6"×9' 3". Non-gangwayed, side doors to each seating bay
Weight: 37 tons 8 cwt
Seats: 2nd, 65

W55020*R	W55026*	W55031*R
W55021	W55027	W55032*
W55022R	W55028*	W55033*
W55023*	W55029*R	W55034*R
W55024*	W55030*	
W55025R		

Class 128 (1)■
Gloucester R. C. & W. Co.
Motor Parcels Van (DMLV)
Introduced: 1959
Engines:
Two B.U.T. (Leyland Albion) 6-cyl. horizontal type of 230 b.h.p.
Body: 64' 6"×9' 3" (Non-gangwayed. From new*)
Weight: 41 tons (40 tons*)
Single car can haul a tail load. Works with Class 130. Gangways have been removed from some vehicles to which they were originally fitted

	W55991	M55994
M55989*	W55992	M55995
M55990*	M55993	

Class 114 (2)■
Derby Works, B.R.
Driving Trailer Composite (L) (DTC)
Introduced: 1956
Body: 64' 6"×9' 3"
Weight: 29 tons 10 cwt
Seats: 1st, 12; **2nd,** 62

E56001	E56006	E56011
E56002R	E56007R	E56012R
E56003R	E56008R	E56013
E56004R	E56009	E56014
E56005R	E56010	E56015R

E56016R	E56027R	E56038R
E56017R	E56028R	E56039R
E56018R	E56029	E56040R
E56019	E56030R	E56041R
E56021R	E56032R	E56042R
E56022R	E56033R	E56043R
E56023R	E56034R	E56044R
E56024	E56035R	E56045R
E56025R	E56036	E56047
E56026R	E56037	E56049R

Class 101 (2)■
Metropolitan-Cammell
Driving Trailer Composite (DTC) (‡Second) (L)
Introduced: 1957
Body: 57' 0"×9' 3"
Weight: 25 tons
Seats: 1st, 12; **2nd,** 53, (45†), ‡2nd, 65

E56050	E56065	M56080R
E56051R	E56066R	E56081
E56052R	E56067R	E56082R
E56053R	E56068R	E56083R
E56054	E56069R	E56084R
M56055	E56070R	E56085
E56056	E56071	E56086R
E56057R	E56072	E56087R
M56058‡R	E56073R	E56088R
E56059R	E56074	E56089R
M56060R	E56075R	E56090*R
E56061R	E56076R	E56091*
E56062R	E56077R	E56092*R
E56063R	E56078R	E56093*
E56064R	E56079R	

Class 100 (2)■
Gloucester R. C. & W. Co.
Driving Trailer Composite (DTC) (*Second) (L)
Introduced: 1957
Body: 57' 6"×9' 3"
Weight: 25 tons
Seats: 1st, 12; **2nd,** 54, *2nd, 66

	M56104*	M56106*
M56103*	M56105*	M56107*

M56108*	M56111*	M56113*
M56109*		

Class 105 (2)■
Cravens
Driving Trailer Composite (DTC)
(*Second DTS) (L)

Introduced: 1956
Body: 57' 6" × 9' 2"
Weight: 23 tons (24 tons†)
Seats: 1st, 12; 2nd, 51, *2nd, 63

E56114	E56126	E56138
E56115*	M56127	E56139*
E56116	M56129	E56140
M56118	E56130	E56141
E56119	E56131*	E56142
M56120	E56132*	E56143
E56121	E56133	E56144
E56122	E56134	M56145
E56123	E56135	M56146
E56124	E56136	M56148
E56125	E56137	M56149

Class 103 (2)■
Park Royal Vehicles
Driving Trailer Composite (L)
(DTC)

Introduced: 1957
Body: 57' 6" × 9' 3"
Weight: 26 tons 10 cwt
Seats: 1st, 16; 2nd, 48

M56150	M56156	M56161
M56151		M56163
M56152	M56158	M56164
M56155	M56159	M56165

Class 104 (2)■
Birmingham R. C. & W. Co.
Driving Trailer Second (DTS)
(*Composite DTC) (L)

Introduced: 1958
Body: 57' 6" × 9' 3"
Weight: 24 tons
Seats: 2nd, 66
*1st, 12; 2nd, 54

M56175	M56180	E56185*
M56176	M56181	E56186*
M56177	M56182	E56187*
M56178	M56183	E56188*
M56179	M56184	E56189*

Class 108 (2)■
Derby Works, B.R.
Driving Trailer Composite (L)
(DTC)

Introduced: 1958
Body: 57' 6" × 9' 2"
Weight: 21 tons (22 tons*)
Seats: 1st, 12; 2nd, 53
†2nd, 65

E56190R	E56198R	E56207R
E56191R	E56199R	E56208R
E56192R	E56200R	E56209R
E56193R	E56201R	E56210R
E56194R	E56202R	M56212
E56195R	E56203R	M56213
E56196R	E56204R	M56214
E56197R	E56205R	

Class 101 (2)■
Metropolitan-Cammell
Driving Trailer Composite (L)
(DTC)

Introduced: 1957
For details see E56050

E56218I	E56219†R	E56220†R

Class 108 (2)■
Derby Works, B.R.
Driving Trailer Composite
(DTC)
(†Second DTS) (L)

Introduced: 1959
For details see E56190

M56221R	M56230R	M56238
M56222R	M56231R	M56239
M56223	M56232R	M56240
M56224	M56233	M56241
M56225R	M56234	M56242
M56227	M56235	M56243
M56228R	M56236	M56244

M56245	M56258R	M56269
M56246	M56259R	M56270
M56247	M56260R	M56271*
M56248	M56261R	M56272*
M56249	M56262R	M56273*R
M56250	M56263R	M56274*
M56251	M56264R	M56275*
M56252R	M56265	M56276*
M56253R	M56266R	M56277*
M56256	M56267†	M56278*R
M56257R	M56268R	M56279*R

Class 121 (2) ■
Pressed Steel Co.
Driving Trailer Second (DTS)
For use with Class 121 and 122
Single Unit cars
Introduced: 1960
Body: 64′ 0″ × 9′ 3″. Non-gangwayed, side doors to each seating bay
Weight: 29 tons 7 cwt
Seats: 2nd, 91

W56280	W56284	W56287R
W56281	W56285R	W56289R
W56283R	W56286R	

Class 122 ■
Gloucester R. C. & W. Co.
Driving Trailer Second (DTS)
For use with Class 121 and 122
Single Unit cars
Introduced: 1958
Body: 64′ 0″ × 9′ 3″. Non-gangwayed, side doors to each seating bay
Weight: 27 tons
Seats: 2nd, 91

M56295	M56296

Class 101 (2) ■
Metropolitan-Cammell
Driving Trailer Composite (DTC)
(‡Second DTS) (L)
Introduced: 1958
For details see E56050

M56332R	M56359R	E56385R
M56333R	M56360	E56386R
M56334	M56361	E56387
M56335R	E56362	E56388
M56336	E56363R	E56389R
M56337R	E56364R	E56390R
M56339R	E56365	E56391
M56340	E56366	E56392R
M56341R	E56367R	E56393
M56342R	E56368R	E56394R
M56343R	E56369R	E56396
M56344R	E56370	E56397R
M56345	E56371R	E56398
M56346R	E56372R	E56399R
M56347R	E56373R	E56400
M56348R	E56374R	E56401R
M56349R	E56375	E56402R
M56350	E56376R	E56403R
M56351R	E56377R	E56404R
M56352	E56378R	E56405
M56353	E56379	E56406R
M56354	E56380	E56407R
M56355	E56381R	E56408R
M56356	E56382R	E56409R
M56357	E56383R	E56410R
M56358	E56384R	M56411‡

Class 105 (2) ■
Cravens
Driving Trailer Composite (DTC)
(*Second DTS) (L)
Introduced: 1958
For details see E56114

E56413*†	E56436†	E56459*†
E56414*†	E56437†	E56460*
E56415*†	E56438*†	E56461†
E56416*†	E56439†	E56462
E56417*†	E56440†	E56463
E56418*†	E56441†	E56464
E56419*†	E56442†	E56465
E56420*†	E56443†	E56466
E56421*†	E56444†	E56467
E56422*†	E56445†	E56468
E56423*†	E56446†	E56469
E56424*†	E56447*†	E56470
E56425*†	E56448*†	E56471
E56426*†	E56449*†	E56472
E56427*†	E56450*†	E56473
M56428*†	E56451*†	E56474
E56429*†	M56452*†	M56475
	E56453*†	
E56431*†	E56454*†	
E56432*†	E56455*†	
E56433*†	M56456*†	
E56434†	E56457*†	E56480
E56435†	E56458*†	M56482

Class 108 (2) ■
Derby Works, B.R.
Driving Trailer Composite (L)
(DTC)
Introduced: 1960
For details see E56190

M56484*R	M56491*R	M56498*R
M56485*R	M56492*R	M56499*R
M56486*R	M56493*	M56500*
M56487*R	M56494*R	M56501*R
M56488*R	M56495*	M56502*
M56489*R	M56496*	M56503*
M56490*R	M56497*	M56504*

Class 116 (3 Suburban) ■
Derby Works, B.R.
Trailer Composite (TC)
(†Second) (TS)
Introduced: 1957
Body: 63' 8¾" × 9' 3". Non-gang-
wayed (*gangwayed), with side
doors to each seating bay

Weight: 28 tons 10 cwt
Seats: 1st, 28; 2nd, 74; †2nd, 102

M59000†R	M59011†	M59021†
M59001†R	M59012†R	M59022†R
M59002†R	M59013†R	M59023†
M59003†R	M59014†R	M59024†
M59004†	M59015†R	M59026†R
M59005†R	M59016†R	SC59027†
M59006†R	M59017†	M59028†R
M59007†R	M59018†	M59029†R
M59008†	M59019†	W59030*R
M59009†R	M59020†R	W59031*R
M59010†R		

Class 116 (3 Suburban) ■
Derby Works, B.R.
Trailer Second (TS)
Introduced: 1957
Body: 63' 8¾" × 9' 3". Gangwayed,
with side doors to each seating bay
Weight: 29 tons
Seats: 2nd, 98

W59032R	W59036R	W59039R
W59033R	W59037R	W59040*R
W59034R	W59038R	W59041R
W59035R		

Class 101 (4) ■
Metropolitan-Cammell
Trailer Second (L) (TS)
Introduced: 1956
Body: 57' 0" × 9' 3"
Weight: 25 tons
Seats: 2nd, 61 (71*)

SC59042	SC59045R	SC59047
SC59043	SC59046R	SC59048R

Class 101 (4) ■
Metropolitan-Cammell
Trailer Brake Second (L) (TBS)
Introduced: 1956
Body: 57' 0" × 9' 3"

Weight: 25 tons
Seats: 2nd, 45 (53*)

E59049	E59052R	E59054R
W59050	SC59053	E59055R

Class 101 (4) ■
Metropolitan-Cammell
Trailer Second (L) (TS)

For details see E59042

SC59060*R	E59065*R	SC59069*R
SC59061*	SC59066*R	E59070*R
E59062*R	SC59067*	SC59071*
E59063*R	SC59068*	SC59072*
E59064*R		

Class 101 (4) ■
Metropolitan-Cammell
Trailer Brake Second (L) (TBS)

Introduced: 1957
For details see E59049

SC59073*R	E59078*R	W59082*
SC59074*	E59079*	E59083*R
E59075*R	SC59080*	E59084*R
E59076*R	SC59081*	E59085*
E59077*		

Class 101 (4) ■
Metropolitan-Cammell
Trailer Second (L) (TS)

Introduced: 1957
For details see E59042

SC59086	SC59088R	SC59090
E59087R	E59089	E59091

Class 101 (4) ■
Metropolitan-Cammell
Trailer Brake Second (L) (TBS)

Introduced: 1957
For details see E59049

E59092	E59094R	W59096
W59093	E59095	E59097R

Class 101 (3) ■
Metropolitan-Cammell
Trailer Second (L) (TS)

Introduced: 1957
Body: 57' 0" × 9' 3"
Weight: 25 tons
Seats: 2nd, 71

E59100R	E59104	E59107R
E59101	E59105R	E59108R
E59102R	E59106	

Class 101 (4) ■
Metropolitan-Cammell
Trailer Brake Second (L) (TBS)

Introduced: 1957
For details see E59049

SC59112*R E59113*R

Class 101 (3) ■
Metropolitan-Cammell
Trailer Composite (TC)
(*Second) (TS) (L)

Introduced: 1958
Body: 57' 0" × 9' 3"
Weight: 25 tons
Seats: 1st, 12; 2nd, 53

M59114*R	M59120*R	M59126*R
M59115*R	M59121*R	M59127*
M59116*	W59122*R	M59128*
M59117*R	W59123*R	M59129*
M59118*	M59124*R	M59130R
M59119*R	M59125*	M59131R

Class 104 (3) ■
Birmingham R. C. & W. Co.
Trailer Composite (TC)
(*Second) (TS) (L)

Introduced: 1957
Body: 57' 0" × 9' 3"
Weight: 24 tons
Seats: 1st, 12; 2nd, 54
*2nd, 66

M59132*	M59150	M59171
M59133*	M59151	M59172
M59134*	M59152	M59173
M59135*	M59153	M59174
M59136*	M59155	M59175
M59137*	M59156	M59176
M59138*	M59157	M59177
	M59158	M59178
M59140*	M59159	M59179
M59141*	M59160	M59180
M59142	M59161	M59181
M59143	M59162*	M59182
M59144	M59163*	M59183
M59145*	M59164	M59184
M59146	M59165	M59185
M59147*	M59166	M59186
M59148*	M59168	M59187
M59149	M59169	

Class 104 (4) ■
Birmingham R. C. & W. Co.
Trailer Second (L) (TS)

Introduced: 1958
Body: 57' 0" × 9' 3"
Weight: 24 tons
Seats: 2nd, 69

M59188	E59194	E59201
E59189	M59195	M59203
E59190	M59197	M59204
E59191	M59198	E59206
M59192	E59199	M59207
M59193	E59200	E59208

Class 104 (4) ■
Birmingham R. C. & W. Co.
Trailer Brake Second (L) (TBS)

Introduced: 1958
Body: 57' 0" × 9' 3"
Weight: 25 tons
Seats: 2nd, 51

E59209	M59210	E59211

E59212	E59218	E59225
E59213	M59219	E59226
E59214	E59220	E59227
E59215	E59221	M59228
M59216	E59223	E59229
E59217	E59224	

Class 104 (4) ■
Birmingham R. C. & W. Co.
Trailer Second (L) (TS)

Introduced: 1958
For details see E59188

M59230	E59232	E59234
E59231	E59233	

Class 123 (3 or 4 Inter-City) ■
Swindon Works, B.R.
Trailer Second (L) (TS)

Introduced: 1963
Body: 64' 6" × 9' 3"
Weight: 31 tons 9 cwt
Seats: 2nd, 64

E59235	E59237	E59239
E59236	E59238	

Class 104 (4) ■
Birmingham R. C. & W. Co.
Trailer Brake Second (L) (TBS)

Introduced: 1958
For details see E59209

E59240	E59242	E59244
E59241	E59243	

Class 108 (4) ■
Derby Works, B.R.
Trailer Brake Second (L) (TBS)

Introduced: 1958
Body: 57' 6" × 9' 2"
Weight: 23 tons
Seats: 2nd, 50

E59245R	E59247R	E59249R
E59246R	E59248R	E59250R

Class 120 (3 Cross Country) ■
Swindon Works, B.R.
Trailer Buffet Second (L) (TRBS)

Introduced: 1958
Body: 64' 6"×9' 3". Open second with miniature buffet at one end
Weight: 31 tons (30 tons 12 cwt*)
Seats: 2nd, 60; Buffet, 4

M59255	M59272	M59287
M59256	M59273	M59288
M59257	M59274	M59289
M59258	M59275	M59290
M59259	M59276	M59291
M59260	M59277	M59292
M59261	M59278	M59293
M59262	M59279	M59294
M59263	M59280	M59295
M59264	M59281	M59296
M59265	M59282	M59297
M59266	M59283	M59299
M59267	M59284	M59300R
M59268	M59285	M59301R
W59269	W59286	

Class 101 (3 or 4†) ■
Metropolitan-Cammell
Trailer Second (L) (TS)

Introduced: 1957
For details see E59040

SC59302*	SC59304*	E59306*†R
SC59303*	SC59305*R	

Class 116 (3 Suburban) ■
Derby Works, B.R.
Trailer Composite (TC) (†Second) (TS)

Introduced: 1957
For details see M59000

M59326†R	M59334†R	M59341†R
M59328†R	E59335*	M59342†
SC59329	M59336†R	M59343†
SC59330	SC59337	SC59344
SC59331	M59338†	SC59345
M59332†R	M59339†R	M59346*†R
M59333†R	W59340*R	SC59347

M59348†	M59358†	SC59367
SC59349	W59359*R	M59368*†R
M59350*R	M59360†R	W59369*R
M59351†R	M59361†R	W59371*R
M59352*†R	W59362*R	M59372*†
E59353*	W59363*R	W59373*R
SC59354R	W59364*R	SC59374*†
W59355*R	M59365*	E59375
W59356*R	M59366*	M59376†R
W59357*R		

Class 108 (3 or 4*) ■
Derby Works, B.R.
Trailer Second (L) (TS)

Introduced: 1958
Body: 58' 1"×9' 3"
*†57' 6"×9' 2"
Weight: 28 tons (22 tons*, 22 tons 10 cwt†)
Seats: 2nd, 71 (68*†)

E59380*	E59384*	E59388†
E59381*R	E59385*	E59389†R
E59382*R	E59386†R	E59390†R
E59383*	E59387†R	

Class 126 (3 or 6 Inter-City) ●
Swindon Works, B.R.
Trailer First (K) (TF)

Introduced: 1959
Body: 64' 6"×9' 3"
Weight: 33 tons 8 cwt
Seats: 1st, 42

SC59391	SC59395	SC59398
SC59392	SC59396	SC59399
SC59393	SC59397	SC59400
SC59394		

Class 126 (3 or 6 Inter-City) ●
Swindon Works B.R.
Trailer Composite (L) (TC)

Introduced: 1959
Body: 64' 6"×9' 3"

Weight: 31 tons 16 cwt
Seats: 1st, 18; **2nd,** 32

SC59402	SC59406	SC59410
SC59403	SC59407	SC59411
SC59404	SC59408	SC59412
SC59405	SC59409	

Class 119 (3 Cross Country) ■
Gloucester R. C. & W. Co.
Trailer Buffet Second (L)
(TRBS)
Introduced: 1958
Body: 64' 6"×9' 3". Open second
with miniature buffet at one end
Weight: 31 tons
Seats: 2nd, 60; **Buffet,** 4

W59413	W59422	W59430
W59414	W59423	W59431
W59415	W59424	W59432
W59416	W59425	W59433
W59417	W59426	W59434
W59418	W59427	W59435
W59419	W59428	W59436
W59420	W59429	W59437
W59421		

Class 116 (3 Suburban) ■
Derby Works, B.R.
Trailer Composite (TC)
(†Second) (TS)
Introduced: 1958
For details see M59000

M59438†R	M59442†R	W59445R
M59439†R	M59443†	W59446R
M59440†	W59444*R	M59448†R
M59441†R		

Class 118 (3 Suburban) ■
Birmingham R. C. & W. Co.
Trailer Composite (L) (TC)
Introduced: 1960

Body: 63' 10"×9' 3". Gangwayed,
with side doors to each seating bay
Weight: 30 tons
Seats: 1st, 22; **2nd,** 48

W59469	W59474	W59479R
W59470	W59475	W59480R
W59471	W59476	W59481
W59472	W59477	W59482
W59473	W59478R	W59483

Class 117 (3 Suburban) ■
Pressed Steel Co.
Trailer Composite (L) (TC)
Introduced: 1959
Body: 63' 10" × 9' 3". Gangwayed,
with side doors to each seating bay
Weight: 30 tons
Seats: 1st, 22; **2nd,** 48

W59484R	W59497R	W59510R
W59485	W59498R	W59511R
W59486R	W59499R	W59512R
W59487R	W59500R	W59513R
W59488R	W59501R	W59514R
W59489R	W59502R	W59515
W59490	W59503R	W59516R
M59491R	M59504R	W59517R
M59492R	W59505R	W59518R
W59493R	W59506R	W69519R
W59494R	W59507R	W59520R
W59495R	W59508R	W59521R
W59496R	W59509	W59522R

Class 101 (3 or 4*) ■
Metropolitan-Cammell
Trailer Composite (L) (TC)
Introduced: 1959
For details see M59114

E59523*R	E69527*	E59531*R
E59524*R	M59528*R	E59532*
E59525*	E59529*	E59533*
E59526*	W59530*	E59534*R

E59535*R	W59547R	SC59558R
	W59548	SC59559R
M59538*†	W59549R	SC59560R
W59539*	W59550R	W59561
E59540*	W59551R	SC59562R
SC59541*R	SC59552R	SC59563R
E59542*	SC59553R	SC59564R
M59543†	SC59554R	SC59565R
SC59544	SC59555R	SC59566
SC59545R	SC59556R	SC59567
W59546R	SC59557R	SC59568R

Class 101   (3) ■
Metropolitan-Cammell
Trailer Second (L) (TS)
Introduced: 1959
For details see E59100

E59569R	E59571	E59572
E59570		

Class 111   (4) ■
Metropolitan-Cammell
Trailer Buffet Second (L) (TRBS)
Introduced: 1960
Body: 57′ 0″ × 9′ 3″ Open second with miniature buffet at one end
Weight: 25 tons
Seats: 2nd, 53

SC59574	SC59577	SC59578

Class 120   (3 Cross Country) ■
Swindon Works, B.R.
Trailer Buffet Second (L) (TRBS)
Introduced: 1960
For details see M59255

W59580*	W59583*	W59587*
W59581*	W59586*	W59588*
W59582*		

Class 127   (4 Suburban) ▲
Derby Works, B.R.
Trailer Second (L*) (TS)
Introduced: 1959
Body: 63′ 10″ × 9′ 3″ (63′ 8¾″ × 9′ 3″*). Non-gangwayed, side doors to each seating bay. (Intermediate lavatories on each side of central passageway*)
Weight: 29 tons (30 tons*)
Seats: 2nd, 106 (90*)

M59589*	M59609*	M59629
M59590*	M59610*	M59631
M59591*	M59611*	M59632
M59592*	M59612*	M59633
M59593*	M59613*	M59634
M59594*	M59614*	M59636
M59595*	M59615*	M59637
M59596*	M59616*	M59638
M59597*	M59617*	M59639
M59598*	M59619	M59640
M59600*	M59620	M59641
M59602*	M59621	M59642
M59603*	M59622	M59643
M59604*	M59623	M59644
M59605*	M59625	M59645
M59606*	M59626	M59646
M59607*	M59627	M59647
M59608*	M59628	M59648

Class 115   (4 Suburban) ■
Derby Works, B.R.
Trailer Second (TS)
Introduced: 1960
Body: 63′ 8¾″ × 9′ 3″. Non-gangwayed, side doors to each seating bay
Weight: 29 tons
Seats: 2nd, 106

M59649	M59654R	M59659R
M59650	M59655	M59660R
M59651R	M59656	M59661
M59652R	M59657	M59662
M59653	M59658	M59663R

Class 115 (4 Suburban) ■
Derby Works, B.R.
Trailer Composite (L) (TC)

Introduced: 1960
Body: 63' 8¾" × 9' 3". Non-gangwayed, side doors to each seating bay
Weight: 30 tons
Seats: 1st, 30; 2nd, 40

M59664	M59669R	M59674
M59665	M59670	M59675
M59666	M59671R	M59676
M59667R	M59672	M59677
M59668	M59673	M59678R

Class 120 (3 Cross Country) ■
Swindon Works, B.R.
Trailer Buffet Second (L) (TRBS)

Introduced: 1959
For details see M59255

W59679*	W59682*R	W59684*R
SC59680*R	W59683*R	SC59685*R
W59681*R		

Class 101 (3) ■
Metropolitan-Cammell
Trailer Composite (L) (TC)

Introduced: 1959
For details see M59114

SC59686R	SC59689R	SC59691R
SC59687R	SC59690R	SC59692R
SC59688		

Class 110 (3) ■
Birmingham R. C. & W. Co.
Trailer Second (L) (TS)

Introduced: 1961
Body: 57' 6" × 9' 3"
Weight: 24 tons (24 tons 10 cwt*)
Seats: 2nd, 72

E59693R	E59699	E59707R
E59694	E59700	E59708
E59695	E59701	E59709
E59696	E59702	E59710
E59697	E59703	E59711
E59698	E59704	E59712

Class 115 (4 Suburban) ■
Derby Works, B.R.
Trailer Second (TS)

Introduced: 1960
For details see M59649

M59713	M59715R	M59717
M59714R	M59716R	M59718

Class 115 (4 Suburban) ■
Derby Works, B.R.
Trailer Composite (L) (TC)

Introduced: 1960
For details see M59664

	M59721	M59723
M59720	M59722	M59724

Class 115 (4 Suburban) ■
Derby Works, B.R.
Trailer Second (TS)

Introduced: 1960
For details see M59649

M59725	M59732	M59738
M59726	M59733	M59739
M59727R	M59734	M59740
M59728	M59735	M59741R
M59729	M59736R	M59743
M59730	M59737	M59744
M59731		

Class 115 (4 Suburban) ■
Derby Works, B.R.
Trailer Composite (L) (TC)

Introduced: 1960
For details see M59664

M59745	M59752	M59759R
M59746R	M59753	M59760R
M59747	M59754	M59761
M59748	M59755R	M59762
M59749	M59756	M59763R
M59750R	M59757	M59764
M59751	M59758	

Class 124 (5 Trans-Pennine) ■
Swindon Works, B.R.
Trailer Second (L) (TS)

Introduced: 1960
Body: 64' 6" × 9' 3"
Weight: 32 tons
Seats: 2nd, 64

E59765	E59768	E59771
E59766	E59769	E59772
E59767	E59770	E59773

Class 107 (3) ■
Derby Works, B.R.
Trailer Second (L) (TS)

Introduced: 1960
For details see E59380

SC59782	SC59791R	SC59800
SC59783R	SC59792	SC59801
SC59784	SC59793R	SC59802R
SC59785	SC59794	SC59803R
SC59786	SC59795R	SC59804R
SC59787R	SC59796	SC59805R
SC59788	SC59797	SC59806R
SC59789R	SC59798R	SC59807R
SC59790	SC59799R	

Class 110 (3) ■
Birmingham R. C. & W. Co.
Trailer Second (L) (TS)

Introduced: 1961
For details see E59693

E59808*	E59812*	E59815*
E59809*	E59813*	E59816*R
E59810*	E59814*	E59817*
E59811*R		

Class 123 (3 or 4 Inter-City) ■
Swindon Works, B.R.
Trailer Composite (K) (TC)

Introduced: 1963
Body: 64' 6" × 9' 3"
Weight: 32 tons 3 cwt
Seats: 1st, 24; 2nd, 24

E59818	E59822	E59825
E59819	E59823	E59826
E59820	E59824	E59827
E59821		

Class 126 (3 or 6 Inter-City) ●
Swindon Works, B.R.
Motor Brake Second (L) (DMBS)

Introduced: 1956
For details see SC51030

SC79088*

Class 126 (3 or 6 Inter-City) ●
Swindon Works, B.R.
Trailer First (K) (TF)

Introduced: 1957
Body: 64' 6" × 9' 3". Side corridor with seven first class compartments and end doors
Weight: 33 tons 8 cwt
Seats: 1st, 42

SC79470

Derby Class 127 four-car unit at Harpenden Junction [*G. D. Griffiths*

Gloucester Class 128 motor parcels van No M55994 with gangways removed [*B. J. Nicolle*

103

WESTERN REGION DIESEL MULTIPLE-UNIT FORMATIONS

Diesel units allocated to the Western Region are marshalled in fixed formations and carry a three-digit unit number on the outer ends of each set. This unit number currently bears a code letter prefix denoting the area to which the set is allocated (L—London, B—Bristol, C—Cardiff, P—Plymouth). It has been proposed that these units be numbered in the BR standard series which is now being applied to all 25 kV a.c. electric units. Thus, for example Pressed Steel unit No L431 would become 117 431. This list shows the composition of the WR units with the prefix letter omitted for clarity. Where gaps exist in the list a unit may be running with only two cars, or the missing vehicle may be replaced by a "spare" car.

120	W55020		132	W55032
121	W55021		133	W55033
122	W55022		134	W55034
123	W55023		280	W56280
124	W55024		281	W56281
125	W55025		283	W56283
126	W55026		284	W56284
127	W55027		285	W56285
128	W55028		286	W56286
129	W55029		287	W56287
130	W55030		289	W56289
131	W55031			

300	W50080	W59030	W50122
301	W50084	W59373	W50126
302	W50086	W59036	W50128
303	W50087	W59037	W50129
304	W50088	W59362	W50130
305	W50089	W59039	W50131
306	W50091	W59041	W50133

312	W50843	W59355	W50896
313	W50847	W59040	W50900
314	W50848	W59356	W50901
315	W50855	W59363	W50908
316	W50856	W59364	W50909
317	W50858		W50911
318	W50864	W59369	W50917
319	W50868		W50918
320	W50869	W59035	W50922

330	W51128	W59357	W51141
331	W51132		W51145
332	W51134	W59444	W51147
333	W51135	W59445	W51148
334	W51139	W59033	W51152

335	W51140	W59032	W51153
400	W51332	W59484	W51374
401	W51333	W59485	W51375
402	W51335	W59487	W51377
403	W51336	W59488	W51378
404	W51337	W59489	W51379
405	W51340	W59491	W51381
406	W51341	W59493	W51383
407	W51342	W59494	W51384
408	W51343	W59495	W51385
409	W51344	W59496	W51386
410	W51345	W59497	W51387
411	W51346	W59498	W51388
412	W51347	W59499	W51389
413	W51349	W59501	W51391
414	W51350	W59502	W51392
415	W51351	W59503	W51393
416	W51353	W59505	W51395
417	W51354	W59506	W51396
418	W51355	W59507	W51397
419	W51356		W51398
420	W51358	W59510	W51400
421	W51359	W59511	W51401
422	W51360	W59512	W51402
423	W51361	W59513	W51403
424	W51362	W59514	W51404
425	W51363	W59515	W51405
426	W51364	W59516	W51406
427	W51365	W59517	W51407
428	W51366	W59518	W51408
429	W51367	W59519	W51409
430	W51368	W59520	W51410
431	W51369	W59521	W51411
432	W51370	W59522	W51412
433	W51371	W59478	W51413
434	W51372	W59479	W51414
435	W51373	W59480	W51415
440	W50083		W51399
450	W51376	W59031	W51334
451	W51338	W59371	W51380
452	W51339	W59492	W51382
453	W51348	W59500	W51390
454	W51352	W59359	W51394
460	W51302	W69469	W51317
461	W51303	W59470	W51318
462	W51304	W59477	W51319
463	W51305	W59472	W51320

464	W51306	W59473	W51321
465	W51307	W59474	W51322
466	W51308	W59475	W51323
467	W51309	W59476	W51324
468	W51310	W59471	W51325
469	W51311		W51326
470	W51313	W59509	W51328
471	W51314	W59481	W51329
472	W51315	W59482	W51330
473	W51316	W59483	W51331
480	W51312		W51327
500	W50647	W59265	W50705
501	W50653	W59268	W50707
502	W50658	W59282	W50711
503	W50659	W59281	W50700
504	W50665	W59588	W50715
505	W50674	W59278	W50723
506	W50661	W59269	W50710
507	W50662	W59260	W50699
508	W50666	W59286	W50712
509	W50691	W59277	W50728
552	W51573	W59285	W51582
553	W51574	W59284	W51583
554	W51575	W59292	W51584
555	W51576	W59582	W51590
556	W51577	W59583	W51586
557	W51578	W59580	W51587
558	W51579	W59264	W51588
559	W51580	W59586	W51589
560	W57581	W59587	W51585
571	W51052		W51080
572	W51054	W59413	W51082
573	W51055	W59417	W51083
574	W51056	W59415	W51084
575	W51060	W59419	W51088
576	W51062	W59421	W51090
577	W51063	W59422	W51091
578	W51064	W59423	W51092
579	W51065	W59424	W51093
580	W51066	W59425	W51094
681	W51067	W59426	W51095
582	W51068	W59427	W51096
583	W51069	W59428	W51097
584	W51070	W59429	W51098
585	W51075	W59434	W51103
586	W51077	W59420	W51105
587	W51078	W59436	W51106

588	W51079	W59437	W51107
600	W50664		W50702
601	W50672		W50722
602	W50649		W50698
603	W50673		W50724
604	W50681		W50701
605	W50686		W50733
615	W51781	W59682	W51788
616	W51782	W59681	W51790
620	W51783	W59683	W51792
621	W51785	W59684	W51793
622	W51786	W59679	W51791
800	W51445	W59549	W51515
801	W51446	W59547	W51517
802	W51449	W59550	W51521
803	W51450	W59546	W51522
804	W51452	W59551	W51523
805	W50304	W59122	W50329
806	W50319	W59123	W50335
810	W51799	W59539	W51808
811	W51519	W59548	W51801
812	W51462	W59530	W51530
813	W51463	W59561	W51533
820	W51500	W59093	W51512
821	W51509	W59050	W51513
822	W51495	W59096	W51510
823	W51505	W59082	W51511

S.R. DIESEL-ELECTRIC MULTIPLE-UNITS

Class 201 (6S) (6)
Hastings Six-Car Units

Gangwayed within set
Built Eastleigh Works BR from 1957
*Unit 1002 is a five-car unit with two
trailer saloon seconds

Motor Saloon Brake Second (DMBS)
Engine:
English Electric 4-cycl type 4SRKT
Mark II of 500 b.h.p. at 850 r.p.m.
Body: 58' 0" × 8' 2½" & 9' 0"
Weight: 54 tons 2 cwt
Seats: 2nd, 22
Transmission:
Electric. Two nose-suspended axle-
hung traction motors
Nos. S60000/1/8–13

Trailer Saloon Second (L) (TS)
Body: 58' 0" × 8' 2½" & 9' 0"
Weight: 29 tons
Seats: 2nd, 52
Nos. S60500–2/11–19

Trailer First (K) (TF)
Body: 58' 0" × 8' 2½" & 9' 0"
Weight: 30 tons
Seats: 1st, 42
Nos. S60700/3–5
Being converted to trailer composite
(TC) with 30 1st class and 12 2nd
class seats

Trailer Saloon Second (L) (TS)
Body: 58' 0" × 8' 2½" & 9' 0"
Weight: 29 tons
Seats: 2nd, 52

Trailer Saloon Second (L) (TS)
Body: 58' 0" × 8' 2½" & 9' 0"
Weight: 29 tons
Seats: 2nd, 52

Motor Saloon Brake Second (DMBS)
(As Above)

1001	1005	1007
1002*	1006	

Class 202 (6L) (6)
Hastings Six-Car Units

Gangwayed within set
Built Eastleigh Works BR from 1957

Motor Saloon Brake Second (DMBS)
Engine:
English Electric 4-cyl type 4SRKT
Mark II of 500 b.h.p. at 850 r.p.m.
Body: 64' 6" × 8' 2½" & 9' 0"
Weight: 55 tons
Seats: 2nd, 30
Transmission:
Electric. Two nose-suspended axle-
hung traction motors
Nos. S60014–35

Trailer Saloon Second (L) (TS) (*Trailer Second (K))
Body: 64' 6" (58' 0"*) × 8' 2½" & 9' 0"
Weight: 30 tons
Seats: 2nd, 60 (56*)
Nos. S60521–49/51/2
(S60701/2*)

Trailer Saloon Second (L) (TS) (*Trailer Second (K)) (TS)
Body: 64' 6" (58' 0"*) × 8' 2½" & 9' 0"
Weight: 30 tons
Seats: 2nd, 60 (56*)

Trailer First (K) (TF)
Body: 64' 6" × 8' 2½" & 9' 0"
Weight: 31 tons
Seats: 1st, 48
Nos. S60707–17
Being converted to trailer composite
(TC) with 36 1st class and 12 2nd
class seats

Trailer Saloon Second (L) (TS)
Body: 64' 6" × 8' 2½" & 9' 0"
Weight: 30 tons
Seats: 2nd, 60

Motor Saloon Brake Second (DMBS)

(As Above)

1011	1015	1019
1012	1016	1031
1013	1017	1032*
1014	1018	

Class 203 (6B) (6)
Hastings Six-Car Units

Gangwayed within set
Built 1958, Eastleigh Works BR

Motor Saloon Brake Second (DMBS)

Engine:
English Electric 4-cyl type 4SRKT
Mark II of 500 b.h.p. at 850 r.p.m.
Body: 64' 6" × 8' 2½" & 9' 0"
Weight: 55 tons
Seats: 2nd, 30
Transmission:
Electric. Two nose-suspended axle-hung traction motors
Nos. S60036–45

Trailer Saloon Second (L) (TS)

Body: 64' 6" × 8' 2½" & 9' 0"
Weight: 30 tons
Seats: 2nd, 60
Nos. S60550/3–61

Trailer Buffet (TRB)

Body: 64' 6" × 8' 2½" & 9' 0"
Weight: 35 tons
Seats: 21
Nos. S60751–4/6
Buffet facilities withdrawn 1980 and equipment removed. Vehicles retained pending reforming of units

Trailer First (K) (TF)

Body: 64' 6" × 8' 2½" & 9' 0"
Weight: 31 tons
Seats: 1st, 48
Nos. S60718–22
Being converted to trailer composite (TC) with 36 1st class and 12 2nd class seats

Trailer Saloon Second (L) (TS)

(As Above)

Motor Saloon Brake Second

(As Above)

1033	1035	1037
1034	1036	

Class 205 Hampshire† and
Berkshire‡ Three-Car Units

Built 1957 Eastleigh Works BR
Non-gangwayed (R-gangwayed within set and refurbished)

Motor Open Brake Second (DMBS)

Engine:
English Electric 4-cyl type 4SRKT
Mark II of 600 b.h.p. at 850 r.p.m.
Body: 64 0" × 9' 3"
Weight: 56 tons
Seats: 2nd, 52 (42‡) (39R)
Transmission:
Electric. Two nose-suspended axle-hung traction motors
Nos. S60100–25/45–51

Trailer Semi-open Second (TS)

Body: 63' 6" × 9' 3"
Weight: 30 tons
Seats: 2nd, 104 (98R)
Nos. S60650–78

Driving Trailer Composite (L) (DTC)

Body: 64' 0" × 9' 3". Non-gangwayed, side doors to each seating bay or compartment. 5-bay 2nd class saloon and 2 1st class compartments with intermediate lavatories, also a 2nd class compartment next to driving compartment. A luggage compartment has been fitted in place of the 2nd class compartment in the Hampshire units

Weight: 32 tons
Seats: 1st, 13; **2nd,** 50 (62*‡) (76R)
Nos. S60800–32

1101†	1112†	1123†
1102†	1113†	1124†
	1114†	1125†
	1115†	1126†
1105†	1116†	1127‡
1106†	1117†	1128‡
1107†	1118†	1129‡
1108†	1119*	1130‡
1109†	1120*	1131‡
1110†		1132‡
1111R		1133‡

Class 206 (3R)   (3)
Reading-Redhill Three-Car Units
Formed 1964 from ex-Hastings motor and trailer cars and ex-EMU driving trailers.

Motor Saloon Brake Second (DMBS)
Engine:
English Electric 4-cyl type 4SRKT Mark II of 500 b.h.p. at 850 r.p.m.
Body: 58' 0" × 8' 2½" & 9' 0"
Weight: 54 tons 2 cwt
Seats: 2nd, 22
Transmission:
Electric. Two nose-suspended axle-hung traction motors
Nos. S60002–7

Trailer Saloon Second (L) (TS)
Body: 58' 0" × 8' 2½" & 9' 0"
Weight: 29 tons
Seats: 2nd, 52
Nos. S60503–6/9/10

Driving Trailer Semi-Compartment Second (DTS)
Body: 63' 11½" × 9' 0" & 9' 3"
Weight: 30 tons
Seats: 2nd, 66
Nos. S77500/3/7–10
1205	1206

Class 207 (3D)   (3)
East Sussex Three-Car Units
Built 1962 Eastleigh Works BR

Motor Open Brake Second (DMBS)
Engine:
English Electric 4-cyl type 4SRKT Mark II of 600 b.h.p. at 850 r.p.m.
Body: 64' 0" × 8' 6" & 9' 0"
Weight: 56 tons
Seats: 2nd, 42
Transmission:
Electric. Two nose-suspended axle-hung traction motors
Nos. S60126–44

Trailer Composite (L) (TC)
Body: 63' 6" × 8' 6" & 9' 0". Non-gangwayed, side doors to each seating bay or compartment. 3-bay 2nd class saloon, 4 1st class compartments, side lavatory and further 2-bay 2nd class saloon connected by side corridors.
Weight: 31 tons
Seats: 1st, 24; **2nd,** 42
Nos. S60600–18

Driving Trailer Semi-Open Second (DTS)
Body: 64' 0" × 8' 6" & 9' 0"
Weight: 32 tons
Seats: 2nd, 76
Nos. S60900–18

1301	1308	1314
1302	1309	1315
1303	1310	1316
1304	1311	1317
1305	1312	1318
1306	1313	1319
1307		

SR Class 203 Hastings line unit No 1037 at Charing Cross

[*Brian Morrison*

SR Class 205 Berkshire area unit No 1130 at Cosham

[*J. Scrace*

111

Class 204 (3T)   (3)
Hampshire Three-Car Units

Formed 1979. Eastleigh Works BR

Motor Open Brake Second (DMBS)

Details as Class 205 units

Trailer Semi-Compartment Second (TS)
Body: 63′ 11½″ × 9′ 0″ & 9′ 3″

Weight: 30 tons
Seats: 2nd, 66
Nos.   S77500/3/7–10.   Formerly Class 206 Driving trailer seconds

Driving Trailer Composite (L) (DTC)

Details as Class 205 units

1401	1403	1404
1402		

SR Class 207 East Sussex area unit No 1306   *[Brian Morrison*

INTER-CITY 125 (HIGH SPEED TRAIN)

Class 253 and 254

Each unit consists of a rake of seven (eight in Class 254) Mk 3 coaches with a lightweight power car at each end. The units can be easily remarshalled as required and the lists below show the vehicles allocated to each unit. The power cars are listed separately in *Abc BR Locomotives* (or the Locomotives section of the Combined Volume). Further units are on order or under construction.

Class 253
Introduced: 1976
Power car (DMB)
Body: 59' 4" × 9' 1"
Engine: Paxman Valenta 12-cyl 12RP200L V-type, super-charged and inter-cooled of 2,250 b.h.p. (1,680 kW)
Weight: 66 tons
Transmission: Four Brush fully suspended traction motors driving through a cardan shaft with flexible couplings and single reduction gearing. Units 253 028–41 have GEC equipment.
Maximum speed: 125 m.p.h.
Trailer first (TF)
Body: 75' 3" × 9' 1"
Seats: 1st, 48
Weight:
Trailer second (TS)
Body: 75' 3" × 9' 1"
Seats: 2nd, 72
Weight: 33 tons
Trailer restaurant second buffet (TRSB)*
Body: 75' 3" × 9' 1"
Seats: 2nd, 35
Weight: 36 tons
Trailer restaurant unclassed buffet (TRUB)
Body: 75' 3" × 9' 1"
Seats: 17
Weight:
Trailer Guard second (TGS)
Body: 75' 3" × 9' 1"
Seats: 2nd

Class 254
Introduced: 1977. 10-car units for Eastern Region. Vehicle details as for Class 253 units but formation includes two catering vehicles. It is expected that these units will be reformed to include a TGS in place of one TS vehicle

Trailer restaurant unclassed kitchen (TRUK)
Body: 75' 3" × 9' 1"
Seats: 24
Weight:

Class 253

Formation:	DMB	TF	TF	TRUB/TRSB*
253 001	43003	41003	41004	40001*
253 002	43005	41005	41006	40300
253 003	43007	41007	41008	40003*
253 004	43009	41009	41010	40301
253 005	43011	41011	41012	40005*
253 006	43013	41013	41014	40302
253 007	43015	41015	41016	40007*
253 008	43017	41017	41018	40303
253 009	43019	41019	41020	40009*
253 010	43021	41021	41022	40010*
253 011	43023	41023	41024	40011*
253 012	43025	41025	41026	40012*
253 013	43027	41027	41028	40013*
253 014	43029	41029	41030	40014*
253 015	43031	41031	41032	40304
253 016	43033	41033	41034	40016*
253 017	43035	41035	41036	40305
253 018	43037	41037	41038	40015*
253 019	43039	41039	41040	40306
253 020	43041	41041	41042	40017*
253 021	43043	41043	41044	40307
253 022	43045	41045	41046	40002*
253 023	43047	41047	41048	40308
253 024	43049	41049	41050	40004*
253 025	43051	41051	41052	40309
253 026	43053	41053	41054	40006*
253 027	43055	41055	41056	40008*
253 028	43125	41121	41122	40322
253 029	43127	41123	41124	40323
253 030	43129	41125	41126	40324
253 031	43131	41127	41128	40325
253 032	43133	41129	41130	40326
253 033	43135	41131	41132	40327
253 034	43137	41133	41134	40328
253 035	43139	41135	41136	40329
253 036	43141	41137	41138	40330
253 037	43143	41139	41140	40331
253 038	43145	41141	41142	40332
253 039	43147	41143	41144	40333
253 040	43149	41145	41146	40334
253 041	43151	41147	41148	40335

Class 253 units on order: 253 042–253 059

Formation:	TS	TS	TS	TGS	DMB
253 001	42003	42004	42005	44008	43002
253 002	42006	42007	42008	44009	43004
253 003	42009	42010	42011	44010	43006
253 004	42012	42013	42014	44011	43008
253 005	42015	42016	42017	44012	43010
253 006	42018	42019	42020	44013	43012
253 007	42021	42022	42023	44014	43014
253 008	42024	42025	42026	44015	43016
253 009	42027	42028	42029	44016	43018
253 010	42030	42031	42032	44017	43020
253 011	42033	42034	42035	44018	43022
253 012	42036	42037	42038	44019	43024
253 013	42039	42040	42041	44020	43026
253 014	42042	42043	42044	44021	43028
253 015	42045	42046	42047	44022	43030
253 016	42048	42049	42050	44023	43032
253 017	42051	42052	42053	44024	43034
253 018	42054	42055	42056	44025	43036
253 019	42057	42058	42059	44026	43038
253 020	52060	42061	42062	44027	43040
253 021	42063	42064	42065	44028	43042
253 022	42066	42067	42068	44029	43044
253 023	42069	42070	42071	44030	43046
253 024	42072	42073	42074	44031	43048
253 025	42075	42076	42077	44032	43050
253 026	42078	42079	42080	44033	43052
253 027	42081	42082	42083	44034	43054
253 028	42251	42252	42253	44035	43126
253 029	42255	42256	42257	44036	43128
253 030	42259	42260	42261	44037	43130
253 031	42263	42264	42265	44038	43132
253 032	42267	42268	42269	44039	43134
253 033	42271	42272	42273	44040	43136
253 034	42275	42276	42277	44007	43138
253 035	42279	42280	42281	44006	43140
253 036	42283	42284	42285	44005	43142
253 037	42287	42288	42289	44004	43144
253 038	42291	42292	42293	44003	43146
253 039	42295	42296	42297	44002	43148
253 040	42299	42300	42301	44001	43150
253 041	42303	42304	42305	44000	43152

Class 254

Formation:	DMB	TF	TF	TRUK	TS
254 001	43057	41057	41058	40501	42111
254 002	43059	41059	41060	40502	42115
254 003	43061	41061	41062	40503	42119
254 004	43063	41063	41064	40504	42123
254 005	43065	41065	41066	40505	42127
254 006	43067	41067	41068	40506	42131
254 007	43069	41069	41070	40507	42135
254 008	43071	41071	41072	40508	42139
254 009	43073	41073	41074	40509	42143
254 010	43075	41075	41076	40510	42147
254 011	43077	41077	41078	40511	42151
254 012	43079	41079	41080	40512	42155
254 013	43081	41081	41082	40513	42159
254 014	43083	41083	41084	40514	42163
254 015	43085	41085	41086	40515	42167
254 016	43087	41087	41088	40516	42171
254 017	43089	41089	41090	40517	42175
254 018	43091	41091	41092	40518	42179
254 019	43093	41093	41094	40519	42183
254 020	43095	41095	41096	40520	42187

Formation:	DMB	TF	TF	TRUB	TS
254 021	43097	41097	41098	40310	42191
254 022	43099	41099	41100	40311	42196
254 023	43101	41101	41102	40312	42201
254 024	43103	41103	41104	40313	42206
254 025	43105	41105	41106	40314	42211
254 026	43107	41107	41108	40315	42216
254 027	43109	41109	41110	40316	42221
254 028	43111	41111	41112	40317	42226
254 029	43113	41113	41114	40318	42231
254 030	43115	41115	41116	40319	42236
254 031	43117	41117	41118	40320	42241
254 032	43119	41119	41120	40321	42246

Note: These units are being reformed with two catering vehicles as in units Nos 254 001–20.

Class 254 units on order: 254 033–254 039

Formation:	TS	TRSB*	TS	TS	DMB
254 001	42112	40018	42113	42114	43056
254 002	42116	40019	42117	42118	43058
254 003	42120	40020	42121	42122	43060
254 004	42124	40021	42125	42126	43062
254 005	42128	40022	42129	42130	43064
254 006	42132	40023	42133	42134	43066
254 007	42136	40024	42137	42138	43068
254 008	42140	40025	42141	42142	43070
254 009	42144	40026	42145	42146	43072
254 010	42148	40027	42149	42150	43074
254 011	42152	40028	42153	52154	43076
254 012	42156	40029	42157	42158	43078
254 013	42160	40030	42161	42162	43080
254 014	42164	40031	42165	42166	43082
254 015	42168	40032	42169	42170	43084
254 016	42172	40033	42173	42174	43086
254 017	42176	40034	42177	42178	43088
254 018	42180	40035	42181	42182	43090
254 019	42184	40036	42185	42186	43092
254 020	42188	40037	42189	42190	43094

Formation:	TS	TS	TS	TS	DMB
254 021	42192	42193	42194	42195	43096
254 022	42197	42198	42199	42200	43098
254 023	42202	42203	42204	42205	43100
254 024	42207	42208	42209	42210	43102
254 025	42212	42213	42214	42215	43104
254 026	42217	42218	42219	42220	43106
254 027	42222	42223	42224	42225	43108
254 028	42227	42228	42229	42230	43110
254 029	42232	42233	42234	42235	43112
254 030	42237	42238	42239	42240	43114
254 031	42242	42243	42244	42245	43116
254 032	42247	42248	42249	42250	43118

DIESEL UNITS UNDER DEVELOPMENT

Class 210

BR Standard design with air-operated sliding doors. Gangwayed throughout

To be introduced
Driving Motor Brake Second
Body:
Seats: 2nd, 45
Weight:
Equipment: Paxman 6RP200L engine of 1,104 h.p. (MTU 12V 396 TC engine)*
Transmission: Electric
Maximum speed: 90 m.p.h.
Trailer Second
Body:
Seats: 2nd, 84
Weight:
Driving Trailer Second
Body:
Seats, 2nd, 74
Weight:
210 001   210 002*

Class 140
Prototype Lightweight
Diesel Unit

BR design incorporating body parts and equipment of Leyland National bus on 4-wheel underframes
Fitted with air-operated doors and gangwayed within units

To be introduced
Driving Motor Second
Body: 52′ 5¾″ × 8′ 2½″
Seats: 2nd, 52
Weight: 19 tons
Equipment: Leyland under-floor mounted engine of 200 h.p.
Transmission: Mechanical
Maximum speed: 75 m.p.h.
Driving Motor Second (L)
Body: 52′ 5¾″ × 8′ 2½″
Seats: 2nd, 50
Weight: 19 tons
Equipment: Leyland under-floor mounted engine of 200 h.p.
Transmission: Mechanical
140 001

Leyland experimental diesel railcar No RDB 975874 (LEV 1)   [*M. J. Collins*]

DEPARTMENTAL DIESEL MULTIPLE-UNITS

Former numbers in brackets

Derby/Cowlairs Works, B.R. (2)

Introduced: 1958 as 2-car battery-electric unit. Now used for signalling research at Railway Technical Centre, Derby
Electrical equipment: Two 100kW Siemens-Schuckert nose-suspended traction motors powered by 216 lead-acid cell batteries of 1070 amp/hour capacity
Body: 57' 6" × 9' 2"

DB975003 (SC79998)
   Laboratory 16
DB975004 (SC79999) Gemini

D. Wickham & Co. (2)

Introduced: 1957 as motor brake second and driving trailer composite*. Converted 1967 for use as General Manager's Saloon
Engines:
Two B.U.T. (Leyland) 6-cyl horizontal type of 150 b.h.p.
Body: 57' 0" × 9' 3" (57' 6" × 9' 3"*)
Transmission:
Mechanical. Standard

DB975005 (E50416)
DB975006* (E56171)

Derby Works, B.R. (2)

Ultrasonic Test Train
Introduced: 1954 as motor brake second and driving trailer composite*
Engines:
Two B.U.T. (A.E.C.) 6-cyl horizontal type of 150 b.h.p.
Body: 57' 0" × 9' 3" (57' 6" × 9' 3"*)
Transmission:
Mechanical. Standard

DB975007 (M79018)
DB975008* (M79612)

Derby Works, B.R. ♦

Introduced: 1956 as motor brake second single-unit
Used for radio system survey work.
Engines:
Two B.U.T. (A.E.C.) 6-cyl horizontal type of 150 b.h.p.
Body: 57' 6" × 9' 2". Non-gangwayed. Driving compartment at each end
Transmission:
Mechanical. Standard

RDB975010 (M79900) Iris

Metropolitan-Cammell (2)♦

Introduced: 1955 as motor brake second. Used for plasma torch research at Railway Technical Centre, Derby
Engines:
Two B.U.T. (A.E.C.) 6-cyl horizontal type of 150 b.h.p.
Body: 57' 0" × 9' 3"
Transmission:
Mechanical. Standard

DB975018 (E79047)
DB975019 (E79053)
   Laboratory 21

Gloucester R.C. & W. Co. ■

Route-learning cars
Introduced: 1958 as motor brake second single-unit Class 122
Engines:
Two B.U.T. (A.E.C.) (Leyland*) 6-cyl horizontal type of 150 b.h.p.
Body: 64' 6" × 9' 3". Non-gangwayed, side doors to each seating bay
Transmission:
Mechanical. Standard

TDB975023 (W55001)*
DB975042 (M55019)
DB975227 (M55017)
TDB975309 (M55008)
TDB975310 (M55010)
TDB975540 (W55016)*
TDB975994 (SC55014)

Park Royal Vehicles (2)■

Introduced: 1957 as motor brake second and driving trailer composite. Now used for instrumentation tests at Railway Technical Centre, Derby
Engines:
Two B.U.T. (A.E.C.) 6-cyl horizontal type of 150 b.h.p.
Body: 57′ 6″ × 9′ 3″
Transmission:
Mechanical. Standard

DB975089 (M50396)
DB975090 (M56162)

Swindon Works, B.R. ■

Introduced: 1963 as trailer buffet second
Body: 64′ 6″ × 9′ 3″

TDB975327 (W59828)

Gloucester R.C. & W. Co. ■

Introduced: 1957 as motor brake second and driving trailer composite* of Class 100
Engines:
Two B.U.T. (A.E.C.) 6-cyl horizontal type of 150 b.h.p.
Body: 57′ 6″ × 9′ 3″
Transmission:
Mechanical. Standard

DB975349 (E51116)
DB975539 (E56101)*
DB975564 (E51122)
DB975637 (E56300)*

Class 129 ♦
Cravens

Introduced: 1958 as motor parcels

van. Used for physics/acoustics research at Railway Technical Centre, Derby
Engines:
Two B.U.T. (A.E.C.) 6-cyl horizontal type of 150 b.h.p.
Body: 57′ 6″ × 9′ 3″
Non-gangwayed
Transmission:
Mechanical. Standard

RDB975385 (M55997)
  Laboratory 9

Class 203
Eastleigh Works, B.R.

Now Laboratory 4 used for tilt tests
Introduced: 1958 as trailer buffet
Body: 64′ 6″ × 8′ 2½″ & 9′ 0″

RDB975386 (S60750)

Swindon Works, B.R. ●

Introduced: 1956 as motor brake second
Engines:
Two B.U.T. (A.E.C.) 6-cyl horizontal type of 150 b.h.p.
Body: 64′ 6″ × 9′ 3″
Transmission:
Mechanical. Standard

ADM975426 (SC79098)

Derby Works, B.R. ■

Introduced: 1955 as driving trailer composite. Subsequently modified internally for use as an inspection saloon including a pantry
Body: 57′ 6″ × 9′ 2″

DB999510 (M79649)

Class 121 (1)■
Pressed Steel Co.

Route-learning car
Introduced: 1960 as motor brake second single-unit
Engines: Two Leyland 6-cyl horizontal type of 150 b.h.p.
Body: 64′ 6″ × 9′ 3″

TDB975659 (W55035)

ELECTRIC MULTIPLE-UNITS
London Midland Region

SYSTEM:
630 VOLTS D.C. 3rd RAIL

Class 501
London District Three-Car Sets

B.R. Standard design
Introduced: 1957

Motor Open Brake Second (DMBS)

Body: 57' 5" × 9' 0" & 9' 6"
Seats: 2nd, 74
Weight: 47 tons
Equipment: Four 185 h.p. G.E.C. traction motors

M61135	M61153	M61174
M61137	M61154	M61176
M61141	M61155	M61177
M61142	M61156	M61178
M61143	M61157	M61179
M61144	M61158	M61180
M61145	M61159	M61181
M61146	M61160	.
M61147	M61163	M61183
M61148	M61164	
M61149	M61168	
M61150	M61169	M61186
M61151	M61170	M61188
M61152	M61171	

Trailer Second (TS)
(*Trailer Open Second
†Trailer Semi-Open Second)
Body: 57' 1" × 9' 0" & 9' 6"
Seats: 2nd, 108 (92*, 94†)
Weight: 29 tons

M70135*	M70142*	M70145†
M70137†	M70143†	M70146†
M70141*	M70144*	M70148*
M70149†	M70161*	M70178*
M70150*	M70163*	M70179*
M70152†	M70164*	M70180*
M70153*	M70167	M70181*
M70154†	M70168†	M70182†
M70155†	M70169†	M70183*
M70156*	M70170*	M70184†
M70157†	M70171*	M70185†
M70158*	M70174*	M70186*
M70159†	M70176*	M70188*
M70160†	M70177*	M70189†

Driving Trailer Open Brake Second (DTBS)

Body: 57' 5" × 9' 0" & 9' 6"
Seats: 2nd, 74
Weight: 30 tons

M75135	M75154	M75174
M75137	M75155	M75176
M75141	M75156	M75177
M75142	M75157	M75178
M75143	M75158	M75179
M75144	M75159	M75180
M75145	M75160	M75181
M75146	M75161	M75182
M75148	M75163	M75183
M75149	M75164	M75184
M75150	M75168	M75185
M75151	M75169	M75186
M75152	M75170	M75188
M75153	M75171	M75189

SYSTEM:
600/750 VOLTS D.C. 3rd RAIL

Class 502
Liverpool-Southport Three- and Five-Car Sets
With air-operated sliding doors
Introduced: 1939

Motor Open Brake Second (MBS)
Body: 66' 6" × 9' 3" & 9' 5"
Seats: 2nd, 88
Weight: 42 tons
Equipment: Four 235 h.p. English Electric traction motors

M28312M	M28334M	M28354M
M28313M	M28335M	M28357M
M28315M	M28337M	M28364M
M28318M	M28338M	M28366M
M28319M	M28340M	M28369M
M28323M	M28347M	
M28332M	M28351M	

Trailer Open Second (TS)
Body: 66' 6" × 9' 3" & 9' 5"
Seats: 2nd, 102
Weight: 24 tons

M29546M	M29561M	M29582M
M29548M	M29562M	M29584M
M29549M	M29564M	M29586M
M29555M	M29565M	M29587M
M29556M	M29566M	M29588M
M29557M	M29567M	M29593M
M29559M	M29574M	

Driving Trailer Open Second (DTS)
Body: 66' 6" × 9' 3" & 9' 5"
Seats: 2nd, 78
Weight: 25 tons

M29867M	M29877M	M29890M
M29870M	M29880M	M29891M
M29872M	M29883M	M29894M
M29874M	M29886M	M29895M
M29875M	M29889M	M29897M

Scheduled for early withdrawal

Class 501 three-car unit at Broad Street

[*M. L. Rogers*

SYSTEM
600/750 VOLTS D.C. 3rd RAIL

Class 503
Wirral and Mersey Three-Car Sets

With air-operated sliding doors
Introduced: 1938 and 1956

Motor Open Brake Second (MBS)

Body: 58' 0" × 8' 8" & 9' 11"
Seats: 2nd, 56
Weight: 36 or 37 tons
Equipment: Four 135 h.p. B.T.H. traction motors

M28371M	M28386M	M28677M
M28372M	M28387M	M28678M
M28373M	M28388M	M28679M
M28374M	M28389M	M28680M
M28375M	M28390M	M28681M
M28376M	M28391M	M28682M
M28377M	M28392M	M28683M
M28378M	M28393M	M28684M
M28379M	M28394M	M28685M
M28380M	M28672M	M28686M
M28381M	M28673M	M28687M
M28382M	M28674M	M28688M
M28383M	M28675M	M28689M
M28384M	M28676M	M28690M
M28385M		

M28371–94M are 1956 cars

Trailer Open Second (TS)
Body: 56' 0" × 8' 8" & 9' 11"
Seats: 2nd, 55
Weight: 20 or 21 tons

M29702M	M29703M	M29704M

M29705M	M29821M	M29834M
M29706M	M29822M	M29835M
M29707M	M29823M	M29836M
M29709M	M29824M	M29837M
M29710M	M29825M	M29838M
M29711M	M29826M	M29839M
M29712M	M29827M	M29840M
M29713M	M29828M	M29841M
M29714M	M29829M	M29842M
M29715M	M29830M	M29843M
M29716M	M29831M	M29844M
M29718M	M29832M	M29845M
M29719M	M29833M	M29846M
M29720M		

M29821–46M are 1956 cars

Driving Trailer Open Second (DTS)
Body: 58' 0" × 8' 8" & 9' 11"
Seats: 2nd, 66
Weight: 21 tons

M29131M	M29146M	M29274M
M29132M	M29147M	M29275M
M29133M	M29148M	M29276M
M29134M	M29149M	M29278M
M29135M	M29150M	M29279M
M29136M	M29151M	M29280M
M29137M	M29152M	M29281M
M29138M	M29153M	M29282M
M29139M	M29154M	M29283M
M29140M	M29155M	M29284M
M29141M	M29156M	M29285M
M29142M	M29271M	M29287M
M29143M	M29272M	M29288M
M29144M	M29273M	M29289M
M29145M		

M29131–56M are 1956 cars

123

Class 504 Manchester–Bury two-car unit at Manchester Victoria [M. Radnedg

Class 304 four-car unit No 007 at Crewe [B. J. Nicol

SYSTEM:
1,200 VOLTS D.C. SIDE CONTACT 3rd RAIL

Class 504
Manchester-Bury Two-Car
Sets
B.R. Standard design
Introduced: 1959

Motor Open Brake Second
(MBS)
Body: 63' 11½ × 9' 0" & 9' 3"
Seats: 2nd, 84
Weight: 49 tons
Equipment: two 141 h.p. English
Electric traction motors

M65436	M65442	M65447
M65437	M65443	M65448
	M65444	M65449
M65439	M65445	M65450
M65441	M65446	M65451

M65452	M65456	M65459
M65453	M65457	M65460
M65454	M65458	M65461
M65455		

Driving Trailer Open Second
(DTS)
Body: 63' 11½ × 9' 0" & 9' 3"
Seats: 2nd, 94
Weight: 32 tons

M77157	M77167	M77175
M77158	M77168	M77176
	M77169	M77177
M77160	M77170	M77178
M77162	M77171	M77179
M77163	M77172	M77180
M77165	M77173	M77181
M77166	M77174	M77182

SYSTEM:
1,500 VOLTS D.C. OVERHEAD

Class 506
Manchester-Glossop-
Hadfield Three-Car Sets
With air-operated sliding doors
Introduced: 1954

Motor Open Brake Second
(MBS)
Body: 60' 4½ × 9' 0" & 9' 3"
Seats: 2nd, 52
Weight: 50 tons 12 cwt
Equipment: Four 185 h.p. G.E.C.
traction motors

M59401	M59404	M59407
M59402	M59405	M59408
M59403	M59406	

Trailer Open Second (TS)
Body: 55' 0½ × 9' 0" & 9' 3"
Seats: 2nd, 62
Weight: 26 tons 8 cwt

M59501	M59504	M59507
M59502	M59505	M59508
M59503	M59506	

Driving Trailer Open Second
(DTS)
Body: 55' 4½" × 9' 0" & 9' 3"
Seats: 2nd, 60
Weight: 27 tons 9 cwt

M59601	M59604	M59607
M59602	M59605	M59608
M59603	M59606	

SYSTEM:
600/750 VOLTS D.C. 3rd RAIL

Class 507
Garston-Liverpool-
Southport Three-Car Units

B.R. Standard design with air-operated sliding doors
Gangwayed throughout
Introduced: 1978

Motor Open Brake Second
(MBS)

Body: 64' 11½" × 9' 3"
Seats: 2nd, 74
Weight:
Equipment: Four 110 h.p. GEC traction motors
Nos: 64367–64460

Trailer Open Second
Body: 65' 4¼" × 9' 3"

Seats: 2nd, 84
Weight:
Nos: 71342–78

Motor Open Brake Second

(As above)

507 001	507 014	507 027
507 002	507 015	507 028
507 003	507 016	507 029
507 004	507 017	507 030
507 005	507 018	
507 006	507 019	
507 007	507 020	
507 008	507 021	
507 009	507 022	
507 010	507 023	
507 011	507 024	
507 012	507 025	
507 013	507 026	

SYSTEM:
25 kV A.C. OVERHEAD

Classes 304/1, 304/2* and 304/3†
Euston, Birmingham, Manchester and Liverpool Four-Car Units

B.R. Standard design
Introduced: 1960

Driving Trailer Open Brake Second (DTBS)

Body: 64' 0⅝" × 9' 0" & 9' 3"
Seats: 2nd, 82
Weight: 31 tons 8 cwt
(32 tons*†)
Nos.: M75645–79, M75858–67

Trailer Composite (L) (TC)

Body: 63' 6⅛" × 9' 0" & 9' 3"
Seats: 1st, 19; 2nd, 60
Weight: 31 tons 5 cwt
Nos.: M70045–59, M70483–502, M70243–52

Non-Driving Motor Brake Second (Open*†) (MBS)

Body: 63' 6⅛" × 9' 0" & 9' 3"
Seats: 2nd, 96 (72*†)
Weight: 53 tons 12 cwt
(54 tons 3 cwt*†)
Equipment: Four A.E.I. 207 h.p. d.c. traction motors
Nos.: M60145–59, M61628–47, M61873–82

Driving Trailer Open Second (DTS) (L)

Body: 64' 0⅝" × 9' 0" & 9' 3"
Seats: 2nd, 80
Weight: 35 tons 12 cwt
Nos.: M75045–59, M75680–99, M75868–77

001	006	011
002	007	012
003	008	013
004	009	014
005	010	015

016*	027*	037†
017*	028*	038†
018*	029*	039†
019*	030*	040†
020*	031*	041†
021*	032*	042†
022*	033*	043†
023*	034*	044†
024*	035*	045†
025*	036†	

046	063	080
047	064	081
048	065	082
049	066*	083
050	067	084
051	068	085
052	069	086
053	070	087
054	072	088
055	073	089
056	074	090
057	075	091
058	076	092
059	077	093
060	078	094
061	079	095
062		

Class 310
Euston, Birmingham, Manchester and Liverpool Four-Car Units

B.R. Standard design
Partially gangwayed within unit
Introduced: 1966

Driving Trailer Open Second (L) (DTS)
Body: 65′ 1⅝″ × 9′ 0″ & 9′ 3″
Seats: 2nd, 80 (*68)
Weight: 36 tons 15 cwt
Nos.: M76130–79

Non-Driving Motor Open Brake Second (MBS)
Body: 65′ 4¼″ × 9′ 0″ & 9′ 3″
Seats: 2nd, 70
Weight: 56 tons 7 cwt
Equipment: Four English Electric 270 h.p. d.c. traction motors
Nos.: M62071–120

Trailer Open Second (TS)
Body: 65′ 4¼″ × 9′ 0″ & 9′ 3″
Seats: 2nd, 100
Weight: 31 tons 4 cwt
Nos.: M70731–80

Driving Trailer Open Composite (L) (DTC)
Body: 65′ 1⅝″ × 9′ 0″ & 9′ 3″
Seats: 1st, 25; 2nd, 43
Weight: 33 tons 16 cwt
Nos: M76180–229

Class 317
Bedford-St Pancras/ Moorgate Four-Car Units

New B.R. Standard design. Gangwayed throughout and fitted with air-operated sliding doors
These units are equipped to work from 750 V d.c. in tunnel sections

Driving Trailer Vestibule Second (DTVS)
Body:
Seats: 2nd, 71
Weight:
Nos.: M77048–95

Motor Second (non-driving) (MS)
Body:
Seats: 2nd, 79
Weight:
Equipment:
Nos.: M62661–62708

Trailer Composite (TC)
Body:
Seats: 1st, 22; 2nd, 46
Weight:
Nos.: M71577–71624

Driving Trailer Second (DTS)
Body:
Seats: 2nd, 74
Weight:
Nos.: M77000–47

317 301	317 317	317 333
317 302	317 318	317 334
317 303	317 319	317 335
317 304	317 320	317 336
317 305	317 321	317 337
317 306	317 322	317 338
317 307	317 323	317 339
317 308	317 324	317 340
317 309	317 325	317 341
317 310	317 326	317 342
317 311	317 327	317 343
317 312	317 328	317 344
317 313	317 329	317 345
317 314	317 330	317 346
317 315	317 331	317 347
317 316	317 332	317 348

Class 370
Advanced Passenger Train

Introduced: 1979. Some vehicles built in 1978

Six units, each comprising six articulated trailer cars plus one power car will be built. Formations may vary but will normally consist of two units and two power cars coupled together

Driving Trailer Seconds: Nos. 48101–7

Trailer Seconds: Nos. 48201–12

Trailer Buffet/Restaurant: Nos. 48401–6

Trailer Firsts: Nos. 48501–6

Trailer Brake Firsts: Nos. 48601–7

Motor Coaches (non-driving): Nos. 49001–6

Unit Numbers

370 001	370 003	370 005
370 002	370 004	370 006

Class 370 Advanced Passenger Train (APT-P) No 370 002   [C. Burnha

Scottish Region

Classes 303 and 311†
Glasgow Area Three-Car
Units
B.R. Standard design with air-operated sliding doors
Introduced: 1960 (1967†)

Driving Trailer Open
Second (DTS)
Body: 63′ 11⅝″ × 9′ 3″ & 9′ 3″
Seats: 2nd, 83
Weight: 34 tons
Nos.: SC75566–600,
SC75746–801, SC76403–21

Non-Driving Motor Open
Brake Second (MBS)
Body: 63′ 6⅛″ × 9′ 3″ & 9′ 3″
Seats: 2nd, 70
Weight: 56 tons
Equipment: Four A.E.I. (MV) 207
h.p. d.c. traction motors
†Four AEI 222 h.p. d.c. traction motors
Nos.: SC61481–515,
SC61812–67, SC62163–81

Driving Trailer Open
Second (DTS)
Body: 63′ 11⅝″ × 9′ 3″ & 9′ 3″
Seats: 2nd, 83
Weight: 38 tons
Nos.: SC75601–35,
SC75802–57, SC76422–40

001	009	017
002	010	018
003	011	019
004	012	020
005	013	021
006	014	022
007	015	023
008	016	024

025	054	083
026	055	084
027	056	085
028	057	086
029	058	087
030	059	088
031	060	089
032	061	090
033	062	091
034	063	092†
035*	064	093†
036	065	094†
037	066	095†
038	067	096†
039	068	097†
040	069	098†
041	070	099†
042	071	100†
043	072	101†
044	073	102†
045	074	103†
046	075	104†
047	076	105†
048	077	106†
049	078	107†
050	079	108†
051	080	109†
052	081	110†
053	082	

*Fitted with thyristor control equipment

Class 314
Glasgow Area Three-Car Units

BR Standard design with air-operated sliding doors. Gangwayed throughout
Introduced: 1979

Motor Open Second (DMS)

No Series: 64583–64614
Body: 64' 11½" × 9' 3"
Seats: 2nd, 74
Weight:
Equipment:

Trailer Open Second (TS)

No Series: 71450–65
Body: 65' 4¼" × 9' 3"
Seats: 2nd, 84
Weight:
Equipment:

Motor Open Second (DMS)

No Series: 64583–64614
Body: 64' 11½" × 9' 3"
Seats: 2nd, 74
Weight:
Equipment:

314 201	314 207	314 212
314 202	314 208	314 213
314 203	314 209	314 214
314 204	314 210	314 215
314 205	314 211	314 216
314 206		

Scottish Region Class 311 three-car unit No 311 092   *[Brian Morriso*

Eastern Region

SYSTEM:
25 kV (originally 6.25 kV) A.C. OVERHEAD

Class 306
Liverpool St.-Shenfield
Three-Car Units

With air-operated sliding doors
Introduced: (for d.c. working)
1949;
Rebuilt: (for a.c. working) 1960

Motor Open Second (DMS)

Body: 60' 4½" × 9' 0" & 9' 6"
Seats: 2nd, 62
Weight: 50 tons 17 cwt
Equipment: Four 157 h.p. d.c.
traction motors
Nos.: E65201–92

Trailer Open Brake Second (TBS)

(with transformer and rectifier)
Body: 55' 0½" × 9' 0" & 9' 6"
Seats: 2nd, 46
Weight: 26 tons
Nos.: E65401–92

Driving Trailer Open Second (DTS)

Body: 55' 4" × 9' 0" & 9' 6"
Seats: 2nd, 60
Weight: 27 tons 10 cwt
Nos.: E65601–92

306 001		306 021
306 002	306 012	306 022
306 003	306 013	306 023
	306 014	306 024
306 005	306 015	306 025
306 006	306 016	306 026
306 007	306 017	306 027
306 008	306 018	306 028
306 009	306 019	306 029
306 010	306 020	306 031

306 032	306 053	306 073
306 033	306 054	306 074
306 034	306 055	306 075
306 035	306 056	306 076
306 036	306 057	306 077
306 037	306 058	306 078
306 038	306 059	306 079
306 039	306 060	306 080
306 040	306 061	306 081
306 041	306 062	306 082
306 042	306 063	306 083
306 043	306 064	306 084
	306 065	306 085
306 045	306 066	306 086
306 046	306 067	306 087
306 047	306 068	306 088
306 048	306 069	306 089
306 049	306 070	306 090
306 050	306 071	306 091
306 051	306 072	306 092
306 052		

Class 307
G.E. Outer Suburban Four-
Car Units

B.R. Standard design
Introduced: (for d.c. working)
1956;
Rebuilt: (for a.c. working) 1960

Driving Trailer Brake Second (DTBS)

(with transformer and rectifier)
Body: 63' 11½" × 9' 0" & 9' 3"
Seats: 2nd, 84
Weight:
Nos.: E75001–32

Non-Driving Motor Second (MS)

Body: 63′ 6″×9′ 0″ & 9′ 3″
Seats: 2nd, 120
Weight:
Equipment: Four G.E.C. 174 h.p. d.c. traction motors
Nos.: E61001–32

Trailer Composite (TC)

Body: 63′ 6″×9′ 0″ & 9′ 3″
Seats: 1st, 19; 2nd, 6
Weight: 30 tons
Nos.: E70001–32

Driving Trailer Open Second (DTS)

Body: 63′ 11½″×9′ 0″ & 9′ 3″
Seats: 2nd, 80
Weight:
Nos.: E75101–32

307 101	307 112	307 123
307 102	307 113	307 124
307 103	307 114	307 125
307 104	307 115	307 126
307 105	307 116	307 127
307 106	307 117	307 128
307 107	307 118	307 129
307 108	307 119	307 130
307 109	307 120	307 131
307 110	307 121	307 132
307 111	307 122	

Trailer Composite (TC)

Body: 63′ 6″×9′ 0″ & 9′ 3″
Seats: 1st, 19; 2nd, 60
Weight: 31 tons
Nos.: E70611–43

Non-Driving Motor Brake Second (MBS)

Body: 63′ 6″×9′ 0″ & 9′ 3″
Seats: 2nd, 96
Weight: 54 tons
Equipment: Four English Electric 200 h.p. d.c. traction motors
Nos.: E61883–915

Driving Trailer Open Second (DTS)

Body: 64′ 0½″×9′ 0″ & 9′ 3″
Seats: 2nd, 80
Weight: 36 tons
Nos.: E75878–86, E75896–919

308 133	308 144	308 155
308 134	308 145	308 156
308 135	308 146	308 157
308 136	308 147	308 158
308 137	308 148	308 159
308 138	308 149	308 160
308 139	308 150	308 161
308 140	308 151	308 162
308 141	308 152	308 163
308 142	308 153	308 164
308 143	308 154	308 165

Class 308/1
G.E. Outer Suburban Four-Car Units

B.R. Standard design
Introduced: 1961

Driving Trailer Second (DTS)

Body: 64′ 0½″×9′ 0″ & 9′ 3″
Seats: 2nd, 108
Weight: 32 tons
Nos.: E75887–93, E75929–52

Class 302
Fenchurch St.- Shoeburyness Four-Car Units

B.R. Standard design
Introduced: 1959

Driving Trailer Second (DTS)

Body: 63′ 11½″×9′ 0″ & 9′ 3″
Seats: 2nd, 108
Weight: 32 tons
Nos.: E75033–84, E75211–77

Class 306 three-car unit No 085 leading a Liverpool Street–Gidea Park train [*M. L. Rogers*

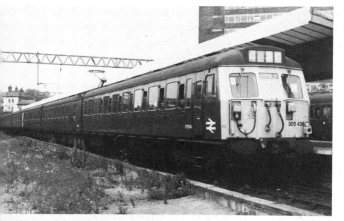

Class 305 three-car unit No 305 428 at Enfield [*M. L. Rogers*

Class 307 four-car unit No 122 entering Ilford

[M. L. Roge

Class 312 four-car unit No 312 711 near Copenhagen Tunnel

[B. J. Nico.

134

Trailer Composite (TC)

Body: 63' 6" × 9' 0" & 9' 3"
Seats: 1st, 19; **2nd,** 60
Weight: 31 tons
Nos.: E70060–220

Non-Driving Motor Brake Second (MBS)

Body: 63' 6" & 9' 0" & 9' 3"
Seats: 2nd, 96
Weight: 56 tons 10 cwt
Equipment: Four English Electric 192 h.p. d.c. traction motors
Nos.: E61060–132, E61190–220

Driving Trailer Open Second (DTS)

Body: 63' 11½" × 9' 0" & 9' 3"
Seats: 2nd, 80
Weight: 36 tons
Nos.: E75085–100, E75190–352

302 201	302 226	302 251
302 202	302 227	302 252
302 203	302 228	302 253
302 204	302 229	302 254
302 205	302 230	302 255
302 206	302 231	302 256
302 207	302 232	302 257
302 208	302 233	302 258
302 209	302 234	302 259
302 210	302 235	302 260
302 211	302 236	302 261
302 212	302 237	302 262
302 213	302 238	302 263
302 214	302 239	302 264
302 215	302 240	302 265
302 216	302 241	302 266
302 217	302 242	302 267
302 218	302 243	302 268
302 219	302 244*	302 269
302 220	302 245	302 270
302 221	302 246	302 271
302 222	302 247	302 272
302 223	302 248	302 273
302 224	302 249	302 274
302 225	302 250	302 275

302 276	302 289	302 301
302 277	302 290	302 302
302 278	302 291	302 303
302 279	302 292	302 304
302 280	302 293	302 305
302 281	302 294	302 306
302 282	302 295	302 307
302 283	302 296	302 308
302 284	302 297	302 309
302 285	302 298	302 310
302 286	302 299	302 311
302 287	302 300	302 312
302 288		

*Unit 244 has one ex-Manchester-Bury Class 504 Driving Trailer Open Second

Class 308/4 Fenchurch St.- Shoeburyness Four-Car Units

B.R. Standard design
Introduced: 1961 (Motor coach rebuilt 1971)

Driving Trailer Second (DTS)

Body: 63' 11½" × 9' 0" & 9' 3"
Seats: 2nd, 108
Weight: 32 tons
Nos.: E75953–6

Trailer Composite (TC)

Body: 63' 6" × 9' 0" & 9' 3"
Seats: 1st, 19; **2nd,** 60
Weight: 31 tons
Nos.: E70644–7

Non-Driving Motor Open Brake Second (MBS)

Body: 63' 6" × 9' 0" & 9' 3"
Seats: 2nd, 76
Weight:
Equipment: Four English Electric 192 h.p. d.c. traction motors
Nos.: E62431–4

Driving Trailer Open Second (DTS)

Body: 63′ 11½″ × 9′ 0″ & 9′ 3″
Seats: 2nd, 80
Weight: 36 tons
Nos.: E75920–3

308 313	308 315	308 316
308 314		

Class 308/2
Fenchurch St.-
Shoeburyness Four-Car
Units

B.R. Standard design
Introduced: 1961

Driving Trailer Second (DTS)
Body: 63′ 11½″ × 9′ 0″ & 9′ 3″
Seats: 2nd, 108
Weight: 32 tons
Nos.: E75957–61

Trailer Composite (TC)
Body: 63′ 6″ × 9′ 0″ & 9′ 3″
Seats: 1st, 19; 2nd, 60
Weight: 31 tons
Nos.: E70648–52

Non-Driving Motor Luggage Van (MLV)
Body: 63′ 6″ × 9′ 0″ & 9′ 3″
Weight: 51 tons 12 cwt
Equipment: Four English Electric 192 h.p. d.c. traction motors
Nos.: E68012/5–8

Driving Trailer Open Second (L) (DTS)
Body: 63′ 11½″ × 9′ 0″ & 9′ 3″
Seats: 2nd, 80
Weight: 36 tons
Nos.: E75924–8

308 317	308 319	308 321
308 318	308 320	

Class 305/1 and *308/3
Liverpool St.-Enfield and
Chingford Three-Car Units

B.R. Standard design
Introduced: 1960 (*1961)

Driving Trailer Open Second (DTS)
Body: 63′ 11½″ × 9′ 0″ & 9′ 3″
Seats: 2nd, 94
Weight:
Nos.: E75462–513, E75741–3

Non-Driving Motor Open Brake Second (MBS)
Body: 63′ 6″ × 9′ 0″ & 9′ 3″
Seats: 2nd, 84
Weight:
Equipment: Four G.E.C. 200 h.p. d.c. traction motors
Nos.: E61429–80, E61689–91
*Four English Electric 200 h.p. d.c. traction motors

Driving Trailer Open Second (DTS)
Body: 63′ 11½″ × 9′ 0″ & 9′ 3″
Seats: 2nd, 94
Weight:
Nos.: E75514–65, E75992–4

305 401	305 420	305 438
305 402	305 421	305 439
305 403	305 422	305 440
305 404	305 423	305 441
305 405	305 424	305 442
305 406	305 425	305 443
305 407	305 426	305 444
305 408	305 427	305 445
305 409	305 428	305 446
305 410	305 429	305 447
305 411	305 430	305 448
305 412	305 431	305 449
305 413	305 432	305 450
305 414	305 433	305 451
305 415	305 434	305 452
305 416	305 435	305 453*
305 417	305 436	305 454*
305 418	305 437	305 455*
305 419		

Class 305/2
G.E. Outer Suburban Four-Car Units

B.R. Standard design
Introduced: 1960

These units are scheduled for major refurbishment. Details marked * show the proposed changes in seating.

Driving Trailer Second (DTS)

Body: 64' 0½" × 9' 0" & 9' 3"
Seats: 2nd, 108 (*88)
Weight: 32 tons
Nos.: E75443–61

Trailer Composite (H) (Second*)
Body: 63' 6" × 9' 0" & 9' 3"
Seats: 1st, 19; **2nd,** 60 (**2nd,** 86*)
Weight: 31 tons
Nos.: E70356–74

Non-Driving Motor Brake Second (MBS)

Body: 63' 6" × 9' 0" & 9' 3"
Seats: 2nd, 96 (*76)
Weight: 54 tons
Equipment: Four G.E.C. 200 h.p. d.c. traction motors
Nos.: E61410–28

Driving Trailer Open Second (DTS) (Composite)*

Body: 64' 0½" × 9' 0" & 9' 3"
Seats: 2nd, 80 (*1st, 24; 2nd, 48)
Weight: 36 tons
Nos.: E75424–42

305 501	305 508	305 514
305 502	305 509	305 515
305 503	305 510	305 516
305 504	305 511	305 517
305 505	305 512	305 518
305 506	305 513	305 519
305 507		

Class 309/1
Liverpool St.-Clacton and Walton Two-Car Units

B.R. Standard design

Gangwayed throughout
Introduced: 1962

Motor Brake Second (MBS)

Body: 64' 9¾" × 9' 0" & 9' 3"
Seats: 2nd, 48
Weight: 59 tons 6 cwt
Equipment: Four G.E.C. 282 h.p. d.c. traction motors
Nos.: E61940–3

Driving Trailer Saloon Second (DTS)

Body: 64' 9¾" × 9' 0" & 9' 3"
Seats: 2nd, 60
Weight: 39 tons 11 cwt
Nos.: E75984–7

309 601	309 603	309 604
309 602		

Class 309/4
Liverpool St.-Clacton and Walton Four-Car Units

B.R. Standard design
Gangwayed throughout
Introduced:
As Class 309/1: 1962;
As Class 309/4: 1974.

Motor Brake Second (MBS)

Body: 64' 9¾" × 9' 0" & 9' 3"
Seats: 2nd, 48
Weight: 59 tons 6 cwt
Equipment: Four G.E.C. 282 h.p. d.c. traction motors
Nos.: E61944–7

Trailer Composite (TC)

Body: 64' 6" × 9' 0" & 9' 3"
Seats: 1st, 24; **2nd,** 24
Weight:
Nos.: E71111–4

Trailer Saloon Second (TS)

Body: 64' 6" × 9' 0" & 9' 3"
Seats: 2nd, 64
Weight:
Nos.: E71107–10

Driving Trailer Saloon Second (DTS)

Body: 64' 9¾" × 9' 0" & 9' 3"
Seats: 2nd, 60
Weight: 39 tons 11 cwt
Nos.: E75988–91

309 605	309 607	309 608
309 606		

Class 309/2
Liverpool St.-Clacton and Walton Four-Car Buffet Units

B.R. Standard design
Gangwayed throughout
Introduced: 1962

Driving Trailer Composite (DTC)

Body: 64' 9¾" × 9' 0" & 9' 3"
Seats: 1st, 18; 2nd, 32
Weight: 39 tons 7 cwt
Nos.: E75637–44

Non-Driving Motor Brake Second (MBS)

Body: 64' 6" × 9' 0" & 9' 3"
Seats: 2nd, 48
Weight: 56 tons 16 cwt
Equipment: Four G.E.C. 282 h.p. d.c. traction motors
Nos.: E61932–9

Trailer Griddle/Buffet Car (TG)

Body: 64' 6" × 9' 0" & 9' 3"
Seats: Buffet, 32
Weight: 35 tons 16 cwt
Nos.: E69100–8

Driving Trailer Saloon Composite (DTC)

Body: 64' 9¾" × 9' 0" & 9' 3"
Seats: 1st, 18; 2nd, 32
Weight: 36 tons 1 cwt
Nos.: E75976–83

309 611	309 614	309 617
309 612	309 615	309 618
309 613	309 616*	

*Unit 616 has an ex-DMU Trailer Buffet Second

Class 309/3
Liverpool St.-Clacton and Walton Four-Car Units

B.R. Standard design
Gangwayed throughout
Introduced: 1962

Driving Trailer Composite (DTC)

Body: 64' 9¾" × 9' 0" & 9' 3"
Seats: 1st, 18; 2nd, 32
Weight: 39 tons 7 cwt
Nos.: E75962–8

Non-Driving Motor Brake Second (MBS)

Body: 64' 6" × 9' 0" & 9' 3"
Seats: 2nd, 48
Weight: 56 tons 16 cwt
Equipment: Four G.E.C. 282 h.p. d.c. traction motors
Nos.: E61925–31

Trailer Saloon Second (TS)

Body: 64' 6" × 9' 0" & 9' 3"
Seats: 2nd, 64
Weight: 34 tons 8 cwt
Nos.: E70253–9

Driving Trailer Saloon Composite (DTC)

Body: 64' 9¾" × 9' 0" & 9' 3"
Seats: 1st, 18; 2nd, 32
Weight: 36 tons 15 cwt
Nos.: E75969–75

309 621	309 624	309 626
309 622	309 625	309 627
309 623		

Class 312/0 GN, 312/1 GE and 312/2 LM
Outer Suburban Four-Car Units

B.R. Standard design. Gangwayed within unit. These units are being renumbered in the 312 700 series
Introduced: 1975

Driving Trailer Open Second (DTS)
Body: 65' 1⅝" × 9' 0" & 9' 3"
Seats: 2nd, 84
Weight: 34 tons 7 cwt
Nos.: 76949–97

Non-Driving Motor Open Brake Second (MBS)
Body: 65' 4¼" × 9' 0" & 9' 3"
Seats: 2nd, 68
Weight: 54 tons 12 cwt
Equipment: Four G.E.C. 270 h.p. d.c. traction motors
Nos.: 62484–528

Trailer Open Second (TS)
Body: 65' 4¼" × 9' 0" & 9' 3"
Seats: 2nd, 98
Nos.: 71168–212/77–80

Driving Trailer Open Composite (DTC)
Body: 65' 1⅝" × 9' 0" & 9' 3"
Seats: 1st, 25; 2nd, 47
Weight: 32 tons 2 cwt
Nos.: 78000–48

Class 312/0

312 701	312 710	312 019
312 702	312 711	312 020
312 703	312 712	312 021
312 704	312 713	312 022
312 705	312 714	312 023
312 706	312 015	312 024
312 707	312 716	312 025
312 708	312 717	312 026
312 709	312 018	

Class 312/1

312 781	312 788	312 794
312 782	312 789	312 795
312 783	312 790	312 796
312 784	312 791	312 797
312 785	312 792	312 798
312 786	312 793	312 799
312 787		

Class 312/2

312 201	312 203	312 204
312 202		

Class 313 GN
Inner Suburban Three-Car Units

B.R. Standard design with air-operated sliding doors
Gangwayed throughout
(These units are also equipped to work from 750 V. d.c. 3rd rail in tunnel sections)
Introduced: 1976

Motor Open Second (MS)
Body: 64' 11½" × 9' 3"
Seats: 2nd, 74
Weight: 35.94 tonnes
Equipment: Four 110 h.p. G.E.C. traction motors
Nos.: 62529–92

Trailer Open Second (TS)
Body: 65' 4¼" × 9' 3"
Seats: 2nd, 84
Weight: 31.76 tonnes
Nos.: 71213–76

Motor Open Second (MS)
Body: 64' 11½" × 9' 3"
Seats: 2nd, 74
Weight: 37.74 tonnes
Equipment: Four 110 h.p. G.E.C. traction motors
Nos.: 62593–628

313 001	313 023	313 044
313 002	313 024	313 045
313 003	313 025	313 046
313 004	313 026	313 047
313 005	313 027	313 048
313 006	313 028	313 049
313 007	313 029	313 050
313 008	313 030	313 051
313 009	313 031	313 052
313 010	313 032	313 053
313 011	313 033	313 054
313 012	313 034	313 055
313 013	313 035	313 056
313 014	313 036	313 057
313 015	313 037	313 058
313 016	313 038	313 059
313 017	313 039	313 060
313 018	313 040	313 061
313 019	313 041	313 062
313 020	313 042	313 063
313 021	313 043	313 064
313 022		

Class 315 GE
Liverpool St.-Shenfield
Inner Suburban Four-Car
Units

B.R. Standard design with air-operated sliding doors
Gangwayed throughout
Introduced: 1980

Motor Open Brake Second (MBS)

Body:
Seats: 2nd, 74
Weight:
Equipment:

Non Driving Motor Open Second (MS)

Body:
Seats: 2nd, 84
Weight:
Equipment:

Trailer Open Second (TS)

Body:
Seats: 2nd, 84
Weight:

Driving Trailer Open Brake Second (DTS)

Body:
Seats: 2nd, 74
Weight:

315 801	315 822	315 842
315 802	315 823	315 843
315 803	315 824	315 844
315 804	315 825	315 845
315 805	315 826	315 846
315 806	315 827	315 847
315 807	315 828	315 848
315 808	315 829	315 849
315 809	315 830	315 850
315 810	315 831	315 851
315 811	315 832	315 852
315 812	315 833	315 853
315 813	315 834	315 854
315 814	315 835	315 855
315 815	315 836	315 856
315 816	315 837	315 857
315 817	315 838	315 858
315 818	315 839	315 859
315 819	315 840	315 860
315 820	315 841	315 861
315 821		

Research Department
Electric Unit
Class 920 Prototype
Suburban Three-Car Unit

B.R. Standard design with air-operated sliding doors. Gangwayed throughout. Now allocated to Railway Technical Centre, Derby
Introduced: 1975

Motor Open Brake Second (MBS)

Body: 64' 11½" × 9' 3"
Seats: 2nd
Weight:
Equipment: Four 100 h.p. English Electric traction motors

Trailer Open Second (TS)

Body: 65' 4¼" × 9' 3"
Seats: 2nd
Weight:

Motor Open Brake Second (MBS)

(As above)
920 001

Class 313 three-car unit No 313 023 passing Hadley Wood

[*Brian Morrison*

Class 315 four-car unit No 315 812 near Romford

[*J. M. Rickard*

141

Southern Region

Class 491
Four-Car Trailer Units (4-TC)
B.R. Standard design
Gangwayed throughout
Introduced: 1966 and 1974*

Driving Trailer Saloon Second (DTS)
Body: 64' 6" × 9' 0" & 9' 3"
Seats: 2nd, 64
Weight: 32 tons
Nos.: S76270–332, S76943–47

Trailer Brake Second (TBS)
Body: 64' 6" × 9' 0" & 9' 3"
Seats: 2nd, 32
Weight: 35 tons
Nos.: S70812–43, S71160/1

Trailer First (TF)
Body: 64' 6" × 9' 0" & 9' 3"
Seats: 1st, 42
Weight: 33 tons
Nos.: S70844–71, S71162–7

Driving Trailer Saloon Second (DTS)
(As above)

401	413	424
402	414	425
403	415	426
404	416	427
405	417	428
406	418	429
407	419	430
408	420	431
409	421	432*
410	422	433*
411	423	434*
412		

Class 430
Four-Car Units (4-REP)
B.R. Standard design
Gangwayed throughout
Introduced: 1967 and 1974*
(These units work in conjunction with 4-TC trailer units and are not normally worked in multiple with other powered units)

Motor Saloon Second (MS)
Body: 64' 6" × 9' 0" & 9' 3"
Seats: 2nd, 64
Weight: 52 tons
Equipment: Four 365 h.p. English Electric traction motors
Nos.: S62141–62, S62476–83

Trailer Buffet (TRB)
Body: 64' 6" × 9' 0" & 9' 3"
Seats: 19
Weight: 34 tons
Nos.: S69319–29, S69022–5

Trailer Brake First (TBF)
Body: 64' 6" × 9' 0" & 9' 3"
Seats: 1st, 24
Weight: 35 tons
Nos.: S70801–11, S71156–9

Motor Saloon Second (MS)
(As above)

3001	3006	3011
3002	3007	3012*
3003	3008	3013*
3004	3009	3014*
3005	3010	3015*

Class 405/2
Four-Car Suburban Units
(4-SUB)
Introduced: 1948/9
Motor Open Brake Second
(MBS)
Body: 62' 6" × 9' 0" & 9' 3"
Seats: 2nd, 82
Weight: 39 tons
Equipment: Two 250 h.p. English
Electric traction motors
Nos.: S10849–58/61–7/9–72/
74–8/80–93. 11323/39S

Trailer Second (Trailer Open
Second*) (TS)
Body: 62' 0" × 9' 0" & 9' 3"
Seats: 2nd, 120, (102*)
Weight: 28 tons
Nos.: S10121–5/7/9–35/7–48/
50/2/3–8/60–5S, S12374/80S

Trailer Open Second (TS)
Body: 62' 0" × 9' 0" & 9' 3"
Seats: 2nd, 102
Weight: 28 tons

Motor Open Brake Second
(MBS)
(As above)

4277*	4285*	4293*
4278	4286	4294*
4279*	4287	4295
4280	4288	4296
4281	4289	4298*
4283	4290	4299*
4284*	4291*	

Class 405/2
Four-Car Suburban Units
(4-SUB)
Introduced: 1949/50
Motor Open Brake Second
(MBS)
Body: 62' 6" × 9' 0" & 9' 3"
Seats: 2nd, 82
Weight: 39 tons

Equipment: Two 250 h.p. English
Electric traction motors
Nos.: Random from S8600S,
S11300S and S12600S series

Trailer Open Second (Trailer
Second*) (TS)
Body: 62' 0" × 9' 0" & 9' 3"
Seats: 2nd, 120 (102†, 108‡)
Weight: 28 tons (27 tons‡)
Nos.: Random mainly from
S8900S, S10200S and S12300S
series

Trailer Open Second (TS)
(As above)

Motor Open Brake Second
(MBS)
(As above).

4617	4656	4696
4618	4657	4697*
4619	4658	4701*
4620	4659	4705*
4621	4660*	4709*
4623		4710
4626	4664*	4714*
4627	4666	4716*
4628*	4668	
4629*	4669*	4719*
4630*	4670	4721*
4631*	4671	4722
4632*	4672	4725
4633	4673*	4726
4635*	4674	4730
4636*	4675*	4732
4637	4677*	4733
4638*	4678	4735*
4639	4679	4738
4641*	4680	4739
4643*	4681*	4742*
4645	4682	4743
4648*	4683*	4747*
4649	4684*	4749
4650*	4687	4750
4651	4689*	4751*
4653*	4692*	
4654	4693*	4754*
4655*	4695*	

Class 405 unit No 4361   [*Brian Morrison*

Refurbished Class 411 four-car unit No 411 605   [*C. J. Marsden*

144

Class 415/1
Four-Car Suburban Units
(4-EPB)
Introduced: 1951–4

Motor Open Brake Second
(Motor Semi-Open Brake
Second‡§■) (MBS)
Body: 62' 6"×9' 0" & 9' 3"
‡63' 11½"×9' 0" & 9' 3"
Seats: 2nd, 82 (84‡■)
Weight: 40 tons
Equipment: Two 250 h.p. English
Electric traction motors
Nos.: S14001–106S and
S14201–465

Trailer Second (Trailer Open
Second■) (TS)
Body: 62' 0"×9' 0" & 9' 3"
Seats: 2nd, 120 (108* 102■)
Weight: 28 tons (27 tons■)
Nos.: Random from S15001–
S15450S series

Trailer Open Second (Trailer
Second †§) (TS)
Body: 62' 0"×9' 0" & 9' 3"
Seats: 2nd, 102 (120†)
Weight: 27 tons (28 tons†)
(Nos. as above)

Motor Open Brake Second
(Motor Semi-Open Brake
Second§■)(MBS)
(As above)

5001	5011	5021
5002	5012	5022
5003	5013	5024
5004	5014	5025
5005*	5015	5026
5006	5016	5027
5007	5017	5028
5008*	5018	5029
5009	5019	5030
5010	5020	5031

5032	5132	5184
5033	5133	5185
5034	5134	5186
5035	5135	5187
5036	5136	5188
5037	5137	5189
5038	5138	5190
5039	5139	5191
5040	5140	5192
5041	5142	5193
5042	5143R	5194
5043	5144	5195
5044	5145	5196
5045	5146	5197
5046	5147	5198
5048	5148	5199
5049	5149	5200
5050	5150	5201
5051	5151	5202
5052	5152	5203
5053	5153	5205
5101	5154	5206
5102	5155	5207
5104	5156	5208
5105	5157	5209
5106	5158	5210
5107	5159	5211
5108	5160	5212
5109	5161	5213
5110	5162	5214
5111	5163	5215
5112	5164	5216
5113	5165	5217
5114	5166	5218
5115*	5168	5219
5116	5169	5220
5117	5170	5221
5118	5171	5222
5119	5172	5223
5120	5173	5224
5121	5174	5225R
5122	5175	5226
5123	5176	5227
5124	5177	5228
5125	5178	5229
5126	5179	5230
5127	5180	5231
5128	5181	5232
5129	5182	5233
5131	5183	5234

145

Refurbished Class 415/1 four-car unit No 5225   [*C. J. Marsden*

Class 414 two-car unit No 6037   [*C. J. Marsden*

5235	5245†	5255
5236	5246‡	5256
5237	5247	5257
5238	5248	5258
5239	5249	5259
5240	5250	5260
5241	5251	5261§
5242	5252	5262‡
5243	5253	5263■
5244	5254	5264■

*Units 5005/8, 5115, 5220 have one nine-compartment trailer second

†Unit 5245 has two trailer compartment seconds

‡Units 5246/62 have one BR standard motor coach

§Unit 5261 has two BR standard motor coaches and two trailer compartment seconds

■ Units 5263/4 have two trailer open seconds

Class 415/2
Four-Car Suburban Units
(4-EPB)
Motor coaches only: B.R. Standard design
Introduced: 1960

Motor Semi-Open Brake Second (MBS)
Body: 63' 11¾" × 9' 0" & 9' 3"
Seats: 2nd, 84
Weight: 40 tons
Equipment: Two 250 h.p. English Electric traction motors
Nos.: S61625–7/S65308S

Trailer Second (TS)
Body: 62' 0" × 9' 0" & 9' 3"
Seats: 2nd, 120
Weight: 28 tons
Nos.: S15043/79S

Trailer Open Second (TS)
Body: 62' 0" × 9' 0" & 9' 3"
Seats: 2nd, 102 (120")
Weight: 27 tons
Nos.: S15121/413S

Motor Semi-Open Brake Second (MBS)
(As above)

5301	5302

Class 415/2
Four-Car Suburban Units
(4-EPB)
B.R. Standard design
Introduced: 1960–4

Motor Semi-Open Brake Second (MBS)
Body: 63' 11½" × 9' 0" & 9' 3"
Seats: 2nd, 84
Weight: 39 tons or 40 tons
Equipment: Two 250 h.p. English Electric traction motors
Nos.: S61516–S61623, S61989–S62016

Trailer Semi-Compartment Second (TS)
Body: 63' 6" × 9' 0" & 9' 3"
Seats: 2nd, 112
Weight: 29 tons
Nos.: S70375–482, S70667–94

Trailer Semi-Compartment Second (TS)
(As above)

Motor Semi-Open Brake Second (MBS)
(As above)

5303*	5311*	5319*
5304*	5312*	5320
5305*	5313*	5321
5306*	5314*	5322
5307*	5315*	5323
5308*	5316	5324
5309*	5317*	5325
5310*	5318*	5326

Class 416/2 two-car unit No 5793 passing Weybridge [*C. J. Marsden*

Class 421 four-car unit No 7350 [*J. Scrace*

5327	5342	5357
5328	5343	5358
5329	5344	5359
5330	5345	5360
5331	5346	5361
5332	5347	5362
5333	5348	5363
5334	5349	5364
5335	5350	5365
5336	5351	5366
5337	5352	5367
5338	5353	5368
5339	5354	5369
5340	5355	5370
5341	5356	

*Fitted with express gear ratio

Class 418/0
Two-Car Units (2-SAP)
Introduced: as Class 414: 1958; as Class 418: 1976

Motor Semi-Open Brake Second (Motor Open Brake Second*) (MBS)
Body: 62′ 6″ × 9′ 0″ & 9′ 3″
Seats: 2nd, 84 (82*)
Weight: 40 tons
Equipment: Two 250 h.p. English Electric traction motors
Nos.: S14521–56

Driving Trailer Second (K) (DTS)
Body: 62′ 6″ × 9′ 0″ & 9′ 3″
Seats: 2nd, 60
Weight: 32 tons
Nos.: S16001–36

5604	5613	5622
5605	5614	5623
5606	5615	5624*
5607	5616	5625
5608	5617	5626
5609	5618	5627
5610	5619	5628
5611	5620	5629
5612	5621	5630

| 5631 | 5633 | 5635 |
| 5632 | 5634 | |

*Unit 5624 has an SR-type 4-EPB open motor coach

Class 416/1
Two-Car Suburban Units (2-EPB)
Introduced: 1953–6

Motor Semi-Open Brake Second (MBS)
Body: 62′ 6″ & 9′ 0″ & 9′ 3″
Seats: 2nd, 84
Weight: 40 tons
Equipment: Two 250 h.p. English Electric traction motors
Nos.: S14557–90

Driving Trailer Semi-Open Second (DTS)
Body: 62′ 6″ × 9′ 0″ & 9′ 3″
Seats: 2nd, 94
Weight: 30 tons
Nos.: S16101–34

5651	5663	5674
5652	5664	5675
5653	5665	5676
5654	5666	5677
5655	5667	5678
5656	5668	5679
5657	5669	5680
5658	5670	5681
5659	5671	5682
5660	5672	5683
5661	5673	5684
5662		

Class 416/2
Two-Car Suburban Units (2-EPB)
B.R. Standard design
Introduced: 1953–6 (*On South Tyneside 1955; modified for SR 1963)

Motor Semi-Open Brake Second (MBS)

Body: 63' 11½"×9' 0" & 9' 3"
Seats: 2nd, 84 (74*)
Weight: 40 tons
Equipment: Two 250 h.p. English Electric traction motors
Nos.: S65301–9/11–92

Driving Trailer Semi-Compartment Second (DTS)

Body: 63' 11½"×9' 0" & 9' 3"
Seats: 2nd, 102
Weight: 30 tons
Nos.: S77501–78, S77100–14

5702	5736	5765
5703	5737	5767
5705	5738	5768
5706	5739	5769
5707	5740	5770
5710	5741	5771
5712	5742	5772
5713	5743	5773
5714	5744	5774
5715	5745	5775
5716	5746	5776
5717	5747	5777
5718	5748	5778
5719	5749	5779
5720	5750	5781*
5721	5751	5782*
5722	5752	5783*
5723	5753	5784*
5724	5754	5785*
5725	5755	5786*
5726	5756	5787*
5727	5757	5788*
5728	5758	5789*
5729	5759	5790*
5730	5760	5791*
5731	5761	5792*
5732	5762	5793*
5733	5763	5794*
5734	5764	5795*
5735		

Classes 414/2* and 414/3 Two-Car Units (2-HAP)

B.R. Standard design
Introduced: 1957* (1958–63)

Motor Semi-Open Brake Second (MBS)

Body: 63' 11½"×9' 0" & 9' 3"
Seats: 2nd, 84
Weight: 40 tons
Equipment: Two 250 h.p. English Electric traction motors
Nos: S61243–303, S61648–88, S61962–88

Driving Trailer Composite (DTC)

Body: 63' 11½"×9' 0" & 9' 3"
Seats: 1st, 19; **2nd,** 50
Weight: 30 tons
Nos: S75363–423, S75700–40, S75995–76021

6001	6026	6051
6002	6027	6052
6003	6028	6053
6004	6029	6054
6005	6030	6055
6006	6031	6056
6007	6032	6057
6008	6033	6058
6009	6034	6059
6010	6035	6060
6011	6036	6061
6012	6037	6062
6013	6038	6063
6014	6039	6064
6015	6040	6065
6016	6041	6066
6017	6042	6067
6018	6043	6068
6019	6044	6069
6020	6045	6070
6021	6046	6071
6022*	6047	6072
6023*	6048	6073
6024	6049	6074
6025	6050	6075

6076	6109	6142
6077	6110	6143
6078	6111	6144
6079	6112	6145
6080	6113	6146
6081	6114	6147
6082	6115	6148
6083	6116	6149
6084	6117	6150
6085	6118	6151
6086	6119	6152
6087	6120	6153
6088	6121	6154
6089	6122	6155
6090	6123	6156
6091	6124	6157
6092	6125	6158
6093	6126	6159
6094	6127	6160
6095	6128	6161
6096	6129	6162
6097	6130	6163
6098	6131	6164
6099	6132	6165
6100	6133	6166
6101	6134	6167
6102	6135	6168
6103	6136	6169
6104	6137	6170
6105	6138	6171
6106	6139	6172
6107	6140	6173
6108	6141	

Units 6001–21 and 6024–52 built 1957/8 and modified to Class 418 in 1974 and re-converted to Class 414 during 1980—6001–21/24–52 formerly 5901–21/22–50 in sequence

Classes 410/1* and 410/2 Four-Car Units (4-BEP)

B.R. Standard design
Gangwayed throughout
Introduced: 1956* (1959)

Refurbishing of these units commenced in 1979

Motor Saloon Brake Second (MBS)

Body: 64′ 6″ × 9′ 0″ & 9′ 3″
Seats: 2nd, 56
Weight: 41 tons (40 tons*)
Equipment: Two 250 h.p. English Electric traction motors
Nos: S61041–4, S61390–408, S61792–811

Trailer Composite (TC)

Body: 64′ 6″ × 9′ 0″ & 9′ 3″
Seats: 1st, 24; **2nd,** 24
Weight: 33 tons (31 tons*)
Nos.: S70041/2, S70346–55, S70601–11

Trailer Buffet (TRB)

Body: 64′ 6″ × 9′ 0″ & 9′ 3″
Seats: Buffet, 21
Weight: 36 tons (35 tons*)
Nos.: S69000–21

Motor Saloon Brake Second (MBS)

(As Above)

7001*	7009	7016
7002*	7010	7017
7003	7011	7018
7004	7012	7019
7005	7013	7020
7006	7014	7021
7007	7015	7022
7008		

Classes 420/1 and 420/2*
Four-Car Units (4-BIG)
B.R. Standard design
Gangwayed throughout
Introduced: 1965 (1970*)

Driving Trailer Composite (DTC)
Body: 64′ 6″ × 9′ 0″ & 9′ 3″
Seats: 1st, 24; **2nd,** 28
Weight:
Nos.: S76058–75, S76571–5/7–80

Trailer Buffet (TRB)
Body: 64′ 6″ × 9′ 0″ & 9′ 3″
Seats: 2nd, 40
Weight:
Nos.: S69301–18, S69330–9

Non-Driving Motor Saloon
Brake Second (MS)
Body: 64′ 6″ × 9′ 0″ & 9′ 3″
Seats: 2nd, 56
Weight:
Equipment: Four 250 h.p. English
Electric traction motors
Nos.: S62053–70, S62277–86

Driving Trailer Composite (DTC)
Body: 64′ 6″ × 9′ 0″ & 9′ 8″
Seats: 1st, 18; **2nd,** 36
Weight:
Nos.: S76112–29, S76561–5/7–70

7031	7041	7050*
7032	7042	7051*
7033	7043	7052*
7034	7044	7053*
7035	7045	7054*
7036	7046	7055*
7037	7047	7056*
7038	7048	7057*
7039	7049*	7058*
7040		

Classes 411/1*, 411/2 and
411/3‡
Four-Car Units (4-CEP)

B.R. Standard design. Gangwayed
throughout
Introduced: 1956*, 1958–63 (rebuilt 1975‡, 1980†)
Refurbishing of these units commenced in 1979. The details marked ‡
are applicable to the refurbished
units, the first of which returned to
traffic in 1980

Motor Saloon Brake Second
(MBS) (Motor Saloon
Second‡)
Body: 64′ 6″ × 9′ 0″ & 9′ 3″
Seats: 2nd, 56 (64‡)
Weight: 41 tons (40 tons*)
Equipment: Two 250 h.p. English
Electric traction motors
Nos.: S61033–40, S61229–389,
S61695–790, S61868/9, 61948–60

Trailer Composite (TC)
(Trailer Brake Composite ‡)
Body: 64′ 6″ × 9′ 0″ & 9′ 3″
Seats: 1st, 24 (24‡), **2nd,** 24 (6‡)
Weight: 33 tons (31 tons‡)
Nos.: S70037–40, S70235–40,
S70303–45, S70552–70600,
S70653–9

Trailer Second (TS)
(Trailer Saloon Second (L) ‡)
Body: 64′ 6″ × 9′ 0″ & 9′ 3″
Seats: 2nd, 64 (†56)
Weight: 32 tons (31 tons*)
Nos.: S70033–6, S70229–34,
S70260–70302, S70503–51,
S70660–66

Motor Saloon Brake Second
(MBS) (Motor Saloon
Second‡)
(As Above)

7101*	7105	7108
7103*	7106	7109
7104*	7107	7110

7112	7149	7182	411 522	411 548	411 573
7113	7150	7183	411 523	411 549	411 574
7114	7151	7184	411 534	411 550	411 575
7115	7152	7185	411 526	411 551	411 576
7116	7153‡	7186	411 527	411 552	411 577
7120	7155	7187	411 528	411 553	411 578
7121	7157	7188	411 529	411 554	411 579
7123	7158	7189†	411 530	411 555	411 580
7124	7159	7190	411 531	411 556	411 581
7125	7161	7191	411 532	411 557	411 582
7127	7162	7192	411 533	411 558	411 583
7128	7164	7193	411 534	411 559	411 584
7130	7165	7194	411 535	411 560	411 585
7132	7166	7195	411 536	411 561	411 586
7134	7167	7196	411 537	411 562	411 587
7135	7168	7198	411 538	411 563	411 588
7136	7170	7199	411 539	411 564	411 589
7137	7171	7200	411 540	411 565	411 590
7138	7172	7201	411 541	411 566	411 591
7139	7173	7202	411 542	411 567	411 592
7140	7174	7203	411 543	411 568	411 593
7143	7175	7205	411 544	411 569	411 594
7144	7176	7206	411 545	411 570	411 595
7145	7177	7207	411 546	411 571	411 596
7146	7178	7208	411 547	411 572	411 597
7147	7179	7209			
7148	7180	7210			

411 598 (7197)
411 599 (7160)
411 600 (7169)
411 601
411 602 (mixed)
411 603
411 604
411 605 (7163)
411 606 (7154)
411 607 (7156)
411 608 (7211)

Class 411

Units refurbished. Introduced 1980

411 501 (7001)
411 502 (7104)
411 503   411 504   **411 505**
411 506 (7133)
411 507 (7140)
411 508 (7111)
411 509 (7126)
411 510 (7141)
411 511 (7142)
411 512 (7119)
411 513 (7129)
411 514 (7122)
411 515 (7131)
411 516 (7118)
411 517 (7117)
411 518 (7125)
411 519 (7009)
411 520 (7135)
411 521 (7132)

Classes 421/1* and 421/2
Four-Car Units (4-CIG)

B.R. Standard design
Gangwayed throughout
Introduced: 1964*, 1970–2

Driving Trailer Composite (DTC)

Body: 64' 6" × 9' 0" & 9' 3"
Seats: 1st, 24; **2nd**, 28
Weight:
Nos.: S76022–57, S76611–40,
S76788–860

7301–7384

Trailer Saloon Second (TS)
Body: 64′ 6″×9′ 0″ & 9′ 3″
Seats: 2nd, 72
Weight:
Nos.: S70695–70730, S70967–96,
S71035–71106

Non-Driving Motor Saloon Brake Second (MS)
Body: 64′ 6″×9′ 0″ & 9′ 3″
Seats: 2nd, 56
Weight:
Equipment: Four 250 h.p. English Electric traction motors
Nos.: S62017–52, S62287–316, S62355–425

Driving Trailer Composite (DTC)
Body: 64′ 6″×9′ 0″ & 9′ 3″
Seats: 1st, 18; **2nd,** 36
Weight:
Nos.: S76076–111, S76581–610, S76717–76787

7301*	7329*	7357
7302*	7330*	7358
7303*	7331*	7359
7304*	7332*	7360
7305*		7361
7306*	7334*	7362
7307*	7335*	7363
7308*	7336*	7364
7309*	7337	
7310*	7338	7366
7311*	7339	7367
7312*	7340	7368
7313*	7341	7369
7314*	7342	7370
7315*	7343	7371
7316*	7344	7372
7317*	7345	7373
7318*	7346	7374
7319*	7347	7375
7320*	7348	7376
7321*	7349	7377
7322*	7350	7378
7323*	7351	7379
7324*	7352	7380
7325*	7353	7381
7326*	7354	7382
7327*	7355	7383
7328*	7356	7384

Class 423 four-car unit No 7704

[*C. J. Marsden*]

			Driving Trailer Composite (H)
7385	7403	7421	(As Above)
7386	7404	7422	

7385	7403	7421
7386	7404	7422
7387	7405	7423
7388	7406	7424
7389	7407	7425
7390	7408	7426
7391	7409	7427
7392	7410	7428
7393	7411	7429
7394	7412	7430
7395	7413	7431
7396	7414	7432
7397	7415	7433
7398	7416	7434
7399	7417	7435
7400	7418	7436
7401	7419	7437
7402	7420	7438

Class 423 Four-Car Units (4-VEP)

B.R. Standard design
Gangwayed throughout
Introduced: 1967–74

Driving Trailer Composite (DTC)

Body: 64′ 6″ × 9′ 0″ & 9′ 3″
Seats: 1st, 24; **2nd,** 38 (30*)
Weight: 34 tons
Nos.: S76230–474, S76475–560, S76642–715, 76862–942

Trailer Open Second (TS)

Body: 64′ 6″ × 9′ 0″ & 9′ 3″
Seats: 2nd, 98 (78*)
Weight: 31 tons
Nos.: S70781–800, S70872–966, S70997–71034, S71115–55

Non-Driving Motor Open Brake Second (MBS)

Body: 64′ 6″ × 9′ 0″ & 9′ 3″
Seats: 2nd, 58 (46*)
Weight: 48 tons
Equipment: Four 250 h.p. English Electric traction motors
Nos.: S62121–40, S62182–223, S62224–76, S62317–354, S62435–75

Driving Trailer Composite (H)
(As Above)

7701	7749	7808
7702	7750	7809
7703	7751	7810
7704	7752	7811
7705	7753	7812
7706	7754	7813
7707	7755	7814
7708	7756	7815
7709	7757	7816
7710	7758	7817
7711	7759	7818
7712	7760	7819
7713	7761	7820
7714	7762	7821
7715	7763	7822
7716	7764	7823
7717	7765	7824
7718	7766	7825
7719	7767	7826
7720	7768	7827
7721	7769	7828
7722	7770	7829
7723	7771	7830
7724	7772	7831
7725	7773	7832
7726	7774	7833
7727	7775	7834
7728	7776	7835
7729	7777	7836
7730	7778	7837
7731	7779	7838
7732	7780	7839
7733	7781	7840
7734	7782	7841
7735	7783	7842
7736	7784	7843
7737	7785	7844
7738	7786	7845
7740	7787	7846
7741	7800	7847
7742	7801	7848
7743	7802	7849
7744	7803	7850
7745	7804	7851
7746	7805	7852
7747	7806	7853
7748	7807	7854

7855	7869	7883
7856	7870	7884
7857	7871	7885
7858	7872	7886
7859	7873	7887
7860	7874	7888
7861	7875	7889
7862	7876	7890
7863	7877	7891
7864	7878	7892
7865	7879	7893
7866	7880	7894
7867	7881	
7868	7882	

Class 423/1
Four-Car Units
(4-VEG)

B.R. Standard design
Gangwayed throughout
Introduced: 1978. Modified from
Class 423 Units 7788–99. With extra
luggage space for Gatwick services

Driving Trailer Composite (DTC)
Body: 64' 6"×9' 0" & 9' 3"
Seats: 1st, 24; **2nd,** 30
Weight: 34 tons
Nos.: 576505–28

Trailer Open Second (TS)
Body: 64' 6"×9' 0" & 9' 3"
Seats: 2nd, 78
Weight: 31 tons
Nos.: S70939–50

Non-Driving Motor Open Brake
Second (MBS)
Body: 64' 6"×9' 0" & 9' 3"
Seats: 2nd, 46
Weight: 48 tons
Equipment: Four 250 h.p. English
Electric traction motors
Nos.: S62249–60

7901	7905	7909
7902	7906	7910
7903	7907	7911
7904	7908	7912

Class 508
Four-car Units

B.R. standard design with air-
operated sliding doors
Introduced: 1979

Motor Open Second (DMS)
Body: 64' 11½"×9' 3"
Seats: 2nd, 74
Weight: 36.15 tonnes
Equipment:
Nos.: 64649–64764

Trailer Open Second (TS)
Body: 65' 4¼"×9' 3"
Seats: 2nd, 86
Weight: 26.72 tonnes
Nos.: 71483–71598

Trailer Open Second (TS)
(As Above)

Motor Open Second
(DMS)
(As Above)

508 001	508 016	508 030
508 002	508 017	508 031
508 003	508 018	508 032
508 004	508 019	508 033
508 005	508 020	508 034
508 006	508 021	508 035
508 007	508 022	508 036
508 008	508 023	508 037
508 009	508 024	508 038
508 010	508 025	508 039
508 011	508 026	508 040
508 012	508 027	508 041
508 013	508 028	508 042
508 014	508 029	508 043
508 015		

Two-Car Departmental De-
Icing Units

(Gangwayed within set)
Introduced: 1967. Converted from
2-HAL motor coaches
Motor Brake De-Icing Van (SU)
Body: 62' 6"×9' 0" & 9' 3"
Weight: 47 tons
Equipment: Two 250 h.p. English
Electric traction motors

Class 430 four-car unit No 3009 at Eastleigh

[Brian Morrison

Class 508 four-car unit No 508 009 at Shepperton

[Chris Leigh

Motor-Brake De-Icing Van (SU)
(As Above)

001	002	003

Introduced: 1977. Converted from 4-SUB motor coaches

004	006	008
005	007	009

Two-Car Departmental De-Icing Units
(Gangwayed within set)
Introduced: 1959

Motor Brake De-Icing Van (SU)
Body: 62′ 6″ × 8′ 6″ & 9′ 0″
Equipment: Two 275 h.p. English Electric traction motors
Weight:

Motor Brake De-Icing Van (SU)
(As Above)

011	013	016

Scheduled for early withdrawal and replacement by ex 4-SUB type units

Two-Car Departmental Stores Units
Introduced: 1970 (1972*)

Motor Brake Stores Van (SU)
Body: 62′ 6″ × 9′ 0″ & 9′ 3″
Equipment: Two 275 h.p. English Electric traction motors
Weight:

Motor Brake Stores Van (SU)
(As Above)

022	023	024*

Class 486 Isle of Wight Three-Car Units (3-TIS)
(Ex-London Transport tube size vehicles with air-operated sliding doors). Refurbished 1967 for BR use

Motor Open Brake Second (MBS)
Body:
Seats: 2nd, 26
Weight: 29 tons
Equipment: Two 240 h.p. traction motors
Nos.: S1/3/5/7/11S

Trailer Open Second (TS)
Body:
Seats: 2nd, 42
Weight: 18 tons 10 cwt
Nos.: S47/92–4/96S

Driving Trailer Open Second (DTS)
Body:
Seats: 2nd, 38
Weight: 17 tons
Nos.: S26/8/30/2/6S

031	033	035
032	034	

Class 485 Isle of Wight Four-Car Units (4-VEC)
(Ex-London Transport tube size vehicles with air-operated sliding doors). Refurbished in 1967 for BR use

Motor Open Brake Second (MBS)
Body:
Seats: 2nd, 26
Weight: 29 tons
Equipment: Two 240 h.p. traction motors
Nos.: S2/4/6/8/9/10/13/15/19–23S

Trailer Open Second (TS)
Body:
Seats: 2nd, 38 or 42
Weight: 17 tons or 18 tons 10 cwt
Nos.: S27/9/31/3/4/41–4/6/9/95S

Trailer Open Second (TS)
(As Above)

Motor Open Brake Second
(MBS)
(As Above)

| 041 | 043* | 045 |
| 042 | 044 | 046 |

*Fitted with de-icing equipment

Four-Car Departmental Instruction Unit

Gangwayed within set
Introduced: 1974
(Formed of stock from withdrawn 4-SUB No. 4367 fitted internally for use as a mobile instruction train)

Motor Brake (SU)
Body: 62' 6" × 9' 0" & 9' 3"
Weight: 43 tons
Equipment: Two 275 h.p. English Electric traction motors

Trailer (SU)
Body: 62' 0" × 9' 0" & 9' 3"
Weight: 28 tons

Trailer (SU)
(As Above)

Motor Brake (SU)
(As Above)
055

Class 419 Single Units

Introduced: 1959–61

Motor Luggage Van (DMLV)
Body: 64' 6" × 9' 0" & 9' 3"
Weight: 45 tons

Equipment: Two 250 h.p. English Electric traction motors

(These vehicles can work singly, hauling a limited load, or in multiple with EP-type stock. They are equipped with traction batteries for working on non-electrified quay lines at Dover and Folkstone)

Coach Nos
S68001	S68005	S68008
S68002	S68006	S68009
S68003	S68007	S68010
S68004		

Trailer Departmental De-Icing Vans

(Withdrawn 4-SUB post-war all-steel trailers fitted with conductor rail scraping and spraying equipment; wired for multiple-unit operation with EP-type stock)

Trailer De-Icing Van (SU)
Body: 62' 0" × 9' 0" & 9' 3"
Weight:

Coach Nos
| ADS70050 | ADS70086 |
| ADS70051 | ADS70087 |

Single Unit

General Manager's Saloon
Trailer
Body: 64' 6" × 8' 2½" & 9' 0"
Weight:

(Double-ended driving trailer rebuilt from Hastings line diesel buffet car; may be used with both multiple-unit stock and locomotives)

Coach No.
DB975025

Four-Car Research Dept. Unit

Former Class 445 (Prototype 4-PEP) suburban unit
B.R. Standard design with air-operated sliding doors. Gangwayed throughout

Motor Brake
Body: 64' 11½" × 9' 3"
Equipment: Four 100 h.p. English Electric traction motors

Non-Driving Motor
Body: 65' 4¼" × 9' 3"
Equipment: Four 100 h.p. English Electric traction motors
Allocated departmental unit No. 057
4002

Single Unit

Experimental Driving Trailer
Body: 64' 6" × 9' 0" & 9' 3"
Weight:

(Single-ended driving trailer converted from 4-VEP driving trailer composite)

Coach No.
DB975081 Hermes

Test Unit

Former Class 501 driving trailer open brake second converted to mobile laboratory
Previous No. M75165
ADB975032

Class 487
Waterloo and City One- or Five-Car Units

(Tube size vehicles with air-operated sliding doors. Trains are formed of a single motor car or up to five-car units comprising two motor cars and three trailers)
Introduced: 1940

Motor Open Brake Second (DMS)
Body: 47' 0" × 8' 7¾"
Seats: 2nd, 40
Weight:
Equipment: Two 190 h.p. English Electric traction motors

Coach Nos.

51	55	59
52	56	60
53	57	61
54	58	62

Trailer Open Second (TS)
Body: 47' 0" × 8' 7¾"
Seats: 2nd, 52
Weight: 18 tons 14 cwt

Coach Nos.

71	77	82
72	78	83
73	79	84
74	80	85
75	81	86
76		

LATE INFORMATION

DIESEL UNITS
Reformed: WR set No 470, 51313, 59478, 51328
Withdrawn: 51784, 56460, 50526, 50182, 50788, 52052, 1033, 1205.

ELECTRIC UNITS
New: 507031/2.
Withdrawn: All Class 502 vehicles. 7736, 303035.
Renumbered: (new number in brackets) 5263 (415401), 5225 (415402), 5143 (415403), 5218 (415404).
It should be noted that some SR units do not carry the first two digits of the six-digit number, thus No 415401 carries only 5401. This also applies to Class 411 units recently outshopped.

PRESERVED LOCOMOTIVES

Although most preserved locomotives will eventually fall into two groups—static preservation by a museum or other official body, and working preservation by a Society or Trust—the present situation is necessarily complex, with locomotives existing under various categories. They may be already on display or awaiting removal to a museum, stored pending restoration, in use on privately-owned lines, privately-owned (in some cases on behalf of a preservation fund), or stored awaiting completion of purchase or removal to a permanent home, to name but few. Secondly, the locomotives may be in regular or occasional use, capable of being steamed, or totally inactive. Thirdly, they may have reached the preservation stage after service with British Railways, withdrawal for preservation before 1948, or private use (having been sold prior to Nationalisation).

The general principle behind compilation of this section is to give full details of all locomotives and other motive power which ran in regular service on British Railways. Among those included, therefore, are the GWR 4–4–0 City of Truro and the two Scottish "veterans" of LMS Group origin. Certain locomotives withdrawn before 1948 which made brief excursions in recent years—such as the GNR Stirling Single and Ivatt Atlantics—are listed at the end with the rest of the locomotives withdrawn for preservation or sold by the "Big Four" companies before 1948 and now preserved by BR or privately. Some exceptions may be found in the lists—the ex-LMS 0–4–0ST No. 11243 has been included with No. 51218, for example—but in these cases, an explanation is given in the class headings.

Locomotives are listed in order of their final BR numbers (shown in brackets where renumbering has subsequently taken place). The number now carried, owner and place of preservation shown are as known at the time of going to press. Where no details of ownership or location are given, the locomotive is generally in store awaiting removal to a permanent site. It should be noted that many preserved locomotives are not available for public inspection; those in museums and at privately-owned railways may be seen at normal viewing times or operating days, however, and certain other locations are open on special occasions.

The Ian Allan publication *Railways Restored* gives full details of all the major preservation sites, including times of public opening, and facilities available.

G.W.R. Steam Locomotives

Corris Railway 0-4-2ST

*Introduced 1878. Falcon Engine and Car Co. design for use on 2' 3" gauge Corris Railway. Built as 0-4-0ST but rebuilt by 1901 as 0-4-2ST. Purchased by GWR with railway in 1930.

†Introduced 1921. Kerr Stuart design for Corris Railway. Purchased by GWR with railway in 1930.
Both sold to the Talyllyn Railway, 1948 and still in service.

Weight: *9 tons, †8 tons
Boiler pressure: 160lb/sq in NS
Cylinders: (O) 7"×12"
Driving wheel diameter: 2' 6", †2' 0"
Tractive effort: *2,665 lb, †3,330 lb
Valve gear: Stephenson (slide valves)
†Modified Hackworth (slide valves)

*3 Sir Haydn †4 Edward Thomas

V of R 2-6-2T

Introduced 1902. Davies and Metcalfe design for Vale of Rheidol 1' 11½" gauge railway.

Introduced 1923. GWR development of Vale of Rheidol design. Converted to oil-firing during 1977/8.
The only steam locomotives in service with British Railways, operating during the summer on the Aberystwyth–Devil's Bridge Vale of Rheidol line.

Weight: 25 tons
Boiler pressure: 165 lb sq in NS
Cylinders:
(O) 11"×17", *(O) 11½"×17"
Driving wheel diameter: 2' 6"
Tractive effort: 9,615 lb, *10,510 lb
Valve gear: Walschaerts (piston valves)

*7 Owain Glyndwr   *8 Llywelyn
9 Prince of Wales

W & L 0-6-0T

Introduced 1902. Beyer-Peacock design for Cambrian Railways Welshpool & Llanfair Section 2' 6" gauge railway.
No. 1 at National Railway Museum, York. No. 2 at Welshpool & Llanfair Railway.

Weight: 19 tons 18 cwt
Boiler Pressure: 150 lb/sq in NS
Cylinders: (O) 11½"×16"
Driving wheel diameter: 2' 9"
Tractive effort: 8,175 lb
Valve gear: Walschaerts (slide valves)

1 (822)   The Earl
2 (823)   The Countess

Cardiff Railway 0-4-0ST

Introduced 1898. Kitson design for Cardiff Railway.
Preserved at Somerset Railway Museum, Bleadon and Uphill Station, but may be moved to Didcot.

Weight: 25 tons 10 cwt
Boiler pressure: 160 lb/sq in NS
Cylinders: (O) 14"×21"
Driving wheel diameter: 3' 2½"
Tractive effort: 14,540 lb
Valve gear: Hawthorn-Kitson

1338

Class 1361 0-6-0ST

Introduced 1910. Churchward GWR design for dock shunting.
Preserved by the Great Western Society. Didcot.

Weight: 35 tons 4 cwt
Boiler pressure: 150 lb/sq in NS
Cylinders: (O) 16"×20"
Driving wheel diameter: 3' 8"
Tractive effort: 14,835 lb
Valve gear: Stephenson (slide valves)

1363

Class 1366   0-6-0PT
Introduced 1934. Collett development of 1361 class.
Preserved by the Dart Valley Railway at Buckfastleigh.
Weight: 35 tons 15 cwt
Boiler pressure: 165 lb/sq in NS
Cylinders: (O) 16″ × 20″
Driving wheel diameter: 3′ 8″
Tractive effort: 16,320 lb
Valve gear: Stephenson (slide valves)

1369

Class 1400   0-4-2T
Introduced 1932. Collett design for light branch work (originally designated 4800). Push-and-pull fitted.
[1] Preserved at the Dart Valley Railway, Buckfastleigh.
[2] Preserved at Tiverton Museum.
[3] Preserved by the Great Western Society, Didcot.
Weight: 41 tons 6 cwt
Boiler pressure: 165 lb/sq in NS
Cylinders: (I) 16″ × 24″
Driving wheel diameter: 5′ 2″
Tractive effort: 13,900 lb
Valve gear: Stephenson (slide valves)

1420 Bulliver[1]	1450 Ashburton[1]
1442[2]	1466[3]

Class 1500   0-6-0PT
Introduced 1949. Hawksworth short-wheelbase design for heavy shunting.
Preserved by the Warwickshire Railway Society at Bridgnorth.
Weight: 58 tons 4 cwt
Boiler pressure: 200 lb/sq in NS
Cylinders: (O) 17½″ × 24″
Driving wheel diameter: 4′ 7½″

Tractive effort: 22,515 lb
Valve gear: Walschaerts (piston valves)

1501

Class 1600   0-6-0PT
Introduced 1949. Hawksworth light branch line and shunting design.
Preserved at the Dart Valley Railway, Buckfastleigh.
Weight: 41 tons 12 cwt
Boiler pressure: 165 lb/sq in NS
Cylinders: (I) 16½″ × 24″
Driving wheel diameter: 4′ 1½″
Tractive effort: 18,515 lb
Valve gear: Stephenson (slide valves)

1638

Class 2301   0-6-0
Introduced 1883. Dean GWR design, later fitted with superheater.
Preserved at Swindon Railway Museum.
Weight:
Locomotive: 36 tons 16 cwt
Tender: 34 tons 5 cwt
Boiler pressure: 180 lb/sq in Su
Cylinders: (I) 17″ × 24″
Driving wheel diameter: 5′ 2″
Tractive effort: 17,120 lb
Valve gear: Stephenson (slide valves)

2516

Class 2800   2-8-0
Introduced 1903. Churchward GWR design.
*Introduced 1938. Collett locomotives, with side-window cabs and detail alterations.
[1] Preserved at the National Railway Museum, York.

ale of Rheidol Class 98 2-6-2T No 7 Owain Glyndwr   [*Brian Morrison*

x-GWR '14xx' 0-4-2T No 1450   [*Brian Morrison*

[2]Preserved by the 2857 Society at the Severn Valley Railway, Bridgnorth.

[3]Preserved by the Great Western Society at Didcot.

[4]Preserved by the GWR Preservation Group at Southall.

Weight:
Locomotive: 75 tons 10 cwt
*76 tons 5 cwt
Tender: 40 tons
Boiler pressure: 225 lb/sq in Su
Cylinders: (0) $18\frac{1}{2}'' \times 30''$
Driving wheel diameter: 4' $7\frac{1}{2}''$
Tractive effort: 35,380 lb
Valve gear: Stephenson (piston valves)

2818[1]
2857[2]
*3822[3]   2885[4]

Class 2251   0-6-0

Introduced 1930. Collett design. Preserved by the Severn Valley Railway Society, Bridgnorth.

Weight:
Locomotive: 43 tons 8 cwt
Tender: 36 tons 15 cwt
Boiler pressure: 200 lb/sq in Su
Cylinders: (I) $17\frac{1}{2}'' \times 24''$
Driving wheel diameter: 5' 2''
Tractive effort: 20,155 lb
Valve gear: Stephenson (slide valves)

3205

Class 5700   0-6-0PT

Introduced 1929. Collett design.
*Introduced 1933 with detail alterations and modified cab.
[1]Preserved by the Great Western Society at Didcot.
[2]Preserved at the Severn Valley Railway, Bridgnorth.
[3]Preserved at the Keighley & Worth Valley Railway, Haworth.
[4]Preserved by the Worcester Locomotive Society at The Bulmer Railway Centre, Hereford.
[5]Preserved by the Quainton Railway Society Ltd at Quainton Road.
[6]Preserved at the Standard Gauge Steam Trust, Tyseley.
[7]Privately preserved at NCB, Maesteg.
[8]Preserved by the Forest Pannier Tank Fund at Norchard Steam Centre, Lydney.
[9]Stored on behalf of Holiday Inns, Cardiff.
[10]Preserved at Llangollen Railway.
Weight: 47 tons 10 cwt, *49 tons
Boiler pressure: 200 lb/sq in NS
Cylinders: (I) $17\frac{1}{2}'' \times 24''$
Driving wheel diameter: 4' $7\frac{1}{2}''$
Tractive effort: 22,515 lb
Valve gear: Stephenson (slide valves)

*3650[1]	7714[2]	9600[6]
*3738[1]	7715[5]	*9642[7]
5764[2]	7752[6]	9629[9]
L89 (5775)[3]	7754[10]	9681[8]
5786[4]	7760[6]	

Class 3440   4-4-0
"City"

Introduced 1903. Churchward GWR design. Withdrawn in 1931 and preserved at York Railway Museum as No. 3717. Returned to service in 1957 as No. 3440 for work on special trains.
Preserved at Swindon Railway Museum.

Weight:
Locomotive: 55 tons 6 cwt
Tender: 36 tons 15 cwt
Boiler pressure: 200 lb/sq in Su
Cylinders: (I) $18'' \times 26''$
Driving wheel diameter: 6' $8\frac{1}{2}''$
Tractive effort: 17,790 lb
Valve gear: Stephenson (slide valves)

3717 (3440)   City of Truro

ex-GWR '57xx' 0-6-0PT No 3738   [*P. Chatman*

ex-GWR '45xx' 2-6-2T No 4566   [*N. E. Preedy*

Class 4000   4-6-0
''Star''

Introduced 1907. Churchward GWR design developed from No. 4000, introduced as 4–4–2 No. 40 in 1906. Preserved at Swindon Railway Museum.

Weight:
Locomotive: 75 tons 12 cwt
Tender: 46 tons 14 cwt
Boiler pressure: 225 lb/sq in Su
Cylinders: Four, 15" × 26"
Driving wheel diameter: 6' 8½"
Tractive effort: 27,800 lb
Valve gear: Inside Walschaerts, with rocking shafts (piston valves)

4003   Lode Star

Class 4073   4-6-0
''Castle''

Introduced 1923. Collett design, developed from "Star"
*Fitted with 4-row superheater and double chimney.
[1] Preserved at the Science Museum, London.
[2] Privately preserved at Dampier, Australia.
[3] Preserved by the Great Western Society, Didcot. This locomotive also bears the name "Drysllwyn Castle" on occasions.
[4] Preserved by 7029 Clun Castle Ltd at Tyseley.

Weight:
Locomotive: 79 tons 17 cwt
Tender: 46 tons 14 cwt
Boiler pressure: 225 lb/sq in Su
Cylinders: Four, 16" × 26"
Driving wheel diameter: 6'·8½"
Tractive effort: 31,625 lb
Valve gear: Inside Walschaerts, with rocking shafts (piston valves)

4073   Caerphilly Castle[1]
4079   Pendennis Castle[2]
5029   Nunney Castle[3]
*5043   Earl of Mount Edgcumbe[4]
5051   Earl Bathurst[3]

5080   Defiant[4]
7027   Thornbury Castle[4]
*7029   Clun Castle[4]

Class 5101 and 6100
2-6-2T

5101. Introduced 1929. Development of Collett 5100 Class.
*6100. Introduced 1931. Development of Collett 5101 class with increased boiler pressure for London suburban area.
[1] Preserved by the GWR Preservation Group at Southall.
[2] Preserved at the Severn Valley Railway, Bridgnorth.
[3] Preserved by the Great Western Society, Didcot.
[4] Preserved at Tyseley.
[5] Preserved at Steamport, Southport.

Weight: 78 tons 9 cwt
Boiler pressure:
220 lb/sq in Su, *225 lb/sq in Su
Cylinders: (O) 18" × 30"
Driving wheel diameter: 5' 8"
Tractive effort: 24,300 lb, *27,340 lb
Valve gear: Stephenson (piston valves)

4110[1]	4150[2]	5193[5]
4141[2]	4160[4]	*6106[3]
4144[3]	5164[2]	

Class 4200 and 5205
2-8-0T

4200. Introduced 1910. Churchward GWR design.
*5205. Introduced 1923. Development of 4200 Class, with larger cylinders and detail alterations.
[1] Preserved at Swansea Maritime Museum.
[2] Preserved by the Dart Valley Railway and used on Torbay line.
[3] Preserved by the Great Central Railway at Loughborough.

Weight: 81 tons 12 cwt, *82 tons 2 cwt
Boiler pressure: 200 lb/sq in Su

x-GWR '42xx' 2-8-0T No 5239 *[J. E. Augustson*

x-GWR 'King' 4-6-0 No 6000 King George V *[G. Wright*

Cylinders: (O) 18½″ × 30″
  *(O) 19″ × 30″
Driving wheel diameter: 4′ 7½″
Tractive effort: 31,450 lb,
*33,170 lb
Valve gear: Stephenson (piston valves)

4270[1]
5224[3]
5239[2] Goliath

Class 4500   2-6-2T

Introduced 1906. Churchward GWR development of 4400 class with larger wheels and increased boiler pressure.
*Introduced 1927. Collett 4575 Class, with detail alterations and increased weight.
[1] Preserved at the Dart Valley Railway, Buckfastleigh.
[2] Preserved by the 4566 Preservation Society at the Severn Valley Railway, Bridgnorth.
[3] Preserved by Forest Prairie Fund at Norchard Steam Centre, Lydney.
[4] Preserved by the Great Western Society at Didcot.
[5] Preserved on the West Somerset Railway.
[6] Preserved by the Dart Valley Railway, Torbay line.
Weight: 57 tons, *61 tons
Boiler pressure: 200 lb/sq in Su
Cylinders: (O) 17″ × 24″
Driving wheel diameter: 4′ 7½″
Tractive effort: 21,250 lb
Valve gear: Stephenson (piston valves)

4555[1]
4561[5]
4566[2]
*4588[6]
*5521[3]
*5541[3]
*5542[5]
*5572[4]

Class 4900   4-6-0
''Hall''

Introduced 1928. Modified design of Collett rebuild with 6′ 0″ driving wheels of ''Saint''.
[1] Preserved by the Dumbleton Hall Preservation Society at the Dart Valley Railway.
[2] Preserved by the Severn Valley Railway, Bridgnorth.
[3] Preserved by the Great Western Society at Didcot.
[4] Preserved at the Standard Gauge Steam Trust, Tyseley.
Weight:
Locomotive: 75 tons
Tender: 46 tons 14 cwt
Boiler pressure: 225 lb/sq in Su
Cylinders: (O) 18½″ × 30″
Driving wheel diameter: 6′ 0″
Tractive effort: 27,275 lb
Valve gear: Stephenson (piston valves)

4920   Dumbleton Hall[1]
4930   Hagley Hall[2]
4942   Maindy Hall[3]
4983   Albert Hall[4]
5900   Hinderton Hall[3]

Class 4300   2-6-0

Introduced 1911. Churchward GWR design.
[1] Preserved by the Great Western Society at Didcot.
[2] Preserved by the Great Western (SVR) Association at the Severn Valley Railway.
Weight:
Locomotive: 62 tons
Tender: 40 tons
Boiler pressure: 200 lb/sq in Su
Cylinders: (O) 18½″ × 30″
Driving wheel diameter: 5′ 8″
Tractive effort: 25,670 lb
Valve gear: Stephenson (piston valves)

5322[1]   9303 (7325)[2]

Class 5600   0-6-2T

Introduced 1924. Collett design for service in Welsh valleys.

[1] Preserved by the Telford Horsehay Steam Trust.

[2] Preserved at Tyseley.

[3] Preserved at Steamtown, Carnforth.

[4] To be preserved by Taff Vale Railway Society.

[5] Preserved by the North Yorkshire Moors Railway 6619 Fund at Grosmont.

[6] Preserved by the Great Western Society at Didcot.

[7] Preserved by Swanage Railway Trust at Swanage.

Weight: 69 tons 6 cwt
Boiler pressure: 200 lb/sq in Su
Cylinders: (I) $18'' \times 26''$
Driving wheel diameter: 4' 7½"
Tractive effort: 25,800 lb
Valve gear: Stephenson (piston valves)

5619[1]	5643[3]	6619[5]
5637[2]	5668[4]	6695[7]
		6697[6]

Class 6000   4-6-0
"King"

Introduced 1927. Collett design. Later modified with 4-row superheater and double chimney.

[1] Part of National Collection; on loan to H.P. Bulmer Ltd, Hereford.

[2] Preserved by the King Preservation Society at Quainton Road.

Weight:
Locomotive: 89 tons
Tender: 46 tons 14 cwt
Boiler pressure: 250 lb/sq in Su
Cylinders: Four, $16\frac{1}{4}'' \times 28''$
Driving wheel diameter: 6' 6"
Tractive effort: 40,285 lb
Valve gear: Inside Walschaerts, with rocking shafts (piston valves)

6000   King George V[1]
6024   King Edward I[2]

Class 6400   0-6-0PT

Introduced 1932. Collett development of 5400 class for light passenger work, with smaller wheels. Push-and-pull fitted.

[1] Preserved at the West Somerset Railway.

[2] Preserved at the Dart Valley Railway, Buckfastleigh.

Weight: 45 tons 12 cwt
Boiler pressure: 180 lb/sq in NS
Cylinders: (I) $16\frac{1}{2}'' \times 24''$
Driving wheel diameter: 4' 7½"
Tractive effort: 18,010 lb
Valve gear: Stephenson (slide valves)

6412   The Flockton Flyer[1]
6430[2]
6435[2]

Class 6959   4-6-0
"Modified Hall"

Introduced 1944. Hawksworth development of "Hall", with larger superheater, one-piece main frames and plate-framed bogie.

[1] Preserved at Severn Valley Railway, Bridgnorth.

[2] Preserved by the Witherslack Hall Society at the Main Line Steam Trust, Loughborough.

[3] Preserved by the Great Western Society, Didcot.

[4] Preserved by members of Quainton Railway Society at Quainton Road.

Weight:
Locomotive: 75 tons 16 cwt
Tender: 46 tons 14 cwt
Boiler pressure: 225 lb/sq in Su
Cylinders: (O) $18\frac{1}{2}'' \times 30''$
Driving wheel diameter: 6' 0"
Tractive effort: 27,275 lb
Valve gear: Stephenson (piston valves)

6960   Raveningham Hall[1]
6989   Wightwick Hall[4]
6990   Witherslack Hall[2]
6998   Burton Agnes Hall[3]

Class 7200   2-8-2T

Introduced 1934. Collett development of Churchward 4200 Class, with extended bunker and additional trailing wheels.
Preserved by the Great Western Society at Didcot.

Weight: 92 tons 2 cwt
Boiler pressure: 200 lb/sq in Su
Cylinders: (O) 19″×30″
Driving wheel diameter: 4′ 7½″
Tractive effort: 33,170 lb
Valve gear: Stephenson (piston valves)

7202

Class 7800   4-6-0
"Manor"

Introduced 1938. Collett design for use on secondary lines, incorporating certain parts of withdrawn 4300 class 2-6-0 locomotives.
[1] Privately preserved at Didcot.
[2] Preserved by the Severn Valley Railway, Bridgnorth.
[3] Preserved by the 7822 Foxcote Manor Society at Oswestry.
[4] Preserved by the Dart Valley Railway, Torbay line.
[5] Preserved by the Gwili Railway at Bronwydd Arms.
Stored at Stourport by Severn Valley Railway, for spare parts only.

Weight:
Locomotive: 68 tons 18 cwt
Tender: 40 tons
Boiler pressure: 225 lb/sq in Su
Cylinders: (O) 18″×30″
Driving wheel diameter: 5′ 8″
Tractive effort: 27,340 lb
Valve gear: Stephenson (piston valves)

7802   Bradley Manor[6]
7808   Cookham Manor[1]

7812   Erlestoke Manor[2]
7819   Hinton Manor[2]
7820   Dinmore Manor[5]
7822   Foxcote Manor[3]
7827   Lydham Manor[4]

Class 9000   4-4-0

Introduced 1936. Collett rebuilt incorporating "Duke" class boiler and "Bulldog" class frames for work on secondary lines. Numbered in 3200–28 series until 1946.
Privately preserved at the Bluebell Railway, Sheffield Park.

Weight:
Locomotive: 49 tons
Tender: 36 tons 15 cwt
Boiler pressure: 180 lb/sq in NS
Cylinders: (I) 18″×26″
Driving wheel diameter: 5′ 8″
Tractive effort: 18,955 lb
Valve gear: Stephenson (slide valves)

3217 (9017)   Earl of Berkeley

Class 9400   0-6-0PT

Introduced 1947. Hawksworth taper boiler design for heavy shunting.
[1] Preserved at Swindon Railway Museum.
[2] Preserved at Quainton Road.

Weight: 55 tons 7 cwt
Boiler pressure: 200 lb/sq in Su
Cylinders: (I) 17½″×24″
Driving wheel diameter: 4′ 7½″
Tractive effort: 22,515 lb
Valve gear: Stephenson (slide valves)

9400[1]   9466[2]

Ex-GWR 'Castle' 4-6-0 No 7029 Clun Castle

[*Brian Morrison*

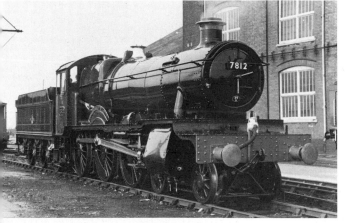

Ex-GWR 'Manor' 4-6-0 No 7812 Erlestoke Manor

[*T. G. Flinders*

S.R. Steam Locomotives

Class USA   0-6-0T

Introduced 1942. US. Army Transportation Corps design, purchased by SR 1946 and fitted with modified cab and bunker and other detail alterations for use in Southampton Docks.

[1] Preserved by Southern Railway Locomotive Preservation Co Ltd at the Bluebell Railway, Sheffield Park.
[2] Preserved by Kent & East Sussex Railway Society at Rolvenden.
[3] Preserved by Keighley & Worth Valley Railway, Haworth.

Weight: 46 tons 10 cwt
Boiler pressure: 210 lb sq/in NS
Cylinders: (O) $16\frac{1}{2}'' \times 24''$
Driving wheel diameter: 4' 6"
Tractive effort: 21,600 lb
Valve gear: Walschaerts (piston valves)

30064[1]
22 (30065 DS 237)   Maunsell[2]
21 (30070 DS 238)   Wainwright[2]
72 (30072)[3]

Class B4   0-4-0T

Introduced 1891. Adams LSWR design for shunting in Southampton Docks.

[1] Preserved by the Bulleid Society Ltd at the Bluebell Railway, Sheffield Park.
[2] Preserved at Bressingham Hall, Diss.

Weight: 33 tons 9 cwt
Boiler pressure: 140 lb/sq in NS
Cylinders: (O) $16'' \times 22''$
Driving wheel diameter: 3' $9\frac{3}{4}''$
Tractive effort: 14,650 lb
Valve gear: Stephenson (slide valves)

30096 Normandy[1]
102 (30102)[2]

Class M7   0-4-4 T

Introduced 1897. Drummond LSWR design.

[1] Preserved at Steamtown, USA.
[2] National Railway Museum York (not on display).

Weight: 60 tons 4 cwt
Boiler pressure: 175 lb/sq in NS
Cylinders: (I) $18\frac{1}{2}'' \times 26''$
Driving wheel diameter: 5' 7"
Tractive effort: 19,755 lb
Valve gear: Stephenson (slide valves)

30053[1]   245 (30245)[2]

Class T9   4-4-0

Introduced 1899. Drummond LSWR design, fitted with superheater and larger cylinders by Urie from 1922. Withdrawn 1962, restored to pregrouping livery and returned to service for use on special trains. National Railway Museum York (not on display).

Weight:
Locomotive: 51 tons 18 cwt
Tender: 44 tons 17 cwt
Boiler pressure: 175 lb/sq in Su
Cylinders: (I) $19'' \times 26''$
Driving wheel diameter: 6' 7"
Tractive effort: 17,675 lb
Valve gear: Stephenson (slide valves)

120 (30120)

Class S15   4-6-0

Introduced 1920. Urie LSWR design; development of N15 class for mixed traffic work.

Ex-LSWR '0415' 4-4-2T No 488   [*J. Scrace*

Ex-LSWR 'T3' 4-4-0 No 563   [*N. E. Preedy*

*Introduced 1936. Maunsell development of the Urie LSWR design with higher boiler pressure, reduced cylinder diameter, modified cab and other detail alterations.
[1] Preserved by the Urie S15 Preservation Group at the Mid-Hants Railway, New Alresford.
[2] Preserved by Essex Locomotive Society at North York Moors Railway, Grosmont.
[3] Preserved by Maunsell Locomotive Society on the Bluebell Railway.

Weight:
Locomotive: 79 tons 16 cwt
*79 tons 5 cwt
Tender: 57 tons 16 cwt
*56 tons 8 cwt
Boiler pressure:
180 lb/sq in Su
*200 lb/sq in Su
Cylinders:
(O) 21″×28″, *(O) 20½″×28″
Driving wheel diameter: 5′ 7″
Tractive effort: 28,200 lb, *29,855 lb
Valve gear: Walschaerts (piston valves)

506 (30506)[1]   30499[1]
*841 (30841) Greene King[2]
*30847[3]

Class Q   0-6-0

Introduced 1938. Maunsell design, later fitted with multiple-jet blastpipe and large-diameter chimney.
Preserved by the Maunsell Locomotive Preservation Society at the Bluebell Railway.
Weight:
Locomotive: 49 tons 10 cwt
Tender: 40 tons 10 cwt
Boiler pressure: 200 lb/sq in
Cylinders: 19″×26″
Driving wheel diameter: 5′ 1″
Tractive effort: 26,160 lb
Valve gear: Stephenson (piston valves)

30541

Class 0415   4-4-2T

Introduced 1882. Adams LSWR design, subsequently reboilered. Sold by LSWR in 1917 but purchased from East Kent Railway by SR in 1946 for use on Lyme Regis branch. Preserved by Bluebell Railway at Sheffield Park.

Weight: 55 tons 2 cwt
Boiler pressure: 160 lb/sq in NS
Cylinders: (O) 17½″×24″
Driving wheel diameter: 5′ 7″
Tractive effort: 14,920 lb
Valve gear: Stephenson (slide valves)

488 (30583)

Class 0298   2-4-0WT

Introduced 1874. Beattie LSWR design, rebuilt by Adams 1884–92, Urie 1921/2 and Maunsell 1931–5. Retained for use on Wenford Bridge china clay trains.
[1] Preserved by the Quainton Railway Society Ltd at Quainton Road.
[2] Part of National Collection; loaned to Dart Valley Railway, Buckfastleigh.

Weight: 37 tons 16 cwt
Boiler pressure: 160 lb/sq in NS
Cylinders: (O) 16½″×20″
Driving wheel diameter: 5′ 7″
Tractive effort: 11,050 lb
Valve gear: Stephenson (slide valves)

E0314 (30585)[1]   30587[2]

Class N15   4-6-0
"King Arthur"

Introduced 1925. Maunsell development of Urie LSWR design with long-travel valves, increased boiler pressure, smaller firebox, modified

Ex-LBSCR 'A1X' 0-6-0T No 8 Freshwater

[*C. P. Boocock*

Ex-SECR 'P' 0-6-0T No 323

[*J. Scrace*

cab to suit Eastern Section loading gauge and with bogie tender.
Part of National Collection, being restored by Humberside Locomotive Preservation Group.

Weight:
Locomotive: 80 tons 19 cwt
Tender: 57 tons 11 cwt
Boiler pressure: 200 lb/sq in Su
Cylinders: (O) $20\frac{1}{2}'' \times 28''$
Driving wheel diameter: 6' 7"
Tractive effort: 25,320 lb
Valve gear: Walschaerts (piston valves)

30777 Sir Lamiel

Class LN 4-6-0
"Lord Nelson"

Introduced 1926. Maunsell design. Fitted with modified cylinders, multiple-jet blastpipe and large-diameter chimney by Bulleid in 1938. National Railway Museum, York. On loan to Carnforth.

Weight:
Locomotive: 83 tons 10 cwt
Tender: 57 tons 19 cwt
Boiler pressure: 220 lb/sq in Su
Cylinders: Four, $16\frac{1}{2}'' \times 26''$
Driving wheel diameter: 6' 7"
Tractive effort: 33, 510 lb
Valve gear: Walschaerts (piston valves)

30850 Lord Nelson

Class V 4-4-0
"Schools"

Introduced 1930. Maunsell design.
[1] National Railway Museum, York. On loan to Dinting Railway Centre.
[2] Preserved by Steamtown, USA; at present on loan to Cape Breton Steam Railway, Canada.

[3] Preserved by East Somerset Railway and on loan to the Bluebell Railway.

Weight:
Locomotive: 67 tons 2 cwt
Tender: 42 tons 8 cwt
Boiler pressure: 220 lb/sq in Su
Cylinders: Three, $16\frac{1}{2}'' \times 26''$
Driving wheel diameter: 6' 7"
Tractive effort: 25,135 lb
Valve gear: Walschaerts (piston valves)

30925 Cheltenham[1]
30926 Repton[2]
928 (30928) Stowe[3]

Class P 0-6-0T

Introduced 1909. Wainwright SECR design for motor train work, subsequently used for light shunting work.
[1] Preserved by Bluebell Railway at Sheffield Park.
[2] Preserved by Kent & East Sussex Railway Society at Rolvenden.
[3] Preserved by Bluebell Railway and on loan to East Somerset Railway.

Weight: 28 tons 10 cwt
Boiler pressure: 160 lb/sq in NS
Cylinders: (I) 12" × 18"
Driving wheel diameter: 3' 9"
Tractive effort: 7,810 lb
Valve gear: Stephenson (slide valves)

27 (31027)[1]
1178 (31178)[1]
323 (31323) Bluebell[3]
11 (31556) Pride of Sussex[2]

Class O1 0-6-0

Introduced 1903. Wainwright rebuild with domed boiler and new cab of Stirling SER O Class.
Privately preserved.

Ex-SR 'S15' 4-6-0 No 841

[*J. R. Broughton*

Ex-SR 'LN' 4-6-0 No 850 Lord Nelson

[*R. W. Hinton*

Weight:
Locomotive: 41 tons 1 cwt
Tender: 28 tons 5 cwt
Boiler pressure: 150 lb/sq in NS
Cylinders: (I) 18″ × 26″
Driving wheel diameter: 5′ 2″
Tractive effort: 17,325 lb
Valve gear: Stephenson (slide valves)

65 (31065)

Class H   0-4-4T

Introduced 1904. Wainwright SECR design.
Preserved by H Class Trust at the Bluebell Railway, Sheffield Park.
Weight: 54 tons 8 cwt
Boiler pressure: 160 lb/sq in NS
Cylinders: (I) 18″ × 26″
Driving wheel diameter: 5′ 6″
Tractive effort: 17,360 lb
Valve gear: Stephenson (slide valves)

263 (31263)

Class C   0-6-0

Introduced 1900. Wainwright SECR design.
Preserved by Wainwright C Preservation Society at the Bluebell Railway, Sheffield Park.
Weight:
Locomotive: 43 tons 16 cwt
Tender: 38 tons 5 cwt
Boiler pressure: 160 lb/sq in NS
Cylinders: (I) 18½″ × 26″
Driving wheel diameter: 5′ 2″
Tractive effort: 19,520 lb
Valve gear: Stephenson (slide valves)

592 (31592)

Class U   2-6-0

Introduced 1928. Maunsell rebuild of SECR K (River) class 2-6-4T.
*New locomotive to same basic design as rebuild, but with detail alterations.
[1] Preserved by the Southern Mogul Preservation Society at Bluebell Railway, Sheffield Park.
[2] Preserved by the Mid-Hants Railway Preservation Society at New Alresford.
[3] Preserved at the Bluebell Railway.
Weight:
Locomotive: 63 tons
*62 tons 6 cwt
Tender: 40 tons 10 cwt
*42 tons 8 cwt
Boiler Pressure: 200 lb/sq in Su
Cylinders: (O) 19″ × 28″
Driving wheel diameter: 6′ 0″
Tractive effort: 23,865 lb
Valve gear: Walschaerts (piston valves)

*31618[1]	31638[3]
31625[2]	31806[2]

Class D   4-4-0

Introduced 1901. Wainwright SECR design with round-top firebox. Preserved at the National Railway Museum, York.
Weight:
Locomotive: 50 tons
Tender: 39 tons 2 cwt
Boiler pressure: 175 lb/sq in NS
Cylinders: (I) 19″ × 26″
Driving wheel diameter: 6′ 8″
Tractive effort: 17,450 lb
Valve gear: Stephenson (slide valves)

737 (31737)

Class N   2-6-0

Introduced 1917. Maunsell SECR mixed traffic design.

Preserved by the Mid-Hants Railway Preservation Society at New Alresford.

Weight:
Locomotive: 61 tons 4 cwt
Tender: 39 tons 5 cwt
Boiler pressure: 200 lb/sq in Su
Cylinders: (O) 19″ × 28″
Driving wheel diameter: 5′ 6″
Tractive effort: 26,035 lb
Valve gear: Walschaerts (piston valves)

31874   Brian Fisk

Class E1   0–6–0T

Introduced 1874. Sold to Cannock & Rugeley Collieries in 1927. Preserved at the East Somerset Railway, Cranmore.
Weight: 44 tons 3 cwt
Boiler pressure: 170 lb/sq in NS
Cylinders: (1) 17″ × 24″
Driving wheel diameter: 4′ 6″
Tractive effort: 18,600 lb
Valve gear: Stephenson (slide valves)

110 (9)   Burgundy

Class E4   0-6-2T

Introduced 1897. R. J. Billinton LBSCR design, development of earlier E3 with larger wheels. Fitted with Marsh boiler and extended smokebox in 1910. Cylinder diameter reduced from 18″ by SR.
Preserved by Bluebell Railway at Sheffield Park.
Weight: 57 tons 10 cwt
Boiler pressure: 170 lb/sq in NS
Cylinders: (I) 17½″ × 26″
Driving wheel diameter: 5′ 6″
Tractive effort: 19,175 lb
Valve gear: Stephenson (slide valves)

473 (32473)   Birch Grove

Class A1 and A1X   0-6-0T "Terrier"

*A1. Introduced 1872. Stroudley LBSCR "Terrier" for suburban work.
●A1. Subsequently fitted with Marsh A1X-type boiler but retaining original smoke-box and other details.
†A1X. Introduced 1911. Marsh rebuild of A1 with new boiler and extended smokebox.
‡A1X. Locomotive with increased cylinder diameter.
§A1X. Transferred to the Isle of Wight by SR but returned to mainland for further use in 1949.
¶A1X. Locomotive acquired by BR from Kent & East Sussex Railway on Nationalisation.
[1] Preserved at the National Railway Museum, York.
[2] Preserved by Bluebell Railway at Sheffield Park.
[3] Preserved by Wight Locomotive Society at Haven Street.
[4] Preserved at Isle of Wight Steam Railway, Haven Street, I.O.W.
[5] Preserved by Borough of Sutton but on loan to Kent & East Sussex Railway Society at Rolvenden.
[6] Preserved at Bressingham Hall, Diss.
[7] Preserved by Kent & East Sussex Railway Society at Rolvenden.
[8] Preserved at West Somerset Railway.
[9] Preserved at Montreal Railway Historical Museum, Canada.

Weight:
*●27 tons 10 cwt
†‡§¶28 tons 5 cwt
Boiler pressure: 150 lb/sq in NS
Cylinders: (I) 12″ × 20″,
‡14 3/16″ × 20″
Driving wheel diameter: 4′ 0″
Tractive effort: 7,650 lb,
‡10,695 lb
Valve gear: Stephenson (slide valves)

*82 (—) Boxhill[1]
‡72 (32636) Fenchurch[2]
†11 (32640) Newport[3]
§46 (32646) Freshwater[4]
†50 (32650) Sutton[5]
†55 (32655) Stepney[2]
†62 (32662) Martello[6]
¶3 (32670) Bodiam[7]
†78 (32678) Knowle[8]
●54 (DS680) Waddon[9]

Class Q1   0-6-0

Introduced 1942. Bulleid "Austerity" design with multiple-jet blastpipe and large diameter chimney.
Preserved by BRB. On loan to Bulleid Society at the Bluebell Railway, Sheffield Park.
Weight:
Locomotive: 51 tons 5 cwt
Tender: 38 tons
Boiler pressure: 230 lb/sq in Su
Cylinders: (I) 19" × 26"
Driving wheel diameter: 5' 1"
Tractive effort: 30,080 lb
Valve gear: Stephenson (piston valves)

33001 (CI)

Class WC & BB 4-6-2
"West Country and Battle of Britain"

*WC. Introduced 1945. Bulleid lightweight development of his Merchant Navy class with air-smoothed casing, high pressure boiler, multiple-jet blastpipe and chain-driven Bulleid valve gear. Boiler pressure subsequently reduced. Originally intended for use in West of England and given a "West Country" name.
†BB. Introduced 1946. Identical in all respects to WC class, but originally intended for use on Eastern Section and given "Battle of Britain" name.

‡Locomotives of both types rebuilt from 1957 with Walschaerts valve gear, multiple-jet blastpipe and large diameter chimney. Air-smoothed casing removed.
[1] Preserved at the Mid-Hants Railway, New Alresford.
[2] Preserved by the Bulleid Society Ltd at the Bluebell Railway, Sheffield Park.
[3] Privately preserved on the Great Central Railway, Loughborough Central.
[4] Part of National Collection. On loan to Great Western Society, Didcot.
[5] Preserved by the Battle of Britain Locomotive Preservation Society at the Nene Valley Railway, Wansford.
[6] Preserved at the Keighley & Worth Valley Railway, Haworth.
[7] Undergoing restoration at Derby for use on proposed Peak Railway, Derbyshire.
[8] Preserved by the Bluebell Railway at Sheffield Park.
[9] Privately preserved at the North York Moors Railway.
[10] Preserved at the Mid-Hants Railway, New Alresford.

Weight:
Locomotive: 86 tons
‡90 tons 1 cwt
Boiler pressure: 250 lb/sq in Su
Cylinders: Three, 16⅜" × 24"
Driving wheel diameter: 6' 2"
Tractive effort: 27,715 lb
Valve gear: Bulleid (piston valves)
‡Walschaerts (piston valves)

*‡34016 Bodmin[1]
*21C123 (34023) Blackmore Vale[2]
*‡34027 Taw Valley[9]
*‡34039 Boscastle[3]
†34051 Winston Churchill[4]
†‡34059 Sir Archibald Sinclair[8]
‡34067 Tangmere[10]
†34081 92 Squadron[5]
*34092 City of Wells[6]
‡34101 Hartland[7]
*34105 Swanage[1]

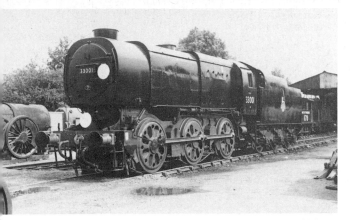

Ex-SR 'Q1' 0-6-0 No 33001

[*J. Scrace*

Rebuilt Ex-SR 'West Country' 4-6-2 No 34016 Bodmin

[*J. Scrace*

Class MN 4-6-2
"Merchant Navy"

Introduced 1941. Bulleid design with air-smoothed casing, high pressure boiler, multiple-jet blastpipe and chain-driven Bulleid valve gear. Rebuilt from 1956 with lower boiler pressure, Walschaerts valve gear, multiple-jet blastpipe and large-diameter chimney. Air smoothed casing removed.

[1] Preserved at Steamtown, Carnforth.
[2] Preserved by Merchant Navy Locomotive Society at Hereford.
[3] Preserved as sectioned exhibit at the National Railway Museum, York.
[4] Preserved at the Mid-Hants Railway.

Weight:
Locomotive: 97 tons 18 cwt
Boiler pressure: 250 lb/sq in Su
Cylinders: Three, 18"×24"
Driving wheel diameter: 6' 2"
Tractive effort: 33, 495 lb

Valve gear: Walschaerts (piston valves)

35005	Canadian Pacific[1]
35018	British India Line[4]
35028	Clan Line[2]
35029	Ellerman Lines[3]

Class O2 0-4-4T

Introduced 1889. Adams LSWR design. Transferred to Isle of Wight in 1925 and fitted with Westinghouse brake. Fitted with enlarged bunker in 1932.

Preserved by Wight Locomotive Society at Havenstreet.

Weight: 48 tons 8 cwt
Boiler pressure: 160 lb/sq in NS
Cylinders: (I) 17½"×24"
Driving wheel diameter: 4' 10"
Tractive effort: 17,235 lb
Valve gear: Stephenson (slide valves)

24 (W24)   Calbourne

Ex-SR 'West Country' 4-6-2 No 34092 City of Wells   [G. Roose

L.M.S. Steam Locomotives

Class 4P 4-4-0

Introduced 1902. Johnson Midland compound, rebuilt 1914 to Deeley design. Subsequently fitted with superheater.
Preserved at the National Railway Museum, York.
Weight:
Locomotive: 61 tons 14 cwt
Boiler pressure: 200 lb/sq in Su
Cylinders: Three:
(O) 21″×26″ (two, low pressure)
(I) 19″×26″ (one, high pressure)
Driving wheel diameter: 7′ 0″
Tractive effort: 21,840 lb (of I.p. cylinders at 80 per cent boiler pressure)
Valve gear: Stephenson (I.p., slide valves; h.p., piston valves)

1000 (41000)

Class 2MT 2-6-2T

Introduced 1946. Ivatt design.
[1] Preserved at the Keighley & Worth Valley Railway, Haworth.
[2] Preserved by the Ivatt Trust at Quainton Road.
[3] Preserved by the Caerphilly Railway Society.
Weight: 63 tons 5 cwt
Boiler pressure: 200 lb/sq in Su
Cylinders:
(O) 16″×24″, *16½″×24″
Driving wheel diameter: 5′ 0″
Tractive effort: 17,410 lb, *18,510 lb
Valve gear: Walschaerts (piston valves)

41241[1]   *41312[3]
*41298[2]   *41313[2]

Class 1F 0-6-0T

Introduced 1878. Johnson Midland design. Rebuilt with Belpaire firebox.
Preserved by the 1708 Locomotive Preservation Trust Ltd, at Midland Railway Trust, Butterley.
Weight: 39 tons 11 cwt
Boiler pressure: 140 lb/sq in NS
Cylinders: (I) 17″×24″
Driving wheel diameter: 4′ 7″
Tractive effort: 15,005 lb
Valve gear: Stephenson (slide valves)

1708 (41708)

Class 3P 4-4-2T

Introduced 1909. Whitelegg LTSR "79" class.
Preserved by BRB. On loan to Bressingham Hall, Diss.
Weight: 71 tons 10 cwt
Boiler pressure: 170 lb/sq in NS
Cylinders: (O) 19″×26″
Driving wheel diameter: 6′ 6″
Tractive effort: 17,390 lb
Valve gear: Stephenson (slide valves)

80 (41966)   Thundersley

Class 4MT 2-6-4T

Introduced 1945. Fairburn development of Stanier design with shorter wheelbase and detail alterations.
Preserved by the Lakeside Railway, Haverthwaite.
[1] Painted in LNWR black livery
[2] Painted in CR blue livery
Weight: 85 tons 5 cwt
Boiler pressure: 200 lb/sq in Su
Cylinders: (O) 19⅝″×26″
Driving wheel diameter: 5′ 9″
Tractive effort: 24, 670 lb
Valve gear: Walschaerts (piston valves)

2073 (42073)[1]   2085 (42085)[2]

Class 4P   2-6-4T

Introduced 1934. Stanier three-cylinder design for LTS line.
Preserved by BRB. On loan to Bressingham Hall, Diss.

Weight: 92 tons 5 cwt
Boiler pressure: 200 lb/sq in Su
Cylinders: Three, 16″×26″
Driving wheel diameter: 5′ 9″
Tractive effort: 24,600 lb
Valve gear: Walschaerts (piston valves)

42500

Class 5MT   2-6-0

Introduced 1926. Hughes LMS design built under Fowler's direction.
[1] Preserved at the National Railway Museum, York.
[2] Privately preserved at Keighley & Worth Valley Railway.

Weight:
Locomotive: 66 tons
Boiler pressure: 180 lb/sq in Su
Cylinders: (O) 21″×26″
Driving wheel diameter: 5′ 6″
Tractive effort: 26,580 lb
Valve gear: Walschaerts (piston valves)

2700 (42700) [1]
42765 [2]

Class 5MT   2-6-0

Introduced 1933. Stanier LMS design.
Preserved by the Stanier Mogul Fund at the Severn Valley Railway, Bridgnorth.

Weight:
Locomotive: 69 tons 2 cwt
Boiler pressure: 225 lb/sq in Su
Cylinders: (O) 18″×28″
Driving wheel diameter: 5′ 6″
Tractive effort: 26,290 lb
Valve gear: Walschaerts (piston valves)

42968

Class 4MT   2-6-0

Introduced 1947. Ivatt design.
Preserved by the Severn Valley Railway, Bridgnorth.

Weight:
Locomotive: 59 tons 2 cwt
Boiler pressure: 225 lb/sq in Su
Cylinders: (O) 17½″×26″
Driving wheel diameter: 5′ 3″
Tractive effort: 24,170 lb
Valve gear: Walschaerts (piston valves)

43106

Class 4F   0-6-0

Introduced 1911. Fowler Midland design.
*Introduced 1924. Post-Grouping development of Midland design, with reduced boiler mountings.
[1] Preserved at the Keighley & Worth Valley Railway, Haworth.
[2] Preserved by BRB, at Midland Railway Trust. Butterley.
[3] Preserved by the North Staffordshire Railway Society at Cheddleton.
[4] Preserved at the Mid-Hants Railway.

Weight:
Locomotive: 48 tons 15 cwt
Boiler pressure: 175 lb/sq in Su
Cylinders: (I) 20″×26″
Driving wheel diameter: 5′ 3″
Tractive effort: 24,555 lb
Valve gear: Stephenson (piston valves)

43924 [1]   44123 [4]
*4027 (44027) [2]   *44422 [3]

Class 5MT   4-6-0

Introduced 1934. Stanier design.
*Introduced 1947. Outside Stephenson link motion and Timken roller bearings.
[1] Preserved at North Yorkshire Moors Railway, Grosmont.

Ex-L&MR 0-4-2 Lion [*K. Smith*

Ex-MR 4-2-2 No 673 [*G. Roose*

[2] Preserved at Steamport Transport Museum, Southport.
[3] Preserved by Steamtown at Carnforth.
[4] Preserved by BRB; on loan to Severn Valley Railway.
[5] Privately preserved at the Strathspey Railway, Boat of Garten.
[6] Preserved by the Stanier Black 5 Locomotive Preservation Society at Severn Valley Railway, Bridgnorth.
[7] Preserved at the Keighley & Worth Valley Railway, Haworth.
[8] Preserved by the Great Central Railway at Loughborough Central.
[9] Preserved by Mr. A. E. Draper, restored by Humberside Locomotive Preservation Group.
[10] Preserved by the Bristol Suburban Railway Society, Bitton.
[11] Preserved by the Stanier Black 5 Preservation Society; at present on loan to the North Yorkshire Moors Railway, Grosmont.

Weight:
Locomotive: 72 tons 2 cwt
*75 tons 6 cwt
Boiler pressure: 225 lb/sq in Su
Cylinders: (O) 18½"×28"
Driving wheel diameter: 6' 0"
Tractive effort: 25,455 lb
Valve gear: Walschaerts (piston valves)
*Stephenson

*4767 (44767) George Stephenson[1]
44806 Magpie[2]
44871[3]
44932[3]
45000[4]
5025 (45025)[5]
45110 RAF Biggin Hill[6]
45212[7]
5231 (45231) 3rd (Volunteer) Battalion The Worcestershire and Sherwood Foresters Regiment[8]
45305[9]
45379[10]
5407 (45407)[3]
5428 (45428) Eric Treacy[11]

Class 6P5F   4-6-0
"Jubilee"

Introduced 1934. Stanier taper boiler development of the "Patriot" class.
*Fitted with double chimney in 1961.
[1] Preserved by 7029 Clun Castle Ltd at Tyseley.
[2] Preserved by the Bahamas Locomotive Society at Dinting Railway Centre.
[3] Privately preserved at Steamtown, Carnforth.
[4] Preserved by Leander Locomotive Ltd at Carnforth.

Weight:
Locomotive: 79 tons 11 cwt
Boiler pressure: 225 lb/sq in Su
Cylinders: Three, 17"×26"
Driving wheel diameter: 6' 9"
Tractive effort: 26,610 lb
Valve gear: Walschaerts (piston valves)

5593 (45593) Kolhapur[1]
*5596 (45596) Bahamas[2]
5690 (45690) Leander[3]
45699 Galatea[4]

Class 7P   4-6-0
"Royal Scot"

Introduced 1943. Stanier rebuild of Fowler locomotives (introduced 1927) with taper boiler, new cylinders and double chimney.
[1] Preserved at Bressingham Hall, Diss.
[2] Preserved at Dinting Railway Centre.

Weight:
Locomotive: 83 tons
Boiler pressure: 250 lb/sq in Su
Cylinders: Three, 18"×26"
Driving wheel diameter: 6' 9"
Tractive effort: 33,150 lb
Valve gear: Walschaerts (piston valves)

6100 (46100) Royal Scot[1]
6115 (46115) Scots Guardsman[2]

Ex-LMSR '4MT' 2-6-0 No 43106

[*N. E. Preedy*

Ex-LMSR '4F' 0-6-0 No 43924

[*M. Hall*

189

Class 7P 4-6-2
"Princess Royal"

Introduced 1933. Stanier design.
*Introduced 1935. Development of original design with modifications to valve gear, boiler and other details.
[1] Preserved by the Princess Elizabeth Locomotive Society at Hereford.
[2] Preserved at the Midland Railway Trust, Butterley.

Weight:
Locomotive: 104 tons 10 cwt
Boiler pressure: 250 lb/sq in Su
Cylinders: Four, $16\frac{1}{4}'' \times 28''$
Driving wheel diameter: 6' 6"
Tractive effort: 40,285 lb
Valve gear: Walschaerts (piston valves)

6201 (46201) Princess Elizabeth[1]
*6203 (46203) Princess Margaret Rose[2]

Class 8P 4-6-2
"Coronation"

Introduced 1937. Stanier enlargement of "Princess Royal" Class.
*Originally streamlined, but casing removed 1946–1949.
[1] Preserved at The National Railway Museum, York (on loan from Butlins Ltd).
[2] Preserved at Bressingham Hall, Diss
[3] Preserved at the Birmingham Museum of Science & Industry.

Weight:
Locomotive: 105 tons 5 cwt
Boiler pressure: 250 lb/sq in Su
Cylinders: Four, $16\frac{1}{2}'' \times 28''$
Driving wheel diameter: 6' 9"
Tractive effort: 40,000 lb
Valve gear: Walschaerts with rocking shafts (piston valves)

*46229 Duchess of Hamilton[1]
6233 (46233) Duchess of Sutherland[2]
*46235 City of Birmingham[3]

Class 2MT 2-6-0

Introduced 1946. Ivatt design.
[1] Preserved by Steamtown at Carnforth.
[2] Preserved by the Severn Valley Railway, Bridgnorth.
[3] Preserved by the Ivatt Trust at Quainton Road.
[4] Preserved by the 46464 Preservation Trust at the Strathspey Railway, Aviemore.
[5] Preserved at the Bulmer Railway Centre, Hereford.

Weight:
Locomotive: 47 tons 2 cwt
Boiler pressure: 200 lb/sq in Su
Cylinders:
(O) $16'' \times 24''$, (O) $16\frac{1}{2}'' \times 24''$
Driving wheel diameter: 5' 0"
Tractive effort: 17,410 lb, *18,510 lb
Valve gear: Walschaerts (piston valves)

6441 (46441)[1]
46443[2]
46447[3]
46464[4]
*46512[5]
*46521[2]

Class 3F 0-6-0T

Introduced 1924. Post-Grouping development of Fowler Midland design with detail alterations.
[1] Preserved by the Liverpool Locomotive Preservation Group at Steamport Transport Museum, Southport.
[2] Preserved by the Midland Railway Trust, Butterley.
[3] Privately preserved at the Severn Valley Railway, Bridgnorth.
[4] Preserved at the East Somerset Railway, Cranmore.
[5] Preserved at Mid-Hants Railway, New Alresford.
[6] Preserved by the South Yorkshire '3F' Fund at Keighley.

x-LMSR '5MT' 4-6-0 No 5000

[*P. J. Skelton*

x-LMSR 'Jubilee' 4-6-0 No 5690 Leander

[*David Eatwell*

46229 Duchess of Hamilton

Weight: 49 tons 10 cwt
Boiler pressure: 160 lb/sq in NS
Cylinders: (I) 18" × 26"
Driving wheel diameter: 4' 7"
Tractive effort: 20,835 lb
Valve gear: Stephenson (slide valves)

47279[6]	47383[3]
47298[1]	47445[2]
47324[5]	47493[4]
47327[2]	47564[2]
16440 (47357)[2]	

Class 8F 2-8-0

Introduced 1935. Stanier design.
[1] Preserved by the Yorkshire Dales Railway Society in store at Wakefield.
[2] Preserved at the Keighley & Worth Valley Railway, Haworth.
[3] Preserved at the Stanier '8F' Locomotive Society Limited.
Weight:
Locomotive: 72 tons 2 cwt
Boiler pressure: 225 lb/sq in Su
Cylinders: (O) 18½" × 28"
Driving wheel diameter: 4' 8½"
Tractive effort: 32,440 lb
Valve gear: Walschaerts (piston valves)

48151[1]	8233 (48773)[3]
8431 (48431)[2]	

Class 7F 0-8-0

Introduced 1921. Beames development of LNWR G2 class, with higher pressure boiler. Later rebuilt with Belpaire boiler.
Preserved by Telford Horsehay Steam Trust at Telford, Shropshire.
Weight:
Locomotive: 62 tons
Boiler pressure: 175 lb/sq in Su
Cylinders: (I) 20½" × 24"
Driving wheel diameter: 4' 5½"
Tractive effort: 28,045 lb
Valve gear: Joy (piston valves)

(485) 49395

Class 2P 2-4-2T

Introduced 1889. Aspinall LYR Class 5.
Preserved at the National Railway Museum, York.
Weight: 55 tons 19 cwt
Boiler pressure: 180 lb/sq in NS
Cylinders: (I) 18" × 26"
Driving wheel diameter: 5' 8"
Tractive effort: 18,955 lb
Valve gear: Joy (slide valves)

1008 (50621)

Class 0F 0-4-0ST

Introduced 1891. Aspinall LYR Class 21.
*Sold by the LMS.
Preserved at the Keighley & Worth Valley Railway, Haworth.
Weight: 21 tons 5 cwt
Boiler pressure: 160 lb/sq in NS
Cylinders: (O) 13" × 18"
Driving wheel diameter: 3' 0⅜"
Tractive effort: 11,335 lb
Valve gear: Stephenson (slide valves)

51218	*19(11243)

Class 2F 0-6-0

Introduced 1887. Barton-Wright LYR Class 25.
Preserved at the Keighley & Worth Valley Railway, Haworth.
Weight:
Locomotive: 39 tons 1 cwt
Boiler pressure: 140 lb/sq in NS
Cylinders: (I) 17½" × 26"
Driving wheel diameter: 4' 6"
Tractive effort: 17,545 lb
Valve gear: Stephenson (slide valves)

957 (52044)

Class 3F　　　　　　0-6-0

Introduced 1889. Aspinall LYR Class 27.
Privately preserved at Steamtown, Carnforth.

Weight:
Locomotive: 42 tons 3 cwt
Boiler pressure: 180 lb/sq in NS
Cylinders: (I) 18″×26″
Driving wheel diameter: 5′ 1″
Tractive effort: 21,130 lb
Valve gear: Joy (slide valves)

1122 (52322)

Class 7F　　　　　　2-8-0

Introduced 1925. Large-boiler development of Fowler SDJR design (introduced 1914). Rebuilt with smaller boiler by BR.
[1] Preserved by the Somerset & Dorset Railway Museum Trust at the West Somerset Railway.
[2] Privately preserved at Midland Railway Centre, Butterley.

Weight:
Locomotive: 64 tons 15 cwt
Boiler pressure: 190 lb/sq in Su
Cylinders: (O) 21″×28″
Driving wheel diameter: 4′ 8½″
Tractive effort: 35,295 lb
Valve gear: Walschaerts (piston valves)

53808[1]
13809 (53809)[2]

Class 2P　　　　　　0-4-4T

Introduced 1900. McIntosh Caledonian "439" or "Standard Passenger" class.
Preserved by the Scottish Railway Preservation Society, Falkirk.

Weight: 53 tons 19 cwt
Boiler pressure: 180 lb/sq in NS
Cylinders: (I) 18″×26″
Driving wheel diameter: 5′ 9″
Tractive effort: 18,680 lb

Valve gear: Stephenson (slide valves)

419 (55189)

Class 3F　　　　　　0-6-0

Introduced 1899. McIntosh Caledonian "812" class.
Preserved at Glasgow Transport Museum. On loan to Strathspey Railway.

Weight:
Locomotive: 45 tons 14 cwt
Boiler pressure: 180 lb/sq in NS
Cylinders: (I) 18½″×26″
Driving wheel diameter: 5′ 0″
Tractive effort: 22,690 lb
Valve gear: Stephenson (slide valves)

828 (57566)

Class 2F　　　　　　0-6-0T

Introduced 1879. Park NLR design.
Preserved by Bluebell Railway at Sheffield Park.

Weight: 45 tons 10 cwt
Boiler pressure: 160 lb/sq in NS
Cylinders: (O) 17″×24″
Driving wheel diameter: 4′ 7″
Tractive effort: 18,140 lb
Valve gear: Stephenson (slide valves)

2650 (58850)

Class 2F　　　　　　0-6-2T

Introduced 1882. Webb LNWR "Coal Tank".
Preserved by the National Trust at Dinting Railway Centre.

Weight: 43 tons 15 cwt
Boiler pressure: 150 lb/sq in NS
Cylinders: (I) 17″×24″
Driving wheel diameter: 4′ 5½″
Tractive effort: 16,530 lb
Valve gear: Stephenson (slide valves)

1054 (58926)

"Jones Goods" 4-6-0

Introduced 1894, Jones Highland Goods design. Withdrawn 1934 as LMS No. 17916 for preservation. Restored to original condition and returned to service for special use 1959–61.

Preserved at Glasgow Transport Museum.

Weight:
Locomotive: 56 tons
Boiler pressure: 175 lb/sq in NS
Cylinders: (O) 20″ × 26″
Driving wheel diameter: 5′ 3″
Tractive effort: 24,555 lb
Valve gear: Stephenson (slide valves)

103

"Caledonian Single" 4-2-2

Introduced 1886. Neilson & Co. design for the Caledonian Railway incorporating Drummond details. Withdrawn as LMS No. 14010 in 1935. Restored to Caledonian livery and returned to service for special use 1958–61.

Preserved at Glasgow Transport Museum.

Weight:
Locomotive and Tender: 75 tons
Boiler pressure: 150 lb/sq in NS
Cylinders: (I) 18″ × 26″
Driving wheel diameter: 7′ 0″
Tractive effort: 12,785 lb
Valve gear: Stephenson (slide valves)

123

x-S&DJR '7F' 2-8-0 No 13809

[G. Roose

L.N.E.R. Steam Locomotives

Class A4   4-6-2

Introduced 1935. Gresley steamlined design. All fitted with double chimney.
*Fitted with corridor tender.
[1] Preserved by the A4 Locomotive Society at Steamtown, Carnforth.
[2] Preserved at Green Bay, Wisconsin, USA.
[3] Privately preserved at Markinch, Fife.
[4] Preserved at Montreal Railway Historical Museum, Canada.
[5] Preserved at Dinting Railway Centre.
[6] Preserved at the National Railway Museum, York.

Weight:
Locomotive: 102 tons 19 cwt
Tender: *64 tons 19 cwt
60 tons 7 cwt
Boiler pressure: 250 lb/sq in Su
Cylinders:
Three, $18\frac{1}{2}'' \times 26''$
Driving wheel diameter: 6' 8"
Tractive effort: 35,455 lb
Valve gear: Walschaerts, with derived motion (piston valves)

*4498 (60007)   Sir Nigel Gresley[1]
60008   Dwight D. Eisenhower[2]
*60009   Union of South Africa[3]
*60010   Dominion of Canada[4]
19 (60019)   Bittern[5]
4468 (60022)   Mallard[6]

Class A3   4-6-2

Introduced 1922. Gresley GNR design, later rebuilt with higher pressure boiler. Fitted witn double chimney in 1959.
Privately preserved with single chimney and corridor tender at Steamtown, Carnforth.

Weight:
Locomotive: 96 tons 5 cwt
Tender: 64 tons 19 cwt
Boiler pressure: 220 lb/sq in Su
Cylinders: Three, $19'' \times 26''$
Driving wheel diameter: 6' 8"
Tractive effort: 32,910 lb
Valve gear: Walschaerts, with derived motion (piston valves)

4472 (60103)   Flying Scotsman

Class A2   4-6-2

Introduced 1947. Peppercorn development of Thompson Class A2/2 with shorter wheelbase. Later rebuilt with double chimney and multiple-valve regulator.
Preserved at Dinting Railway Centre.

Weight:
Locomotive: 101 tons
Tender: 60 tons 7 cwt
Boiler pressure: 250 lb/sq in Su
Cylinders: Three, $19'' \times 26''$
Driving wheel diameter: 6' 2"
Tractive effort: 40,430 lb
Valve gear: Walschaerts (piston valves)

532 (60532)   Blue Peter

Class V2   2-6-2

Introduced 1936. Gresley design. Preserved at the National Railway Museum, York.

Weight:
Locomotive: 93 tons 2 cwt
Tender: 52 tons
Boiler pressure: 220 lb/sq in Su
Cylinders: Three, $18\frac{1}{2}'' \times 26''$
Driving wheel diameter: 6' 2"
Tractive effort: 33,730 lb
Valve gear: Walschaerts with derived motion (piston valves)

4771 (60800)   Green Arrow

Class B1   4-6-0

Introduced 1942. Thompson design.
[1]Preserved by the Thompson B1 Locomotive Society at the Great Central Railway, Loughborough.
[2]Privately preserved at the Great Central Railway, Loughborough.

Weight:
Locomotive: 71 tons 3 cwt
Tender: 52 tons
Boiler pressure: 225 lb/sq in Su
Cylinders: (O) 20″×26″
Driving wheel diameter: 6′ 2″
Tractive effort: 26,880 lb
Valve gear: Walschaerts (piston valves)

1264 (61264)[1]
1306 (61306)   Mayflower[2]

Class B12   4-6-0

B12/3 Introduced 1932. Gresley rebuild of Holden B12/1 (introduced 1911) with large round-topped boiler.
Preserved by the Midland & Great Northern Preservation Society, Sheringham.

Weight:
Locomotive: 69 tons 10 cwt
Tender: 39 tons 6 cwt
Boiler pressure: 180 lb/sq in Su
Cylinders: (I) 20″×28″
Driving wheel diameter: 6′ 6″
Tractive effort: 21,970 lb
Valve gear: Stephenson (piston valves)

61572

Class K4   2-6-0

Introduced 1937. Gresley design.
Preserved at the Severn Valley Railway, Bridgnorth.
Weight:
Locomotive: 68 tons 8 cwt
Tender: 44 tons 4 cwt

Boiler pressure: 200 lb/sq in Su
Cylinders: Three, 18½″×26″
Driving wheel diameter: 5′ 2″
Tractive effort: 36,600 lb
Valve gear: Walschaerts, with derived motion (piston valves)

3442 (61994)   The Great Marquess

Class K1   2-6-0

Introduced 1949. Peppercorn development of Thompson K1/1 (rebuilt from Gresley K4) with increased length.
Preserved by the North Eastern Locomotive Preservation Group at the North Yorkshire Moors Railway, Grosmont.

Weight:
Locomotive: 66 tons 17 cwt
Tender: 44 tons 4 cwt
Boiler pressure: 225 lb/sq in Su
Cylinders: (O) 20″×26″
Driving wheel diameter: 5′ 2″
Tractive effort: 32,080 lb
Valve gear: Walschaerts (piston valves)

2005 (62005)

Class D40   4-4-0

Introduced 1920. Heywood GNSR superheated development of Pickersgill 1899 design. Restored to original condition and returned to service for special use 1959–61.
Preserved at Glasgow Transport Museum.

Weight:
Locomotive: 48 tons 13 cwt
Tender: 37 tons 8 cwt
Boiler pressure: 165 lb/sq in Su
Cylinders: (I) 18″×26″
Driving wheel diameter: 6′ 1″
Tractive effort: 16,185 lb
Valve gear: Stephenson (slide valves)

49 (62277)   Gordon Highlander

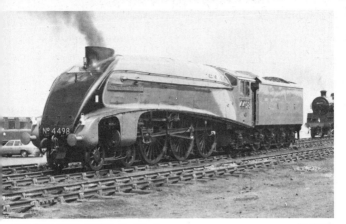

x-LNER 'A4' 4-6-2 No 4498 Sir Nigel Gresley   [*G. Roose*

x-LNER 'A3' 4-6-2 No 4472 Flying Scotsman   [*Marion Canning*

199

Class D34   4-4-0

Introduced 1913. Reid NBR design.
Restored to NBR livery and returned
to service for special use. 1959–61.
Preserved at Glasgow Transport
Museum.

Weight:
Locomotive: 57 tons 4 cwt
Tender: 46 tons 13 cwt
Boiler pressure: 165 lb/sq in Su
Cylinders: (I) 20" × 26"
Driving wheel diameter: 6' 0"
Tractive effort: 20,260 lb
Valve gear: Stephenson (piston valves)

256 (62469)   Glen Douglas

Class D11   4-4-0

D11/1 Introduced 1920. Robinson
GCR "Large Director" development
of D10.
Preserved by the BRB; on loan to the
Great Central Railway, Lough-
borough.

Weight:
Locomotive: 61 tons 3 cwt
Tender: 48 tons 6 cwt
Boiler pressure: 180 lb/sq in Su
Cylinders: (I) 20" × 26"
Driving wheel diameter: 6' 9"
Tractive effort: 19,645 lb
Valve gear: Stephenson (piston valves)

506 (62660)   Butler-Henderson

Class D49   4-4-0

D49/1 Introduced 1927. Gresley
design.
Preserved by the Royal Scottish
Museum, Edinburgh; on loan to the
Scottish Railway Preservation
Society, Falkirk.

Weight:
Locomotive: 66 tons
Tender: 48 tons 6 cwt

Boiler pressure: 180 lb/sq in Su
Cylinders: Three, 17" × 26"
Driving wheel diameter: 6' 8"
Tractive effort: 21,555 lb
Valve gear: Walschaerts, with de-
rived motion (piston valves)

246 (62712)   Morayshire

Class E4   2-4-0

Introduced 1891. J. Holden GER
design.
Preserved at the National Railway
Museum, York.

Weight:
Locomotive: 40 tons 6 cwt
Tender: 30 tons 13 cwt
Boiler pressure: 160 lb/sq in NS
Cylinders: (I) 17½" × 24"
Driving wheel diameter: 5' 8"
Tractive effort: 14,700 lb
Valve gear: Stephenson (slide valves)

490 (62785)

Class Q6   0-8-0

Introduced 1913. Raven NER design.
Preserved by the North Eastern Locomotive Preservation Group at the
North York Moors Railway, Grosmont.

Weight:
Locomotive: 65 tons 18 cwt
Tender: 44 tons 2 cwt
Boiler pressure: 180 lb/sq in Su
Cylinders: (O) 20" × 26"
Driving wheel diameter: 4' 7¼"
Tractive effort: 28,800 lb
Valve gear: Stephenson (piston valves)

3395 (63395)

Class Q7   0-8-0

Introduced 1919. Raven NER design.
Preserved by the National Railway
Museum, on loan to North Eastern
Locomotive Preservation Group at
the North York Moors Railway,
Grosmont.

Weight:
Locomotive: 71 tons 12 cwt
Tender: 44 tons 2 cwt
Boiler pressure: 180 lb/sq in Su
Cylinders: Three, $18\frac{1}{2}'' \times 26''$
Driving wheel diameter: $4'\ 7\frac{1}{4}''$
Tractive effort: 36,965 lb
Valve gear: Stephenson (piston valves)

63460

Class O4   2-8-0

O4/1 Introduced 1911. Robinson
GCR design.
Preserved by BRB. On loan to
Dinting Railway Centre.

Weight:
Locomotive: 73 tons 4 cwt
Tender: 48 tons 6 cwt
Boiler pressure: 180 lb/sq in Su
Cylinders: (O) $21'' \times 26''$
Driving wheel diameter: 4' 8"
Tractive effort: 31,325 lb
Valve gear: Stephenson (piston valves)

102 (63601)

Class J21   0-6-0

Introduced 1886. T. W. Worsdell
NER design.
Part of National Collection. Pre-
served at the North of England Open
Air Museum, Beamish.

Weight:
Locomotive: 43 tons 15 cwt
Tender: 36 tons 19 cwt
Boiler pressure: 160 lb/sq in Su
Cylinders: (I) $19'' \times 24''$
Driving wheel diameter: $5'\ 1\frac{1}{4}''$

Tractive effort: 19,240 lb
Valve gear: Stephenson (piston valves)

876 (65033)

Class J36   0-6-0

Introduced 1888. Holmes NBR de-
sign.
Preserved by the Scottish Railway
Preservation Society, Falkirk.

Weight:
Locomotive: 41 tons 19 cwt
Tender: 33 tons 9 cwt
Boiler pressure: 165 lb/sq in NS
Cylinders: (I) $18\frac{1}{4}'' \times 26''$
Driving wheel diameter: 5' 0"
Tractive effort: 19,690 lb
Valve gear: Stephenson (slide valves)

673 (65243) Maude

Class J15   0-6-0

Introduced 1883. T. W. Worsdell
GER design.
Preserved by the Midland & Great
Northern Preservation Society, Sher-
ingham.

Weight:
Locomotive: 37 tons 2 cwt
Tender: 30 tons 13 cwt
Boiler pressure: 160 lb/sq in NS
Cylinders: (I) $17\frac{1}{2}'' \times 24''$
Driving wheel diameter: 4' 11"
Tractive effort: 16,940 lb
Valve gear: Stephenson (slide valves)

564 (65462)

Class J17   0-6-0

Introduced 1902. J. Holden GER
design.
Prescrved by BRB; at present on loan
to Bressingham Hall, Diss.

Weight:
Locomotive: 45 tons 8 cwt
Tender: 38 tons 5 cwt

Ex-NER 'Q6' 0-8-0 No 2238   [*Brian Morrison*

Ex-NER 'P3' 0-6-0 No 2392   [*J. Hunt*

Boiler pressure: 180 lb/sq in Su
Cylinders: (I) 19" × 26"
Driving wheel diameter: 4' 11"
Tractive effort: 24,340 lb
Valve gear: Stephenson (slide valves)

1217E (65567)

Class J27   0-6-0

Introduced 1921. Raven NER superheated development of W. Worsdell design (introduced 1906) with superheater and piston valves. Superheater later removed.
Preserved by the North Eastern Locomotive Preservation Group. On loan to National Railway Museum, York.

Weight:
Locomotive: 47 tons
Tender: 36 tons 19 cwt
Boiler pressure: 180 lb/sq in NS
Cylinders: (I) 18½" × 26"
Driving wheel diameter: 4' 7¼"
Tractive effort: 24,640 lb
Valve gear: Stephenson (piston valves)

2392 (65894)

Class J94   0-6-0ST

Introduced 1943. Riddles Ministry of Supply design, purchased by LNER, 1946.
[1] Preserved at the East Somerset Railway, Cranmore.
[2] Preserved at the Keighley & Worth Valley Railway, Haworth.
Weight: 48 tons 5 cwt
Boiler pressure: 170 lb/sq in NS
Cylinders: (I) 18" × 26"
Driving wheel diameter: 4' 3"
Tractive effort: 24,870 lb
Valve gear: Stephenson (slide valves)

68005[1]   68077[2]

Class Y7   0-4-0T

Introduced 1888. T. W. Worsdell NER design.
*Sold by LNER.
[1] Preserved by the Y7 Preservation Society at the Great Central Railway, Loughborough.
[2] Preserved by the Middleton Railway Trust, Hunslet, Leeds.
Weight: 22 tons 14 cwt
Boiler pressure: 140 lb/sq in NS
Cylinders: (I) 14" × 20"
Driving wheel diameter: 3' 6¼"
Tractive effort: 11,040 lb
Valve gear: Stephenson (slide valves)

68088[1]   *1310[2]

Class Y9   0-4-0ST

Introduced 1882. Neilson & Co. design for NBR.
Preserved at Lytham Motive Power Museum, Helical Springs Ltd., Lytham St. Annes.
Weight: 27 tons 16 cwt
Boiler pressure: 130 lb/sq in NS
Cylinders: (O) 14" × 20"
Driving wheel diameter: 3' 8"
Tractive effort: 9,845 lb
Valve gear: Stephenson (slide valves)

42 (68095)

Class Y1   0-4-0T

Y1/2 Introduced 1927. Single-speed geared Sentinel Wagon Works design.
Preserved by the Middleton Railway Trust, Hunslet.
Weight: 19 tons 16 cwt
Boiler pressure: 275 lb/sq in Su

x-LNER 'N2' 0-6-2T No 4744

[*G. Wignall*

x-BR Standard '4MT' 4-6-0 No 75027

[*J. Scrace*

Cylinders: (l) $6\frac{3}{4}'' \times 9''$
Driving wheel diameter: 2' 6"
Sprocket gear ratio: 11:25
Tractive effort: 7,260 lb
Valve gear: Sentinel (poppet valves)

59 (54, 68153)

Class J69   0-6-0T

Introduced 1902. J. Holden GER development of J67 (introduced 1890) with higher boiler pressure.
Preserved at the National Railway Museum, York.

Weight: 40 tons 9 cwt
Boiler pressure: 180 lb/sq in NS
Cylinders: (l) $16\frac{1}{2}'' \times 22''$
Driving wheel diameter: 4' 0"
Tractive effort: 19,090 lb
Valve gear: Stephenson (slide valves)

87 (68633)

Class J52   0-6-0ST

J52/2 Introduced 1897. Ivatt GNR design.
Preserved by Captain W. G. Smith; at present on loan to the National Railway Museum, York.

Weight: 51 tons 14 cwt
Boiler pressure: 170 lb/sq in NS
Cylinders: (l) $18'' \times 26''$
Driving wheel diameter: 4' 8"
Tractive effort: 21,735 lb
Valve gear: Stephenson (slide valves)

1247 (68846)

Class J72   0-6-0T

Introduced 1949. Development of W. Worsdell NER 1898 design.
Preserved at the National Railway Museum, York.

Weight: 38 tons 12 cwt
Boiler pressure: 140 lb/sq in NS
Cylinders: (l) $17'' \times 24''$
Driving wheel diameter: 4' $1\frac{1}{4}''$
Tractive effort: 16,760 lb
Valve gear: Stephenson (slide valves)

69023 Joem

Class N2   0-6-2T

N2/2 Introduced 1920. Gresley GNR design. Fitted with condensing apparatus and small chimney for working over Metropolitan line to Moorgate.
Preserved at the Great Central Railway, Loughborough.

Weight: 70 tons 5 cwt
Boiler pressure: 170 lb/sq in Su
Cylinders: (l) $19'' \times 26''$
Driving wheel diameter: 5' 8"
Tractive effort: 19,945 lb
Valve gear: Stephenson (piston valves)

4744 (69523)

Class N7   0-6 2T

N7/4 Introduced 1940. Rebuild of Hill GER design (introduced 1914) with round-topped boiler.
Preserved at the Stour Valley Railway, Chappel & Wakes Colne.

Weight: 61 tons 16 cwt
Boiler pressure: 180 lb/sq in Su
Cylinders: (l) $18'' \times 24''$
Driving wheel diameter: 4' 10"
Tractive effort: 20,515 lb
Valve gear: Walschaerts (piston valves)

999E (69621)

B.R. Standard Locomotives

Class 7P6F   4-6-2

Introduced 1951. Designed at Derby.
[1]Preserved by the Britannia Locomotive Company at the Severn Valley Railway, Bridgnorth.
[2]Preserved by BRB. On loan to Bressingham Hall, Diss.

Weight:
Locomotive: 94 tons 4 cwt
Tender: 49 tons 3 cwt
Boiler pressure: 250 lb/sq in Su
Cylinders: (O) 20" × 28"
Driving wheel diameter: 6' 2"
Tractive effort: 32,150 lb
Valve gear: Walschaerts (piston valves)

70000 Britannia[1]
70013 Oliver Cromwell[2]

Class 8P   4-6-2

Introduced 1954. Designed at Derby. Preserved by Duke of Gloucester (71000) Locomotive Trust at the Great Central Railway, Loughborough.
Weight:
Locomotive: 101 tons 5 cwt
Tender: 53 tons 14 cwt
Boiler pressure: 250 lb/sq in Su
Cylinders: Three, 18" × 28"
Driving wheel diameter: 6' 2"
Tractive effort: 39,080 lb
Valve gear: Caprotti (poppet valves)

71000 Duke of Gloucester

Class 5MT   4-6-0

Introduced 1951. Designed at Doncaster.
[1]Preserved by the Peterborough Railway Society at the Nene Valley Railway, Wansford.
[2]Preserved by the Midland Railway Trust Ltd, Butterley.

[3]Preserved by Camelot Society at the Bluebell Railway, Sheffield Park.
Weight:
Locomotive: 76 tons 4 cwt
Tender: 52 tons 10 cwt
Boiler pressure: 225 lb/sq in Su
Cylinders: (O) 19" × 28"
Driving wheel diameter: 6' 2"
Tractive effort: 26,120 lb
Valve gear: Walschaerts (piston valves)
*Caprotti (poppet valves)

73050 City of Peterborough[1]
73082 Camelot[3]
*73129[2]

Class 4MT   4-6-0

Introduced 1951. Designed at Brighton.
*Introduced 1957. Fitted with double chimney.
[1]Privately preserved at the Bluebell Railway, Sheffield Park.
[2]Preserved by the Shepherd Locomotive Trust at the East Somerset Railway, Cranmore.
[3]Preserved by the Severn Valley Railway, Bridgnorth.
[4]Preserved by the Standard 4 Locomotive Preservation Society at the Keighley & Worth Valley Railway, Haworth.
Weight:
Locomotive: 69 tons
Tender: 42 tons 3 cwt
Boiler pressure: 225 lb/sq in Su
Cylinders: (O) 18" × 28"
Driving wheel diameter: 5' 8"
Tractive effort: 25,100 lb
Valve gear: Walschaerts (piston valves)

75027[1]
*75029 The Green Knight[2]
*75069[3]
*75078[4]

Class 4MT   2-6-0

Introduced 1953. Designed at Doncaster.
[1] Preserved at Mid-Hants Railway, New Alresford.
[2] Preserved by Frogstone Ltd at Steamport Transport Museum, Southport.

Weight:
Locomotive: 59 tons 2 cwt
Boiler pressure: 225 lb/sq in Su
Cylinders: (O) $17\frac{1}{2}" \times 26"$
Driving wheel diameter: 5' 3"
Tractive effort: 24,170 lb
Valve gear: Walschaerts (piston valves)

76017[1]   76079[2]

Class 2MT   2-6-0

Introduced 1953. Designed at Derby.
[1] Preserved by the Severn Valley Railway, Bridgnorth.
[2] Preserved by the Standard Locomotive Preservation Society at the Keighley & Worth Valley Railway, Haworth.
[3] Preserved at Market Bosworth Light Railway.

Weight:
Locomotive: 49 tons 5 cwt
Boiler pressure: 200 lb/sq in
Cylinders: (O) $16\frac{1}{2}" \times 24"$
Driving wheel diameter: 5' 0"
Tractive effort: 18,515 lb
Valve gear: Walschaerts (piston valves)

78018[3]   78019[1]   78022[2]

Class 4MT   2-6-4T

Introduced 1951. Designed at Brighton.
[1] Preserved at the Keighley & Worth Valley Railway, Haworth.
[2] Preserved at the Dart Valley Railway, Buckfastleigh.
[3] Preserved by the Southern Steam Trust at Swanage.
[4] Preserved by the Severn Valley Railway, Bridgnorth.

[5] Preserved by the Locomotive Owners Group (Scotland) Ltd.
[6] Preserved at the North Yorkshire Moors Railway, Grosmont.
[7] Preserved by the Stour Valley Railway Preservation Society.
[8] Preserved on the Bluebell Railway.
[9] Privately preserved at Cheddleton.

Weight: 88 tons 10 cwt
Boiler pressure: 225 lb/sq in Su
Cylinders: (O) $18" \times 28"$
Driving wheel diameter: 5' 8"
Tractive effort: 25,100 lb
Valve gear: Walschaerts (piston valves)

80002[1]	80079[4]	80135[6]
80064[2]	80100[8]	80136[9]
80078[3]	80105[5]	80151[7]

Class 9F   2-10-0

Introduced 1954. Designed at Brighton.
[1] Preserved at the East Somerset Railway, Cranmore.
[2] Preserved at the National Railway Museum, York.
[3] Preserved at the Bluebell Railway, Sheffield Park.
[4] Preserved at Great Central Railway, Loughborough.
[5] Preserved by the Peak Railway Society.
[6] Preserved at the North York Moors Railway.

Weight:
Locomotive: 86 tons 14 cwt
Tender: 52 tons 10 cwt
Boiler pressure: 250 lb/sq in Su
Cylinders: (O) $20" \times 28"$
Driving wheel diameter: 5' 0"
Tractive effort: 39,670 lb
Valve gear: Walschaerts (piston valves)

92134[6]
92203   Black Prince[1]
92212[4]
92214[5]
92220   Evening Star[2]
92240[3]

Ex-BR Standard '4MT' 2-6-4T No 80079

[*G. Roose*

Ex-BR Standard '9F' 2-10-0 No 92220 Evening Star

[*G. Roose*

Diesel Locomotives

Class 02
Yorkshire Engine Co. 0-4-0 Shunter

Introduced 1960. Yorkshire Engine Co. diesel-hydraulic shunting locomotive.
Preserved at the National Railway Museum, York.

Engine:
Rolls-Royce C6NFL of 179 h.p. at 1,800 r.p.m.

Weight: 28 tons

Maximum tractive effort:
15,000 lb

Transmission:
Hydraulic. Rolls-Royce 3-stage torque converter, Series 10,000. Axlehung double-reduction final drive with reversing mechanism

Driving wheel diameter: 3′ 6″
D2860

Class 03
British Railways 0-6-0 Shunter

Introduced 1957. Standard BR 204 b.h.p. diesel-mechanical shunting locomotive.
[1] Preserved at the National Railway Museum, York.
[2] Preserved by the Lakeside Railway, Haverthwaite.
[3] Preserved by the Dart Valley Railway, Buckfastleigh.
[4] Privately preserved at Steamtown, Carnforth.

Engine:
Gardner 8L3 of 204 b.h.p. at 1,200 r.p.m.

Weight: 30 tons

Maximum tractive effort:
15,650 lb

Transmission:
Mechanical. Vulcan-Sinclair type 23 fluid coupling. Wilson-Drewry C.A.5 type five-speed epicyclic gearbox. Type RF II spiral bevel reverse and final drive unit.

Driving wheel diameter: 3′ 7″

03 090[1]	D2192[3]
8 (D2117)[2]	D2381[4]

Class 04
Drewry 0-6-0 Shunter

Introduced 1952 (*1955). Drewry 204 b.h.p. diesel-mechanical shunting locomotive.
[1] Preserved by the North Yorkshire Moors Railway, Grosmont.
[2] Preserved by the Midland Railway Trust Ltd, Butterley.
[3] Shackerstone Railway, Leicestershire.

Engine:
Gardner 8L3 of 204 b.h.p. at 1,200 r.p.m.

Weight: 30 tons (*32 tons)

Maximum tractive effort:
16,850 lb (*15,650 lb)

Transmission:
Mechanical. Vulcan-Sinclair type 23 fluid coupling. Wilson-Drewry C.A.5 type five-speed epicyclic gearbox. Type RF II spiral bevel reverse and final drive unit.

Driving wheel diameter:
3′ 3″ (*3′ 6″)

2207[1]	*2271[2]	2(2245)[3]

Class 14
British Railways 0-6-0

Introduced 1964. The last B.R. diesel-hydraulic design. A type intended for short trip workings. Preserved by Diesel & Electric Group on West Somerset Railway.

Engine:
Paxman 6-cyl Ventura 6YJX of 650 b.h.p. at 1,500 r.p.m.
Weight: 50 tons
Maximum tractive effort: 30,910 lb
Transmission:
Hydraulic. Voith L217U
Driving wheel diameter: 4' 0"

D9526

Class 24/0
British Railways Bo-Bo
Type 2

Introduced 1958. Standard Sulzer-engined Type 2 locomotive built by British Railways workshops. Preserved at the North Yorkshire Moors Railway, Grosmont.

Engine:
Sulzer 6-cyl. 6LDA28 of 1,160 b.h.p. at 750 r.p.m.
Weight: 80 tons
Brake force: 38 tonnes
Maximum tractive effort: 40,000 lb
Transmission:
Electric. Four B.T.H. axle-hung nose-suspended traction motors of 213 h.p. (continuous rating)
Driving wheel diameter: 3' 9"
Route availability: 6
Maximum speed: 75 m.p.h.

D5032 (24 032)

Class 28
Metropolitan Vickers Co-Bo

Introduced 1958. Type 2 locomotive of unusual wheel arrangement, and the only Crossley-engined main line type on B.R. Preserved by Diesel Traction Group at BREL Swindon Works.

Engine:
Crossley 8-cyl. HST V8 of 1,200 b.h.p. at 625 r.p.m.
Weight: 97 tons
Maximum tractive effort: 50,000 lb
Transmission:
Electric. Five Metropolitan Vickers axle-hung nose-suspended traction motors
Driving wheel diameter: 3' 3½"

D5705 (TDB 968006)

Class 31/0
British Railways AIA-AIA
Type 2

Introduced 1957.

Preserved by the National Railway Museum, York, on loan to North York Moors Railway, Grosmont.

Engine:
English Electric 12-cyl. 12SV of 1,470 b.h.p.
Weight: 109 tons
Brake force: 49 tonnes
Maximum tractive effort: 42,000 lb
Transmission:
Electric. Four Brush traction motors, single reduction gear drive
Driving wheel diameter: 3' 7"
Route availability: 5
Maximum speed: 80 m.p.h.
Fitted with electro-magnetic control equipment
D5500 (31018)

Class 35
Beyer Peacock (Hymek)
B B
Type 3

Introduced 1961. Medium-power diesel-hydraulic type for the Western Region.

211

[1] Preserved by the Diesel and Electric Group at the West Somerset Railway.
[2] Privately preserved by D & EG at Didcot.
[3] Preserved by Diesel Traction Group at Swindon.

Engine:
Bristol-Siddeley/Maybach MD870 of 1,700 b.h.p.
Weight: 75 tons
Brake force: 33 tonnes
Maximum tractive effort: 49,700 lb
Transmission:
Hydraulic. Stone-Maybach Mekydro type 6184U
Driving wheel diameter: 3′ 9″
Route availability: 6
Maximum speed: 90 m.p.h.

7017[1]   7018[2]   7029[3]

Class 42
British Railways ''Warship''
B-B
Type 4

Introduced 1958. Swindon-built version of the ''Warship'', with four-wheeled bogies and Maybach engines.
[1] Privately preserved at Swindon.
[2] Privately preserved at Bury Transport Museum.

Engines:
Two Bristol Siddeley-Maybach MD 650 V-type of 1,152 b.h.p. at 1,530 r.p.m.
Weight: 78 tons
Maximum tractive effort: 52,400 lb
Transmission:
Hydraulic. Two Mekydro type K104 hydraulic transmissions containing permanently filled single torque converter and four-speed automatic gearbox
Driving wheel diameter: 3′ 3½″

821   Greyhound[1]
D832   Onslaught[2]

Class 52
British Railways C-C
Type 4

Introduced 1961.

[1] Privately preserved at Merehead. To be renamed Western Yeoman.
[2] Preserved by the Western Locomotive Association on the Severn Valley Railway.
[3] Preserved on the Severn Valley Railway.
[4] Preserved at the National Railway Museum, York.
[5] Preserved at Bury Transport Museum.
[6] Preserved at North York Moors Railway.
[7] Preserved by Diesel Traction Group at Swindon.

Engines:
Two Maybach MD655 12-cyl. V-type of 1,350 b.h.p. at 1,500 r.p.m.
Weight: 109 tons
Brake force: 50 tonnes.
Maximum tractive effort: 72,600 lb.
Transmission:
Hydraulic. Two Voith-North British L630rV hydraulic transmissions, each containing three torque converters
Driving wheel diameter: 3′ 7″
Route availability: 6
Maximum speed: 90 m.p.h.
All dual braked

D1010   Western Campaigner[1]
D1013   Western Ranger[3]
D1015   Western Champion[7]
D1023   Western Fusilier[4]
D1041   Western Prince[5]
D1048   Western Lady[6]
D1062   Western Courier[2]

English Electric Co-Co
Type 5

Introduced 1955. Experimental high horse power locomotive. Ran trials on West Coast and East Coast expresses until 1960.

Preserved at the Science Museum, London.

Engines:
Two 18-cyl. Napier "Deltic" 18-25 of 1,650 b.h.p. at 1,500 r.p.m.

Weight: 106 tons

Maximum tractive effort:
60,000 lb

Transmission:
Electric. Six English Electric EE750 25G axle-hung nose-suspended traction motors

Driving wheel diameter: 3' 7"

Deltic

English Electric 0-6-0 Shunter

Introduced 1957. One of two similar locomotives used for comparative trials between electric and hydraulic transmission.
Preserved at the Keighley & Worth Valley Railway, Haworth.

Engine:
English Electric 6RKT of 500 b.h.p. at 750 r.p.m.

Weight: 48 tons

Maximum tractive effort:
33,000 lb

Transmission:
Electric. One English Electric traction motor coupled to double reduction gear-box final drive

Driving wheel diameter: 4' 0"

D0226

Class 07
Ruston & Hornsby 0-6-0 Shunter

Introduced 1962 for shunting in Southampton Docks. Privately preserved on West Somerset Railway.

Engine: Paxman 6-cyl RPHL

Weight: 42 tons

Brake force: 21 tonnes

Maximum tractive effort:
28,240 lb

Transmission:
Electric. AEI type RTA 6652 traction motor

Driving wheel diameter: 3' 6"

07 010 (D2994)

Hudswell-Clarke 0-6-0 Shunter

Introduced 1956. Sold from capital stock to NCB Brodsworth Colliery. Preserved on Keighley & Worth Valley Railway.

Engine: Gardner 8L3 of 204 b.h.p. at 1,200 r.p.m.

Weight: 36 tons 7 cwt

Maximum tractive effort:
16,100 lb

Transmission:
Mechanical. SCR 5 type, size 23 scoop control fluid coupling. Three-speed "SSS Power-flow" double-syncro type gearbox and final drive.

Driving wheel diameter: 3' 6"

D2511

Class 31/0 A1A-A1A No D5500

Class 42 'Warship' B-B No D832 Onslaught

Multiple Units

Class 100 (2) ■
Gloucester R. C. & W. Co.
Motor brake Second

Introduced 1957.
Preserved by the North Yorkshire Moors Railway, Grosmont.
Engines:
Two B.U.T. (A.E.C.) 6-cyl. horizontal type of 150 b.h.p.
Body: 57′ 6″ × 9′ 3″
Weight: 30 tons 5 cwt
Seats: 2nd, 52
Transmission:
Mechanical. Standard

D10 (50341)   D11 (51118)

Class 103 (2) ■
Park Royal Vehicles
Motor Brake Second

Introduced 1957.
Preserved by the West Somerset Railway.
[2]Preserved at the Shackerstone Railway.
Engines:
Two B.U.T. (A.E.C.) 6-cyl. horizontal type of 150 b.h.p.
Body: 57′ 6″ × 9′ 3″
Weight: 33 tons 8 cwt
Seats: 2nd, 52
Transmission:
Mechanical. Standard

M50397[2]   W50413   W50414

Class 100 (2) ■
Gloucester R. C. & W. Co.
Driving Trailer Composite (L)

Introduced 1957.
[1]Preserved by the North Yorkshire Moors Railway, Grosmont.
[2]Preserved by the Chacewater Light Railway Co.
[3]Preserved by the Gwili Railway Company Ltd.

Body: 57′ 6″ × 9′ 3″
Seats: 1st, 12; 2nd, 54
Weight: 25 tons

D12 (56097)   E56301[2]   E56317[3]
D13 (56099)

Class 103 (2) ■
Park Royal Vehicles
Driving Trailer Composite (L)

Introduced 1957
Preserved by the West Somerset Railway.
[2]Preserved at the Shackerstone Railway.
Body: 57′ 6″ × 9′ 3″
Seats: 1st, 16; 2nd, 48
Weight: 26 tons 7 cwt

M56160[2]   W56168   W56169

Swindon Works, B.R.
(Inter-City) ■
Trailer Buffet First (L)

Introduced 1961.
Preserved at the North Yorkshire Moors Railway, Grosmont.

SC59098

Class 165 (4) ■
Metropolitan-Cammell
Trailer Buffet Second (L)

Introduced 1960.
Preserved by the Keighley & Worth Valley Railway Haworth.
Body: 57′ 0″ × 9′ 3″ Open second with miniature buffet at one end.
Weight: 25 tons
Seats: 2nd, 53

24 (E59575)

Swindon Works, B.R.
(Inter-City) ●

Trailer Buffet First (K)

Introduced 1957.
[1]Preserved at the Strathspey Railway, Boat of Garten.
[2]Preserved by the North Yorkshire Moors Railway, Grosmont.
Body: 64' 6" × 9' 3". Side corridor with seven first class compartments and end doors.
Weight: 33 tons 9 cwt
Seats: 1st, 42

SC79441[1]   SC79443[2]

G.W.R. Railcars

Introduced 1934; *1940.
[1]Preserved at the National Railway Museum, York.
[2]Preserved at the Kent & East Sussex Railway, Rolvenden.
[3]Preserved by the Great Western Society at Didcot Railway Centre.
Engines:
Two A.E.C. 121 b.h.p.
*Two A.E.C. 105 b.h.p.
Seats: 2nd, 44; *48

W4W[1]   *W20W[2]   *W22W[3]

Waggon und Maschinenbau
Four-Wheel Railbus

Introduced 1958.
[1]Preserved by the Midland & Great Northern Preservation Society, Sheringham.
[2]Preserved at the Keighley & Worth Valley Railway, Haworth.
Engine:
Buessing 150 b.h.p. at 1,900 r.p.m.
*A.E.C. A220X type
Transmission:
Mechanical. Cardan shaft to ZF electro-magnetic six-speed gearbox

Body: 41' 10" × 8' 8$\frac{5}{16}$"
Non-gangwayed
Weight: 15 tons
Seats: 2nd, 56

E79960[1]   *E79963[1]   *M79964[2]
62(E79962)[2]

A.C.Cars
Four-Wheel Railbus

Introduced 1958.
[1]Preserved at the Somerset Railway Museum, Bleadon and Uphill station.
[2]Preserved by the Kent & East Sussex Railway.
[3]To be preserved at Strathspey Railway, Aviemore.
Engine:
B.U.T. (A.E.C.) 6-cyl horizontal type of 150 b.h.p.
Transmission:
Mechanical. Standard
Body: 36' 0" × 8' 11"
Non-gangwayed
Weight: 11 tons
Seats: 2nd, 46

W79976[1]   W79978[2]   SC79979[3]

Derby Works, B.R.   (4)
Advanced Passenger Train

Introduced: 1972. Experimental four-car articulated unit, with a power car at each end
Preserved at the National Railway Museum, York
Engine:
Eight Leyland 350 automotive gas-turbines, rated at a nominal 298 h.p.
Transmission:
Four G.E.C. traction 253AY nose-suspended traction motors on the leading bogie only of each power car
APT–E

Electric Multiple Units

This list shows only those vehicles which are preserved as complete units. A number of other emu vehicles are preserved and these include individual cars on static display in museums, and Pullman cars from the 6-PUL and 5-BEL (Brighton Belle) units. In the case of the latter vehicles sufficient cars exist to form a complete unit, but these are widely scattered and some are in use as static restaurants, etc.

Class 401 (2-BIL) Two-car unit

Introduced 1937. Southern Railway (750 V d.c. 3rd rail) semi-fast stock. Stored at Brighton pending preservation.

Motor Brake Second
Body: 62' 6" × 9' 0" & 9' 3"
Weight: 43 tons 10 cwt
Seats: 2nd, 52
Equipment: Two 275 h.p. English Electric traction motors

Driving Trailer Composite
Body: 62' 6" × 9' 0" & 9' 3"
Weight: 31 tons 5 cwt
Seats: 1st, 24; **2nd,** 32

2091

Class 404/2 (4-COR) Four-car unit

Introduced 1937. Southern Railway (750 V d.c. 3rd rail) gangwayed express passenger stock. Preserved by the Southern Electric Group on the Nene Valley Railway.

Motor Saloon Brake Second
Body: 63' 6" × 9' 0" & 9' 4½"
Weight: 46 tons 10 cwt
Seats: 2nd, 52
Equipment: Two 225 h.p. English Electric traction motors

Trailer Second
Body: 63' 6" × 9' 0" & 9' 3"
Weight: 32 tons 13 cwt
Seats: 2nd, 68

Trailer Composite
Body: 63' 6" × 9' 0" & 9' 3"
Weight: 32 tons 12 cwt
Seats: 1st, 30; **2nd,** 24

Motor Saloon Brake Second
(details as above)

3142

Class 502 Two-car unit

Introduced 1939. London Midland and Scottish Railway (630 V d.c. 3rd rail) Liverpool-Southport suburban stock. Preserved by the National Railway Museum. On loan to Steamport, Southport.

Motor Open Brake Second
Body: 66' 6" × 9' 3" & 9' 5"
Weight: 41 tons
Seats, 2nd, 88
Equipment: Four 235 h.p. English traction motors

M29361M

Driving Trailer Open Composite
Body: 66' 6" × 9' 3" & 9' 5"
Weight: 25 tons
Seats: 1st, 53; **2nd,** 25

M29896M

Electric Locomotives

Siemens Bo

Introduced 1898. Former Waterloo & City line shunting locomotive.
Preserved at National Railway Museum, York.

System:
750 V d.c. 3rd rail

DS75

Brush Bo-Bo

Introduced 1904. One of two Class ES1 locomotives for shunting duties on the NER North Tyneside system. Preserved at the National Railway Museum, York.

Equipment:
Four B.T.H. nose suspended traction motors
System:
630 V d.c. overhead and 3rd rail

Total h.p.: 640
Weight: 46 tons
Maximum tractive effort:
25,000 lb

26500

Battery Electric Bo

Introduced 1917. North Staffordshire Railway.
Preserved at the Staffordshire Industrial Museum, Shugborough Hall.

Equipment:
Two B.T.H. traction motors
Driving wheel diameter: 3' 1"
Total h.p.: 82
Weight: 17 tons

BEL 2

British Railways   Bo-Bo
Class 71

Introduced 1958 for Southern Region. Third rail 750 V d.c. collection and fitted pantograph for 750 V d.c. overhead in yards. Preserved at National Railway Museum, York.
Equipment: Motor generator booster set and four English Electric 532 traction motors.
Maximum rail h.p.: 3,000 h.p.
Mechanical parts: BR
Weight: 77 tons
Brake force: 41 tons. Dual braked
Maximum tractive effort:
43,000 lb
Route availability: 6
Maximum speed: 90 m.p.h.

E5001 (71 001)

British Railways   Bo-Bo
Class 76

Introduced 1950 for Manchester–Wath electrification.
Preserved at the National Railway Museum, York.
Equipment:
Four 467 h.p. Metropolitan-Vickers nose suspended traction motors.
Driving wheel diameter: 4' 2"
System: 1,500 V d.c. overhead
Total h.p. 1,868
Weight: 89 tons
Brake force: 43 tons
Maximum tractive effort:
45,000 lb.
Route availability: 8
Maximum speed: 65 m.p.h.

26020 (76020)

British Railways   Bo-Bo
Class 84

For details see Class 84 in Electric Locomotives Section. Preserved at the National Railway Museum, York.

84 001

OTHER PRESERVED LOCOMOTIVES

Date built	Previous owner	Type	Locomotive	Place of preservation
1813	Wylam Colliery	0-4-0	Wylam Dilly	Scottish Museum Edinburgh
1814	Wylam Colliery	0-4-0	Puffing Billy	Science Museum, Kensington
1822	Hetton Colliery	0-4-0	No. 1	Beamish Museum
1825	Stockton & Darlington	0-4-0	Locomotion	Darlington, North Road Museum
1829	Liverpool & Manchester	0 2-2	Rocket	Science Museum, Kensington
1829	Bolton & Leigh	0-4-0	Sanspareil	Science Museum Kensington
1829	Shutt End Rly	0-4-0	Agenoria	Nat. Rly Museum
1830	Canterbury & Whitstable	0-4-0	Invicta	Westgate Gardens, Canterbury
1830	Killingworth Colliery	0-4-0	Billy	Newcastle Museum
1837	GWR	2-2-2 Full-sized replica of the original	North Star	Swindon Museum
1838	Liverpool & Manchester	0-4-2	Lion	Restored to working order. Based at Liverpool Museum
1845	Grand Junction	2-2-2	No. 49 Columbine	Nat. Railway Museum
1845	Stockton & Darlington	0-6-0	No. 25 Derwent	Darlington North Road Museum
1846	Furness	0-4-0	No. 3 Coppernob	Nat. Railway Museum
1847	LNWR	2-2-2	No. 3020 Cornwall	On loan to Severn Valley Railway
1857	Wantage Tramway	0-4-0WT	No. 5 Shannon	Didcot
1865	LNWR	18" gauge	Pet	Narrow Gauge Museum, Towyn
1865	LNWR	0-4-0ST	No. 1439	Shugborough Hall
1866	MR	2-4-0 Class 1	No. 158A	Mid. Rly Trust
1866	Metropolitan	4-4-0T Class A	No. 23	London Transport Museum
1868	South Devon	Broad gauge 0-4-0T	Tiny	National Collection, on loan to DVR Museum, Buckfastleigh
1869	NER	2-2-4T	No. 66 Aerolite	Nat. Railway Museum
1870	GNR	4-2-2	No. 1	Nat. Rly Museum
1872	Oxford & Aylesbury	0-4-0 Tram Locomotive	No. 807	London Transport Museum
1874	NER	0-6-0	No. 1275	Darlington Railway Museum
1875	NER	2-4-0 901 Class	No. 910	Nat. Railway Museum
1878	Gwendraeth Valleys	0-6-0ST	Margaret	Dyfed Museum, Haverfordwest
1882	LBSCR	0-4-2 Class B1	No. 214 Gladstone	Nat. Railway Museum

Date built	Previous owner	Type	Locomotive	Place of preservation
1885	Mersey Railway	0-6-4T	No. 5 *Cecil Raikes*	Steamport, Southport
1885	NER	2-4-0	No. 1463	Darlington Railway Museum
1887	LYR	18″ gauge 0-4-0T	*Wren*	Nat. Railway Museum
1892	LNWR	2-4-0 Precedent Class	No. 790 *Hardwicke*	Nat. Railway Museum
1893	NER	4-4-0 Class M1	No. 1621	Nat. Railway Museum
1893	LSWR	4-4-0 Class T3	No. 563	Nat. Railway Museum
1893	Shrop. and Mont.	0-4-2WT	*Gazelle*	Nat. Railway Museum
1896	Metropolitan	0-4-4T	No. 1 (London Transport L44)	Quainton Road
1896	LYR	0-6-0ST	No. 752	K & WVR
1897	TVR	0-6-2T	No. 28	Caerphilly
1897	Alexandra Docks (GWR)	0-4-0ST	No. 1340 *Trojan*	Didcot
1898	GNR	4-4-2	No. 990 *Henry Oakley*	Nat. Railway Museum
1899	TVR	0-6-2T	No. 52	K & WVR
1899	MR	4-2-2 115 Class	No. 673	Mid. Railway Trust
1900	Burry Port and Gwendraeth Valley	0-6-0ST	*Pontyberem*	Didcot
1902	GNR	4-4-2 Class C1	No. 251	Nat. Railway Museum
1906	GWR	0-4-0ST	No. 921	Leicester Corporation
1917	GSWR	0-6-0T	No. 9	Glasgow Transport Museum
1922	NSR	0-6-2T	No. 2	Shugborough Hall

REPLICA LOCOMOTIVES

Date built	Previous owner	Type	Locomotive	Place of preservation
1979 (1829)	L&MR	0-2-2	*Rocket*	Part of National Collection
1980 (1829)		0-4-0	*Sanspareil*	Part of National Collection
1980 (1829)		0-2-2	*Novelty*	Part of National Collection

LOCOMOTIVES OF PRINCIPAL NARROW GAUGE RAILWAYS NOT FORMING CONSTITUENTS OF THE BR SYSTEM

Talyllyn Railway (Opened 1965)
Steam locomotives

No.	Name	Type	Built
1	Talyllyn	0-4-0ST	1864
2	Dolgoch	0-4-0WT	1865
3	Sir Haydn	0-4-2ST	1878
4	Edward Thomas	0-4-0ST	1921
6	Douglas	0-4-0WT	1918
7	Irish Pete	0-4-2WT	1949

Festiniog Railway (Originally built 1836 for conveyance of slate. Steam traction introduced 1863)
Steam locomotives

1	Princess	0-4-0ST	1863
2	Prince	0-4-0ST	1863
3	Earl of Merioneth	0-4-4-0T Fairlie	1979
10	Merddin Emrys	0-4-4-0T Fairlie	1886
	Blanche	2-4-0ST with tender	1893
	Linda	2-4-0ST with tender	1893
5	Welsh Pony	0-4-0ST	1867
3.23	Mountaineer	2-6-2T Alco	1916

Also diesel locos

Isle of Man Railway (Opened 1873)

1	Sutherland	2-4-0T	1873
4	Loch	2-4-0T	1874
9	Douglas	2-4-0T	1896
10	G. H. Wood	2-4-0T	1905
11	Maitland	2-4-0T	1905
12	Hutchinson	2-4-0T	1908
13	Kissack	2-4-0T	1910
15	Caledonia	0-6-0T	1885
16	Mannin	2-4-0T	1926

Snowdon Mountain Railway (Mountain rack railway. Opened 1896)

2	Enid	0-4-2T	1895
3	Wyddfa	0-4-2T	1895
4	Snowdon	0-4-2T	1896
5	Moel Siabod	0-4-2T	1896
6	Padarn	0-4-2T	1922

7	Ralph Sadler	0-4-2T	1923
8	Eryri	0-4-2T	1923

Welshpool & Llanfair Railway (Opened 1902)

1	The Earl	0-6-0T	1902
2	The Countess	0-6-0T	1902
6	Monarch	0-4-0+0-4-0T	1953
10	Sir Drefaldwyn	0-8-0T	1944
12	Joan	0-6-2T	1927
14		2-6-2T	1954

Ravenglass & Eskdale Railway (Opened 1915. Originally 3 ft 0 in gauge line opened 1875)

	River Esk	2-8-2	1923
	River Mite	2-8-2	1966
	River Irt	0-8-2	1927
	Northern Rock	2-6-2	1976
	Royal Anchor	Bo-Bo Diesel	1956
	Shelagh of Eskdale	Diesel	1969

Fairbourne Railway, Merioneth (Opened 1916. Originally 1890 as 2 ft 0 in horse tramway)

	Count Louis	4-4-2	1924
	Ernest W. Twining	4-6-2	1949
	Katie	2-4-2	1954
	Siân	2-4-2	1963

Also diesel locos

Romney Hythe & Dymchurch Railway (Opened 1927)

1	Green Goddess	4-6-2*	1925
2	Northern Chief	4-6-2*	1925
3	Southern Maid	4-6-2*	1925
4	The Bug	0-4-0	1928
5	Hercules	2-8-2	1926
6	Samson	2-8-2	1926
7	Typhoon	4-6-2*	1926
8	Hurricane	4-6-2*	1926
9	Winston Churchill	4-6-2†	1931
10	Doctor Syn	4-6-2†	1931
11	Black Prince	4-6-2	1937

* Based on LNER Gresley Pacific design.
† Based on Canadian Pacific design.

LATE INFORMATION

Ex-GWR '57xx' 0-6-0PT No 4612 to Keighley.

BR Standard '4MT' 4-6-0 No 75014 to Grosmont.

BR Standard '4MT' 2-6-4T No 80104 to Swanage.

Ex-GWR 'Hall' 4-6-0 No 4979 *Wootton Hall* acquired privately.

Ex-GWR 'Hall' 4-6-0 No 5972 *Olton Hall* acquired privately.

Ex-GWR 'Manor' 4-6-0 No 7828 *Odney Manor* acquired by GW Steam Locomotive Group.

Ex-GWR 'Hall' 4-6-0 No 7903 *Foremarke Hall* acquired by Foremarke Hall Locomotive Ltd.

Ex-SR 'S15' 4-6-0 No 30828 to Eastleigh.

TRANSPORT TRACKERS

We regret, that due to lack of sufficient interest, this scheme has been cancelled.

This edition published 1981

ISBN 0 7110 1127 3

Published by Ian Allan Ltd, Shepperton, TW17 8AS and printed in the United Kingdom by Jarrold & Sons Ltd, Norwich